T0333881

SURVIVING BIAFRA

S. ELIZABETH BIRD

ROSINA UMELO

Surviving Biafra

A Nigerwife's Story

HURST & COMPANY, LONDON

First published in the United Kingdom in 2018 by
C. Hurst & Co. (Publishers) Ltd.,
41 Great Russell Street, London, WC1B 3PL
© S. Elizabeth Bird and Rosina Umelo, 2018
All rights reserved.
Printed in the United Kingdom by Bell & Bain Ltd, Glasgow

Distributed in the United States, Canada and Latin America by
Oxford University Press, 198 Madison Avenue, New York, NY 10016,
United States of America.

The right of S. Elizabeth Bird and Rosina Umelo to be identified as the
author of this publication is asserted by them in accordance with the
Copyright, Designs and Patents Act, 1988.

A Cataloguing-in-Publication data record for this book
is available from the British Library.

ISBN: 9781849049580

This book is printed using paper from registered sustainable
and managed sources.

www.hurstpublishers.com

In memory of those who did not survive

CONTENTS

CONTENTS

MAPS

(All four maps cartography by Bill Nelson, © Bill Nelson, 2018)

ILLUSTRATIONS

(Unless noted otherwise, photos are provided by the Umelo family, or prepared from memorabilia owned by the family)

ILLUSTRATIONS

ACKNOWLEDGEMENTS

Thanks go from both of us to Michael Dwyer and the staff at Hurst, especially Daisy Leitch, for believing in the project and guiding it from proposal to completion. We also thank the two anonymous reviewers, both for their encouraging comments and their helpful suggestions for improvement. In addition, we each have those we would like to thank:

Rosina Umelo: Many thanks are due to the Imperial War Museum Department of Documents for taking in the typescript in 1979 for safe-keeping, and many more to Prof. Liz for bringing it out again. At the time of writing, staring into an uncertain future, I didn't risk mention-ing names but now I thank God for the friendship of sister-Nigerwives, Mary, Isobel, Wendy and Leslie, the support of Fr O'Sullivan and Fr O'Connell, Sr Mary Thomas and Dr Anne Seymour, memories of my husband John and mother-in-law Ukwa, and the love of my children.

Elizabeth Bird: Most important, I thank Rosina Umelo for her wel-come and willingness to share her story and her memories. For me this has been a delightful and rewarding collaboration. I would also like to thank her six children for their help in facilitating our meetings and finding family photos and memorabilia that are used in this book. I acknowledge the support of the American Council of Learned Societies and the University of South Florida, who funded archival and interview research for my earlier book, some of which proved useful for this project. Thanks to Amy Staples and the National Museum of African Art, Smithsonian Institution; Don Davis and the Archives of the American Friends Services Committee, Philadelphia; and Al Venter, all of whom provided photos for use in this book, and to Bill Nelson for

ACKNOWLEDGEMENTS

his excellent cartography. Thanks to Fraser Ottanelli, co-author of my previous Nigeria-related book, for his encouragement and friendship, and to my Nigerian friends, especially Chuck Nduka-Eze, Renny Nwosa, Richie Omo, Louis and Marcella Odogwu, and Ify and Mary Uraih. Special thanks to Dili Ezughah, a former schoolmate of Eze Umelo, who put me in touch with the Umelo family, to Simon Achuzia, who shared some of his experience as the son of a Nigerwife, and to the members of the social media site, Nigeria Nostalgia Project. And thanks to Nigerwives Wendy Ijioma, for her thoughts and insights, and Leslie Mitchell (Ofoegbu), for sharing a wartime list of Nigerwives. Finally, I thank my husband Graham Tobin and my sons Tom Tobin and Daniel Bird Tobin, for their never-failing love and support.

PART I

THE ROAD TO BIAFRA

S. Elizabeth Bird

PROLOGUE

LIVING FROM HOPE TO HOPE

One cold morning in 1950s London, Rosina ('Rose') Martin struck up a conversation with a young Nigerian on a station platform—Royal Oak, she recalls. The two were worlds apart; John Umelo, born in Eastern Nigeria, had come to London in the waning days of colonialism, 'thinking the streets were paved with gold'. Rose was born and raised in Frodsham, Cheshire, a small market town of barely 5,000, about sixteen miles south of Liverpool. Over the next days and weeks, their relationship grew; defying social norms, they first lived together, had a son, and then married in 1961.

Nigeria had gained independence from Britain in 1960, and was poised to become the 'Lion of Africa'—a thriving, resource-rich nation feeling a surge of optimism and pride. Many Nigerians returned home to share in this hope for the future, and in 1964, the Umelos and their three children left for Eastern Nigeria. Rose began teaching Latin in Enugu, the region's capital, and the family enjoyed a quiet, pleasant life, soon welcoming their fourth child. Two years later, they found themselves caught in Nigeria's brutal Civil War, following the secession of the predominantly Igbo Eastern Region of Nigeria, renamed Biafra.

The war broke out in July 1967, and by October, Nigerian Federal troops were poised to take Enugu. Like many others, the Umelo family fled to John's ancestral home to the south. From there, they moved from place to place as the war closed in. When it ended in 1970, with Biafra's surrender, over a million people had died, most from starvation.

Throughout the war, Rose kept notes and started crafting a narrative that captured the day-to-day reality of living in Biafra—from excitement at the beginning to despair at the end. She completed her account soon after the war. While she went on to a successful career as a novelist and editor, her war account was never published, and eventually she loaned the manuscript to the Imperial War Museum in London, hoping that one day, 'perhaps in 100 years', someone would want to read it.

It was a little sooner—just a few years shy of fifty years—when I came across Rose's manuscript. It was early in a project that would consume several years and eventually result in a book on a little-known civilian massacre that happened early in the Nigerian Civil War, across the Niger River from Biafra.[1] Rose's vivid account of life in the East didn't fit that project, but it stuck with me. Some years later, I returned to it, with the idea of finally getting her work published. The IWM had no records of where Rose might be, and suggested it was unlikely she was still living. I turned to the twenty-first century world of social media, hoping to prove them wrong. An enquiry on Nigeria Nostalgia Project, a popular Facebook site, revealed a generation of Nigerians who had fond memories of Rose's young-adult novels. And then came the message I'd been hoping for—from a Nigerian who had been a classmate of Rose and John's eldest son, Eze. Before long, I was talking to Rose by email, learning that, though widowed, she was very much alive, and now living in East London, with several of her six children nearby. We soon met, and our collaboration was born.[2]

Her account, which I have edited and annotated, is the centre of this book. To frame her story for today's readers, I offer background on the war, with special attention to Britain's involvement. I then turn to the circumstances that led to her unlikely move to Nigeria as a 'Nigerwife', using information from our email conversations and meetings at her home, and I conclude with a brief account of Rose's post-war life and career, with reflections on Biafra after five decades. From the beginning, Rose insisted she had never wanted to write 'a steamy white-woman-in-war-torn-jungle' account, and her narrative reflects that desire. As she describes it, 'I began to record what I saw around me, hoping one day someone would ask of Biafra, "How was it? What was it like?"'

It was that impulse that spoke to me as an anthropologist. Perhaps more than any other scholars, we anthropologists find purpose in capturing the stories and experiences of others. We do it in all sorts of ways—observation, interviews, surveys, letters, diaries—basically anything that will offer a window into those experiences. Sometimes, we engage with many stories in an attempt to create a kind of composite picture; this is the approach I took in the dozens of interviews conducted to reconstruct the history of the Asaba Massacre. At other times, the experience of one person provides the core, and here Rose's story stands alone.

The story of Biafra has long been dominated by 'big picture' histories and war memoirs of male politicians and military leaders: 'more than two-thirds of those who recorded their experiences of the Nigerian Civil War are male. In addition, of about 55 memoirs and non-fiction accounts written on the war, only two are by women.'[3] And most of these male authors had a political axe to grind. In contrast, Rose's story is apolitical; like other civilians caught up in the war, she found herself in a situation not of her own making, just having to make the best of it. As she noted later, 'it wasn't a factual account of day-by-day action, more like glimpses through the fog of war', adding that 'the manuscript was never about me!' Whether she knew it or not, in many ways Rose took the stance of an anthropologist herself. She was an outsider, and this stance made her acutely aware of mundane things that any local would have taken for granted. Her experience could never perfectly mirror that of the villagers around her; she knew that her identity automatically brought special attention and sometimes benefits. But as the war dragged on, she gradually became less and less the outsider, as she struggled to survive alongside her in-laws and neighbours. Step by step, she 'became' a Biafran; she planted, harvested, mended, and helped care for the sick and dying. And while the war raged around her, she gave birth in a makeshift camp under a roof of palm-fronds, tended by a traditional midwife and surrounded by her family. As she commented, after re-reading the manuscript after so many years, 'it moved from being about "them" to being about "us"'.

The authors of the only major 'bottom up' history of the war, which captured the memories of dozens of Biafrans thirty years after the war, argued for the importance of listening to the voices of ordinary people, which at that time had mostly been addressed in fictional accounts.[4] At the same time, they noted that studies based on memory can suffer from 'feedback': 'published sources, autobiographies, and more or less fictional accounts ... have influenced the way the war is remembered, and they are continuing to do so'.[5] Rose was writing her account during the war, completing the final chapter immediately afterwards. As she says, 'the war was so much more than the big events that catch the news'; rather it was a mundane, day-to-day slog, punctuated with moments of pain and hope. But if daily life seemed mundane, Rose's writing most certainly is not. As an anonymous reviewer commented, 'Her prose is calm, clear, informative and in places also very beautiful.' As a newcomer, she noticed not only the everyday details that locals might overlook, but also the unexpected flashes of beauty—the rich exuberance of scarlet flowers or 'The glow-worms in the grass ... hundreds of tiny yellow-green lights'.

And so our intention in bringing this book together was not just to tell the story of the Umelo family but also to offer readers the opportunity to understand the experience of a war that, while it changed the history of Nigeria, has often been forgotten elsewhere. Her story is unusual, offering a direct insight into experience, without benefit of hindsight. And that is how she wanted it presented today; she decided not to revisit the text, while allowing me to edit and annotate it in order to explain some points to the contemporary reader. We do not take a political position on the rights or wrongs of Biafran secession, although we do take issue with the way some of those involved conducted the conflict.

As a white foreigner, Rose did not experience the war in the same way as many others, but as she put it, she was indeed one of the millions 'living from hope to hope'. And as she shows, women in particular faced the heavy burden of keeping their children alive and families together. Rose's story is unique in its details, yet universal in its focus on how civilians, buffeted by the decisions of ambitious men, suffer and survive.

1

FROM COLONIALISM TO WAR

In Britain, the United States, and elsewhere, the Nigerian Civil War entered national consciousness in mid-1968, when print and broadcast media were flooded with searing images of starving children, swollen with the tell-tale signs of severe kwashiorkor. Biafra became a byword for starvation, sparking everything from food drives to sick jokes. The relatively new medium of television was at the forefront, showcasing urgent reports from hospitals and feeding stations across Biafra.

Yet many were (and probably still are) unaware of how and why this tragedy had happened. Journalistic accounts of the war often described it as a 'tribal conflict', which safely consigned it to the world of the 'other'—Africans killing Africans for reasons that were probably unfathomable. It was as if Nigeria, a newly-independent country with rich resources and a promising future, had somehow turned upon itself, driven purely by 'tribal' hatred. For the Umelo family, the promise of Nigeria was very real; when they arrived in Enugu, ready to start a new life, they could not know that within two years their home would be engulfed in a brutal war, which seemed destined to tear the new nation apart.

Yet the seeds for secession and war had been sown many years before, and to understand how the tragedy of Biafra unfolded, we need to take a longer view of Nigerian history from colonial times to the war itself, which had been raging for months before the world fully came to grips with it. My intent is not to offer a full account of Nigeria's complex history, but rather to sketch it in broad strokes, showing first how the country spiralled into war in 1967, and then how the war progressed to the point of mass starvation and defeat for Biafra.[1] As we shall see, the histories of Nigeria, Biafra—and the Umelo family itself—are tied inextricably to that of Britain.

The Colonial Legacy

Nigeria, a nation of almost 924,000 square kilometers, is of course a colonial creation, cobbled together by the British from many independent West African territories. Although the number of distinct cultures indigenous to modern Nigeria is still debated, there are well over 250 ethno-linguistic groups, stretching from the Atlantic coast to the edge of the Sahara desert. There had long been clear cultural differences between the Northern and the Southern territories of what became Nigeria, and to this day, the North and South co-exist uncomfortably.

Before colonisation, the Southern territories included the dominant Yoruba people to the west and the Igbo to the east, along with many other cultures, such as the ancient Edo kingdom of Benin, one of the most highly developed states in West Africa. The Yoruba had a political structure led by chiefs of different areas, while the Igbo lived in clustered village groups presided over by councils of senior men. European powers had made incursions into the coastal areas of the Southern territories for centuries, mainly to exploit rich natural resources and obtain slaves. European merchants established trade routes to the Atlantic coast in the sixteenth century, with slave trading as a central component. The slave trade was abolished by Britain in 1807, and was gradually replaced by palm oil, the main cash crop of the colonial era, and other forms of commerce. In a bid to protect its commercial interests from other European powers, Britain annexed the important port of Lagos as a Crown Colony in 1861, and in 1886 granted the recently-formed Royal Niger Company a monopoly over trade in the Niger River basin, opening the door to more extensive, inland incursions.

The 1884–5 Berlin Conference had set off the colonial 'Scramble for Africa', and Britain set out to consolidate its influence. If faced with resistance, it used punitive solutions; for instance, Britain had long traded with the kingdom of Benin, but when Benin resisted the expansion of British influence, a military force sacked the city in 1897, razed it to the ground, looted its magnificent artworks, and removed the Oba (king). In 1900 Britain revoked the charter of the Royal Niger Company; its Niger Coast Protectorate, added to Lagos Colony in 1906, was renamed the Protectorate of Southern Nigeria. Meanwhile, the long history of trade in the South had led to the beginning of missionary activities as early as the fifteenth century, with the arrival of the Portuguese. By the mid-nineteenth century, missionaries from several orders flowed into to the area, building churches and establishing mission schools, dedicated to sweeping away 'pagan' religions.

In contrast, the North had little in common with the South, having been linked for centuries with Muslim North Africa, the Middle East, and Southern Europe, through trade routes across the Sahara. Islam spread through the majority Hausa population between the eleventh and fourteenth centuries, while the Fulani pastoral nomads moved into the area around the same time. By the nineteenth century, the Fulani dominated the seven existing Hausa kingdoms, and had established the highly-centralised Sokoto Caliphate, one of the most significant African empires of its day. After the Berlin Conference, the British began looking to expand trade in the North through the Royal Niger Company, and by the late nineteenth century, these ambitions were transformed into a plan to 'pacify' the North and bring it into the Empire. In 1902, troops under Frederick Lugard moved on the Caliphate, which soon conceded to British rule and was reorganised as the Northern Nigeria Protectorate.

In 1914 the British Colonial Office merged the two Protectorates into a new entity, dubbed 'Nigeria', with Lugard as Governor-General. Rather than facilitating true unity between the disparate regions, Lugard's governing style effectively consolidated their differences. His policy of 'indirect rule' co-opted local rulers, who, in return for prestige, security, and limited interference in internal matters gave up control of trade, taxation, and finance.[2] This cemented the autocratic style of the existing Islamic power, and the British found it a comfortable fit. Colonial authorities discouraged Christian evangelising and missionary schools, for fear of alienating these local leaders, so literacy remained extremely low.

In the South, indirect rule was never a good fit, especially in Igboland, with its long tradition of (male) egalitarianism and resistance to centralised authority. As Chinua Achebe wryly noted, 'Those who visit the Igbo in their home or run into them abroad or in literature are not always prepared for their tense and cocky temperament. The British called them argumentative.'[3] But they saw opportunities, and the Igbo quickly embraced British models of commerce, education, and religion in the first half of the twentieth century. By the 1950s, while 2 million children were enrolled in schools in the South, the number was only 238,000 in the North.[4] By 1966, almost half of the 4,500 graduates of Nigerian universities were Igbo, and many of the more affluent sought higher education in Europe.[5] And while there was initial resistance to missionaries, Roman Catholicism and Anglicanism, the vehicles through which education and literacy were spread, came to dominate the South.

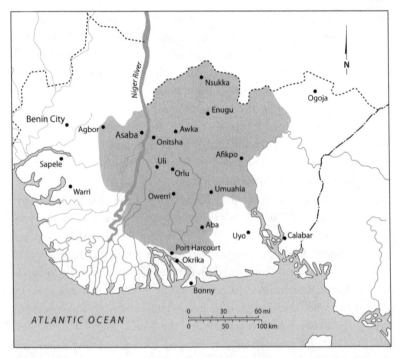

Map 1: The borders of traditional Igboland (shaded), mostly located to the east of the Niger river, but extending west. Cartography by Bill Nelson.

For years, the Igbo flocked into business, government, and the professions, spreading throughout the country, including the North, which had a shortage of qualified people. By the 1960s, Igbos held two-thirds of the senior jobs in the Nigerian Railway Corporation, as well as 75 percent of diplomatic positions.[6] Indeed, as Independence approached, the British needed the Igbo to 'indigenise' the civil services and commerce throughout the country. However, although they performed crucial functions, in the North the Igbo lived in segregated *Sabon Gari* or 'strangers' quarters', and distrust and resentment were always just under the surface. Effectively, British policies had exacerbated existing differences, rather than fostering the common Nigerian identity that Britain officially espoused.

By the mid-twentieth century, in anticipation of Independence, the colonial authorities were trying to foster the development of a representative, constitutional Nigerian government, while maintaining British interests. But the various iterations continued to favour the North over other areas, leading to the formation of political parties that each represented a region and its dominant ethnic group. At Independence, there were three official Regions (North, West, and East), with Southern Nigeria divided by the River Niger between the Yoruba-dominated West and the Igbo-dominated East, and three major, ethnically-based parties. Nationalist leaders Herbert Macaulay and Nnamdi Azikiwe argued ardently for a pan-Nigerian identity, creating a party (the NCNC, National Council of Nigerian Citizens) to further this goal, but it eventually evolved into an organisation supported mainly by Easterners.

Independence and Afterwards

At Independence in 1960, with its population at just over 60 million, Nigeria seemed poised for greatness. As Chinua Achebe wrote in his memoir of Biafra,

> We had no doubt where we were going. We were going to inherit freedom ... Nigeria was enveloped by a certain assurance of an unbridled destiny, of an overwhelming excitement about life's promise ...[7]

Yet the political structure left in place by the British soon showed its flaws. Beginning as a three-region Federal state, the country added a fourth region, the Midwest, in 1963. Benin City was its capital, and although the Edo were its major ethnic group, the Midwest was the most multi-ethnic region, with substantial populations of Igbo and other ethnic groups. [MAP 2]. Each region—and by extension its dominant party—was allocated seats in the Federal Government based on population, laying the groundwork for continued political division. The North had about 50 percent of the population, and thus the largest representation, as well as the support of Britain.

The importance of population numbers set the scene for major conflicts around national censuses, especially in 1962–3, when there was

Map 2: The four Regions of Nigeria, before the Civil War. Cartography by Bill Nelson.

extensive evidence of fraud. In effect, Northern dominance produced a situation in which a coalition was the only way to form a government, and this led to constantly shifting alliances. The elections of 1964 were rife with violence and intimidation; they were followed by another contested election in the Western Region in October 1965, producing major violence and deaths, and serious fears for the stability of the West. As Bourne notes, the nation 'was becoming a deadly combination of zero-sum game and roulette. The honeymoon joy of Independence was the prologue to a deepening crisis.'[8]

The volatile combination of regional/ethnic tensions and widespread fraud and corruption prompted the first of the coups that would eventually lead to the East's decision to secede. On 15 January 1966, a group of military officers attempted to overthrow civil rule, citing the need to defeat corruption. The coup leaders killed several prominent Northern leaders, including the Federal Prime Minister and the premiers of the Northern and Western Regions. The coup failed, and most of its leaders were arrested, but many Northerners believed it to be an Igbo power grab, since many of the coup leaders were Igbo, and significant Igbo politicians were spared, including the President, Nnamdi Azikiwe, who was out of the country. The commanding officer of the Nigerian army, Maj.-Gen. Johnson Aguiyi-Ironsi, who played a central role in putting down the coup in the South, became the new Head of State.

However, suspicions turned toward Ironsi, also an Igbo, when he began putting in place measures advocated by the coup leaders. These were intended to undermine regionalism and corruption, and nurture national unity; Ironsi abolished the Federal system, placing the regions under the direct control of the government in Lagos, and amalgamated the regions' civil services. Political activity was banned for two years, in an attempt to undermine the influence of the ethnically-based parties, and military governors were appointed to run each region, among them the Igbo governor of the East, Lt.-Col. Chukwuemeka ('Emeka') Odumegwu Ojukwu.

While many welcomed these measures as significant reforms, some in the North and West were furious about the brutal murder of their leaders, and Northerners resented the threat to their dominance. The failed coup, along with Ironsi's actions, provided the opportunity to act on a long-festering animosity against the Igbo; mob riots directed against them broke out in Northern and Western Nigeria in May 1966. This was followed by a second military coup, this time led by Northern officers. Scores of Igbo soldiers were captured and killed, and Ironsi was abducted. He was killed, along with Lt.-Col. Francis Fajuyi, the first military governor of the Western Region, who although a Yoruba, was a hero in the East, because it was said he had refused to hand over his guest, Ironsi, and thus died with him. On 29 July 1966, the coup leaders agreed on Lt.-Col. Yakubu Gowon, a thirty-one-year-old Christian Northerner from an ethnic minority, as Supreme Commander of the Nigerian Armed forces and Head of a new Federal Military Government (FMG).

It was expected by many that Gowon would announce the secession of the North, but, probably urged against it by Britain, he instead re-instated the Federal system.[9] But Gowon was unable or unwilling to control the escalation of violence, mostly directed against Igbos, and in the North, killing and looting escalated into systematic massacres, which continued for months during the autumn of 1966. At times soldiers turned a blind eye or even actively joined civilian mobs in slaughtering Igbos.[10] These 'pogroms', as they became known by the Igbo, caused thousands to flee to their ancestral homes in the East and Midwest, by train, plane, or any other transport they could find. Many left everything behind them, and had to rely on their extended families to take them in, as Rose Umelo describes in her narrative. While definitive figures are elusive, many estimates suggest that at least 30,000 Igbos were killed, and more than a million fled.[11] And, as Irish writer/politician Conor Cruise O'Brien noted, this massive death toll and population movement received little coverage in Britain and else-where; he concluded that Africans killing Africans failed to arouse the 'humanitarian rhetoric' that would stir action.[12]

By early 1967, Nigerian unity was increasingly precarious. Leaders of both the Western and Northern Regions had at times pondered seces-sion, but were now in an uneasy alliance. Fuelled by the pogroms, the grievances of the East were the most serious. A two-day summit of Federal authorities and the country's regional governors in Aburi, Ghana, raised hopes for a more loose confederate structure, but an apparent compromise fell apart, and on 27 May 1967, Gowon declared a state of emergency and announced that the country would be divided into twelve new states. This would break the East into three separate units; only one would be Igbo-dominated. The division could separate the Igbos from control of the oil-producing areas of the Niger Delta, which had begun to loom large in the nation's economy. Faced with the trauma of the pogroms, the failure of Aburi, and this political restructuring, Ojukwu decided to secede, announcing the establishment of the sovereign state of Biafra on 30 May 1967.[13] While the new Biafra was predominantly Igbo, it also included many other ethnic groups, such as the Ibibio, Efik, Ijaw, and Ogoni, whose commitment to the new entity varied.[14]

The ambitious Ojukwu, then only thirty-three years old, believed that Biafra's oil riches and highly-educated elite would sustain the new nation, and that it would find allies internationally. The new Biafran leaders contrasted themselves with a Nigeria beset by outmoded traditions and corruption: 'The image they presented to the world was of a new nation that confidently and unapologetically embodied key characteristics of modernity'.[15] Meanwhile, Federal authorities insisted that the unity of the nation must be preserved, and that they would be supported by an international community that would see the dissolution of Nigeria as a threat to Africa's stability. And both sides were very aware that the country's rich oil resources were located in the newly-named Biafra, and the only refinery was in Port Harcourt.[16] Britain, although also on the side of unity, was taking a 'wait and see' attitude before making any major commitment.

Nigeria at War

At this point, Gowon and his FMG believed that a 'police action', backed up by an economic blockade, would quickly put down secession; no-one imagined it would take almost three years for Biafra to capitulate. Accounts and discussions of the thirty-month Nigerian Civil War have filled thousands of pages of scholarly and journalistic analysis.[17] Once again, my intent here is only to outline the progress of the war, offering a larger context to Rose Umelo's personal account of survival.

When hostilities began, Biafra was densely populated, supporting about 14 million people, including 9 million Igbo and many smaller ethnic groups. This population density, and the resulting pressure on natural resources, had been one factor in the migrations that had long taken Igbo people into other parts of Nigeria, and it was a key weakness that Ojukwu failed to understand at the outset. Driven out by the pogroms, between one and two million had now returned to their homeland, putting additional pressure on farmland and other resources, which had always been supplemented by the import from other areas of Nigeria of protein sources like cattle. The sudden population increase, coupled with an economic blockade placed by the FMG, prevented the import of all goods and resources, and set the stage for the tragic famine that eventually followed.

The first shots were fired on 6 July 1967, with an advance by the Federal First Infantry Division into the northeastern corner of Biafra, and a few days later, Ogoja, a largely ethnic-minority town near the border with Cameroon, was captured. Ogoja was one of Biafra's few meat-producing areas, and its capture began the slow process of cutting off the Igbo heartland from established sources of food. Other neighbouring areas also fell quickly; by the end of the month, the university town of Nsukka was captured. Meanwhile, Federal forces of the Third Division took the island of Bonny, off the Biafran coast, by sea. This was a dangerous blow to Biafra, since it brought the Federal forces within striking distance of Port Harcourt, Biafra's main port and site of its only oil refinery. At this point, it looked as if the FMG's predictions of a 'quick kill' would come true.

However, the Biafrans responded on 9 August with an unexpected and audacious move—sending 3,000 troops over the recently-constructed Niger Bridge from the important Eastern market town of Onitsha into the Midwest town of Asaba. Facing little opposition, they fanned out southwest, and westwards to Benin City, capital of the Midwest Region, finally reaching the crossroads town of Ore in the Western Region, within striking distance of Lagos. There they were stopped by the hastily-raised Federal Second Division, under the command of Col. Murtala Muhammed. By early October, the Biafrans had been pushed back to the Niger River where they crossed the bridge into Onitsha, before blowing up the eastern spans behind them.

Much has been written about Ojukwu's motivations for invading the Midwest—whether it was simply a diversion from the main action to the north, or perhaps part of a grandiose plan to enlist the West into the secession battle, or even to conquer Nigeria itself. In any event, the invasion was a major turning point, with the FMG abandoning any idea of a 'police action' and launching all-out war. During their occupation of the Midwest, the Biafrans had not been welcomed by the non-Igbo majority, and with the retaking of the territory by the Federal troops, civilians turned on the Igbo-speaking minority, killing thousands in Benin City and elsewhere.[18]

After Muhammed's troops pushed on to the Niger River, the worst atrocity against Midwest Igbo-speakers took place in Asaba, on the west bank of the river. Muhammed had planned to send troops across the bridge to take the strategic town of Onitsha, but was prevented by the destruction of the bridge. Over the course of several days, Federal troops slaughtered over 1,000 civilians, including around 700 men and boys in a single, bloody massacre on 7 October.[19] These extensive civilian deaths, added to the devastation of the pogroms, confirmed for the Biafrans their belief that defeat would inevitably result in genocide, setting the war on its doomed path.

As Muhammed reached Asaba in October, the First Division was taking the Biafran capital, Enugu, prompting thousands of Biafrans, including the Umelos, to flee. The Third Marine Commando Division captured the important Eastern city of Calabar that same month, subsequently sealing off Biafra's border with Cameroon. With the island of Bonny, controlling access to the Atlantic, also in federal hands, the Igbo heartland in Biafra was now encircled and landlocked. At this point, the international expectation was that the war would be over by Christmas. A report in *Newsweek*, declaring that 'the sun was setting' on Biafra, was typical of press pronouncements in October 1967.[20]

Meanwhile, Britain had come down firmly on the side of the FMG, and rapidly became its largest arms supplier. It was expected that Murtala Muhammed's forces would now execute the coup de grâce by swiftly taking Onitsha and linking up with the First Division (under Mohammed Shuwa) in the East. However his poorly-trained troops now found themselves stuck on the wrong side of the Niger, from where Murtala Muhammed launched a series of river assaults, using flotillas of commandeered ferries and small boats. The result was a disaster, with thousands of Federal troops slaughtered by Biafran bombardment, or drowning.

This created a stalemate, and the opportunity for a quick end to the war was lost. Indeed, the Biafrans, fuelled by fears of genocide stoked by the Midwestern massacres, as well as their decimation of the Second Division, fought with new vigour. Muhammed eventually crossed the Niger further north, and captured Onitsha—but not before a fierce Biafran ambush had killed many more of his troops at Abagana on 31 March 1968, when a homemade rocket missile (known as *ogbunigwe*) hit a truck carrying gasoline, setting off a deadly chain reaction.

Abagana was the last major military success for the Biafrans, and by May 1968, the crucial oil town of Port Harcourt had fallen, and all supplies, including arms and food, were being flown into Uli, where a road had been converted into an airstrip. By mid-1968, Biafra had lost

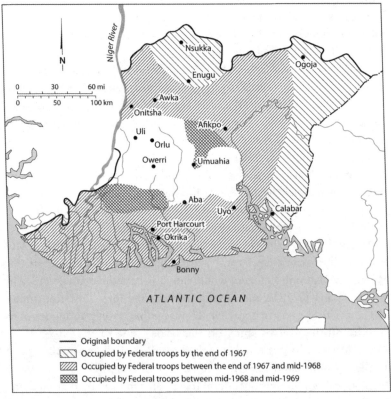

Map 3: The changing boundaries of Biafra, 1967–69, as the territory shrank from the entire former Eastern Region into a small enclave in the Igbo heartland. Cartography by Bill Nelson.

most of the land controlled by non-Igbo groups, which had included almost all of the main food-producing areas. The country had shrunk from 29,484 square miles to an Igbo heartland of 3,600 square miles; it was in that small enclave that the Umelo family and many like them were struggling to survive. Food shortages were hitting everyone—and children most of all. Once again, predictions were rife that surrender was inevitable. [MAP 3]

And yet Biafra fought on. Engineers and scientists, committed to the Biafran cause, had achieved remarkable success, creating ingenious home-made weapons and establishing makeshift oil refineries that supplied the army.[21] The government bureaucracy continued to function, and the civilian population pitched in by recycling everything, putting every available piece of land to farming, and developing their own small refineries to provide fuel. From the beginning, Ojukwu's government had insisted that the aim of the Gowon regime was to wipe out the Igbo, and the actions of Nigerian 'liberating' troops often served to bolster that narrative, strengthening patriotic fervour. The civilian killings in the Midwest were followed by the slaughter of over 300 worshippers in the cathedral at Onitsha, and reports of more massacres when troops took Calabar. And in spite of Federal denials that civilians were targeted by air strikes, bombing raids on markets, hospitals, and residential areas were becoming a regular, terrifying reality. To most Biafrans, surrender was assumed to mean certain death.

The Ojukwu government worked to make an international case for genocide, hoping to bring international support. They listed multiple atrocities in a document sent to the UN Committee on Human Rights, in February 1968, starting with the 1966 pogroms,[22] and a follow-up letter to UN General Secretary U Thant argued that the pogroms and other outrages constituted 'a genocide of an enormity only equaled in recent times by the experience of Jews from the Nazis'.[23] However, this argument gained little traction. Although some of the bombing raids and other incidents were reported in the international press, coverage was spotty and there was little clear sense that this was anything but a local, 'tribal' fight. The 'humanitarian rhetoric' that had failed to emerge after the pogroms remained elusive. Serious malnutrition had been appearing in Biafra by late 1967, and was reaching crisis proportions by 1968, but the world's gaze was elsewhere—on the Middle East, Czechoslovakia, Vietnam.

All that changed in June 1968. Lasse Heerten describes the moment, when 'a new icon of the Third World was born':

> That day, the British daily newspaper *Sun* devoted most of its first three pages to articles and images that Michael Leapman and his photographer Ronald Burton had sent home ... For the first time, a large British and international public was confronted with the ghastly images of Biafra's starving children. That evening, the British television station, Independent Television News (ITN), aired the pictures that Alan Hart shot at the Holy Ghost Fathers missionary station—the first TV images of the humanitarian crisis to be broadcast ... In the ensuing months, Western media feverishly reported about the West African conflict. The images of the 'Biafran babies', tiny, malformed human beings doomed to die of hunger, lodged 'Biafra' in the mental landscapes of people around the globe.[24]

As I discuss in the next chapter, this new awareness finally sparked a debate, especially in Britain, about the morality of supporting a government that was apparently using starvation as a weapon of war. But mostly, it served to mobilise that dormant 'humanitarian rhetoric' in ways that ultimately did not serve the Biafran political cause. Ojukwu's attempts to enlist international support for his cause had been fairly unsuccessful from the outset. In 1963, the Organisation of African Unity (OAU) had committed to maintaining colonial boundaries, and was reluctant to recognise Biafra for fear this would start a rush of unrest and secession throughout Africa. Tanzania recognised Biafra in April 1968, followed shortly by Zambia, and some other states like Gabon and Ivory Coast were sympathetic. Outside Africa, only Haiti officially recognised the country, but not until March 1969. From early in the war, France had expressed sympathy; it never offered formal recognition but did provide both the arms and relief supplies that helped keep Biafra going.

After mid-1968, international efforts focused on bringing humanitarian relief to Biafran children, rather than debating the political positions of each side. Large-scale airlifts of food and medicines began from many nations, using volunteer and mercenary pilots who flew into the now-famous airstrip at Uli. For those civilians trapped in the shrinking Biafra, a war that began in such hopeful expectation was becoming simply a matter of survival; their cause was effectively lost. The Biafran military had small successes as the surviving enclave expanded and contracted; the town of Owerri, which features so prominently in Rose Umelo's account, changed hands three times before it was all over. In this constantly shifting landscape, civilians might encounter both Biafran and Federal troops; both could be very dangerous. American Red Cross volunteer John Sherman worked in the Biafran area of Elele (about 50 km. south of Owerri), after it had been re-occupied by the FMG. He described a young boy named Pius, who had 'adopted our medical team':

> He should be the poster child of this war. His father was peacefully living in his village when the Nigerians captured it and lost it almost immediately. When he came out of hiding after the Biafrans had regained control, the Biafran soldiers were angry that he and some other men had not joined the army, so they accused them of being spies. They shot them right in front of their families. Pius' mother, after more battles and more wins and losses, was taken captive by the Nigerians. Pius last saw her as she was screaming and struggling in the back of an army lorry headed north. The soldiers were laughing and pulling off her clothes.[25]

The Biafran leader Ojukwu had always maintained a cult of personality, refusing to listen to the advice of those who had come to believe that surrender was the only way to end the suffering of his people.[26] In the last year of the war, the Biafran government became increasingly paranoid and authoritarian. Reversals were blamed on saboteurs or 'sabos'; in particular, non-Igbo people were widely believed to be subverting the Biafran cause and were harassed and killed.[27] Civilians endured endless roadblocks, searches and interrogations, and discipline among troops began to break down: 'Soldiers began to steal crops from farms and to kill animals belonging to the people they were supposed to protect.'[28] The military was running out of volunteers, and aggressive conscription tactics left families terrorised. Alfred Obiora, who was a young child during the war, later recalled that boys as young as fourteen were taken by force, and beaten if they resisted:

> Young boys no longer had the freedom to roam the villages, because they would immediately be taken away and sent to war. A typical conscription exercise consisted of three or four soldiers, armed to the teeth, suddenly swooping on the village ... while some went from house to house in search of men of army age, others would hang outside the compounds, hoping to catch those attempting to escape.[29]

In mid-1969, Biafran forces made one final land offensive, in which they were supported by foreign mercenary pilots, who were not only flying in food and medical supplies but also weapons, many coming from France. The five-plane Biafran Air Force had some success in disrupting Nigerian air operations, but it was short-lived. Meanwhile, the plight of civilians had grown increasingly dire: 'towards the end of the war, up to or even more than one-third of the Biafran population consisted of refugees in camps'.[30]

As 1970 began, Federal troops had almost completely overrun the remaining Biafran enclave. Refugees streamed into Owerri, but the beleaguered town was quickly recaptured by Federal troops, and there was nowhere left to flee. On 11 January, Ojukwu abruptly announced that he was leaving the country, ostensibly to explore peace options. He flew to Ivory Coast with his family and entourage, leaving his deputy, Philip Effiong, to order Biafran troops to lay down their arms. The dream of Biafra ended with formal surrender on 15 January; the name of Biafra was officially expunged from the map of Nigeria.

And although many Biafran Igbo had been terrified that defeat would mean their total annihilation, this did not happen. Gowon made his famous 'No Victor, No Vanquished' statement, and a slow process of rebuilding and reintegration began. Families like the Umelos gradually returned to towns and villages that had been almost completely destroyed, and slowly tried to rebuild their lives.

2

BIAFRA AND BRITAIN

A POSTCOLONIAL TRAGEDY

In the autumn of 1968, Rosina Umelo managed to get a letter out of Biafra to her mother, who passed it to her home-town newspaper, the *Runcorn Weekly News*. It wasn't her first, but it seemed to mark a change. Previous letters had been optimistic; even as she described the terror of bombing raids and the growing food shortage, Rose had painted a picture of strength and unity:

Everyone in the village works extremely hard. The usual idea of life in the tropics as a day-long drowse in the palm tree shade is quite wrong ... As well as farming, many people also have other jobs—sewing, shoe mending, bicycle or general repairs ...Life goes on as normally as it does because of the amazing resilience and resourcefulness of the people ...[1]

The more recent letter, used in an October story, was bleaker, describing the starvation that was spreading through the beleaguered territory:

They were all ages, from teenagers to tiny babies, whose skin looked several sizes too big for their withered bodies. The very sick were too weak to cry noisily, but the tears often welled out of their eyes, and rolled silently down their patient faces.[2]

23

As we shall see, Rose's letters sparked action in her own small English community, representing a small piece of a movement that was growing throughout Britain, following the June 1968 media revelations of a humanitarian crisis. A war that had been raging for almost a year suddenly began to loom large in Britain, and Rose Umelo's story points to the web of connections that tied Biafra and Britain together. People around the world had also woken up to the horrors of what was happening; in the United States, which remained officially neutral (although in practice, pro-FMG), grass-roots movements developed, and citizen opinion was internationally mobilised.[3] But the shock of Biafra was felt most deeply in Britain, where the long record of colonial and postcolonial ties left a much greater sense of responsibility. The legacy of Britain was engrained in Nigeria's educational and bureaucratic institutions, and indeed in its military—the Civil War pitted the Sandhurst-trained Gowon against the Oxford-educated Ojukwu. Before the war, there were about 15,000 British citizens in Nigeria, many of them in the East as teachers, business people, and medical personnel. Regarded as a peaceful and promising country, Nigeria had been a popular posting for idealistic young Britons with Voluntary Services Overseas (and their US counterpart, the Peace Corps). Meanwhile, the children (or more often the sons) of more affluent Nigerians streamed into Britain for training as doctors, lawyers, and scientists, while those with fewer resources, like John Umelo, also went to Britain to work in blue-collar jobs. Some met and married British women; wives of Nigerians married to foreign women in the immediate postcolonial years were most likely to be British.[4]

The British Policy: Realpolitik

In spite of these strong connections, it was only after 1968 that Biafra suddenly became 'the most consistently significant foreign policy issue facing the [British] government'[5] of Labour Prime Minister Harold Wilson. History's verdict on the Wilson government's handling of the issue has not been kind; even in the immediate aftermath of the war, it was described as at worst an 'extraordinarily disgusting episode',[6] and at best, 'confused, guilt-ridden and deceptive',[7] bearing a significant degree of responsibility for the tragedy that befell so many civilians.

To understand that failure, we must revisit the early days of the war, tracing Britain's role; the eleven months of neglect was not an accident. When hostilities began, Britain was officially neutral, although in principle there was a prevailing sentiment to support the integrity of a nation the British had created. It was not long before Britain's more economic interests moved to the fore. As George Thomas, Minister of State for Commonwealth Affairs, noted,

> the sole immediate British interest in Nigeria is that the Nigerian economy should be brought back to a condition in which our substantial trade and investment in the country can be further developed, and particularly so we can regain access to important oil installations.[8]

Oil had become an especially pressing issue following the Six-Day Arab-Israeli War of June 1967, after which several Arab nations cut off oil supplies to Britain and the United States. To make up the shortfall, Britain wanted to increase Nigeria's share of its oil imports from 10 percent to 25 percent, and initially did not rule out the possibility of dealing with an oil-producing Biafra if secession prevailed.[9] However, after the Biafrans' failed incursion into the Midwest, and once it was apparent that the Federal Military Government (FMG) had the upper hand, the government settled into a clear, pro-Federal stance.[10] In itself, this was a legitimate choice, and one embraced by most other nations, since Biafra's secession was seen as a potential threat to the stability of Africa. But the implementation of the policy became deeply problematic, often characterised by deception and unwillingness to grasp and intervene in the unfolding humanitarian disaster.

Moral and economic support of the FMG quickly led to Britain's key role as arms supplier, justified early in the war as fulfilling its role as the 'traditional' source of arms to Nigeria.[11] It declined to provide jet fighters and bomber aircraft (which were later obtained from the Soviet Union), and heavy tanks, but did supply infantry weapons, light artillery, anti-aircraft guns, and armoured cars. The government started by defining its arms shipments as 'defensive' weaponry:

> We are justified in claiming that we could not reasonably withhold normal replacements. In the last resort, if the supply of the anti-aircraft guns becomes public knowledge, we would, of course, say that they are defensive weapons.[12]

Even this position was soon abandoned as the arms shipments escalated; indeed, the basic premise was untrue. Britain had provided less than 40 percent of Nigeria's armaments in the years 1964–5, about half by 1967, but almost 98 percent by 1969.[13] As early as the end of 1967, the Head of the Commonwealth Office news department was advising on how to head off press scrutiny, since 'If the actual facts become known such a line would undoubtedly damage our reputation for credibility with the Press'.[14]

However, the British government succeeded in heading off public scrutiny for almost a year after the outbreak of war. Key to this was a consistent denial of civilian casualties; the government knew that public opinion could swing against them if extensive abuses against civilians became known, and touted Gowon's Operational Code of Conduct, designed to govern troops' interaction with civilians.[15] Numerous reports of atrocities against civilians in the first nine months of the war—first the Midwest massacres, then further killing as Federal troops swept through Biafra, and then bombing raids on civilian targets—were publicly dismissed.

Yet Foreign Office records show that the government knew full well that there were serious problems with the conduct of the war. They knew that the FMG was 'indiscriminately bombing Eastern churches, schools and hospitals',[16] including the Mary Slessor hospital at Itu, which was bombed three times on 23 January 1968.[17] That February, the British High Commissioner noted the importance of warning the FMG about 'serious damage such bombings could create in alienating influential sectors of opinion abroad'.[18] Relief efforts, coordinated by the Red Cross, were underway in areas recently reoccupied by Federal troops, but local people were proving reluctant to come to the camps to receive food and medicine. The Red Cross was reporting that most villages around the recaptured Enugu and Nsukka were deserted after residents fled into the bush, terrified of expected massacres as troops arrived. These fears were not unreasonable; the Red Cross reported 'a good deal of indiscriminate killing of people who happened to be in the line of the Federal advance', as well as the removal of people from the camps for execution.[19]

Indeed, Gowon's goal of peaceful reintegration was constantly thwarted by some of his field commanders. Second Division

Commander Murtala Muhammed, who had presided over the carnage in the Midwest, was well known to have an 'ugly reputation', and fears about Third Division Commander Benjamin Adekunle (known as the 'Black Scorpion') were growing in London, especially after the occupation of Calabar in October 1967: 'the Red Cross believe that hundreds of people, including some Efiks, were rounded up and shot, including "all the male inmates of the mental hospital."' British officials reported that Adekunle was 'widely believed to be mentally unbalanced', while concluding that all the Divisional Commanders were abusing their authority.[20]

Yet Britain continued to state publicly that not only was the war going well, but it was being conducted honorably, and that the Biafrans were refusing to capitulate only because of deceitful propaganda that convinced them they had no choice. Generally the British press did not question this; most newspapers were content to take a pro-Federal stance. And as Jonathan Derrick, then a reporter for *West Africa* magazine, noted, the fact that the BBC accommodated the government's wishes was especially important, since BBC radio was by far the most influential news source internationally, including in both Nigeria and Biafra.[21] Early in the war, BBC reporter Frederick Forsyth had filed reports that contradicted the government position, enraging High Commissioner David Hunt and resulting in a reprimand from the BBC, followed by Forsyth's resignation. He recalls, 'I knew there was a conspiracy of silence way back in October 1967 ... There was a brutal and callous cynicism operated by my government...'[22] Forsyth later returned to Biafra, writing an influential, pro-Biafran book.[23]

By early 1968, a few were breaking ranks and writing unwelcome stories. For instance Matthew Rosa of the *Observer* described the bombing of many civilian targets, such as schools and hospitals.[24] In a confidential memo, Hunt, known for his strongly pro-Federal views, notes, 'I have never heard of Matthew Rosa ... His article reports what has become standard Biafran propaganda ...'.[25] He goes on to give talking points to be used when asked.

And so, in spite of regular predictions about the impending demise of Biafra, the war dragged on, with Britain supplying more and more of the arms needed, partly to counter both Soviet arms sales to Nigeria and growing French support for Biafra, which was interpreted as an attempt to damage British interests in West Africa. By April 1968, some journalists were venturing further into Biafra; four prominent British journalists witnessed (and wrote about) a bombing raid on the market-place at Aba, in which at least eighty people were killed. The *Times* correspondent William Norris later described the effect on the 'bustling market town':

> Now it was a scene of carnage such as I had never seen, and hope never to see again. Bodies and parts of bodies lay everywhere. Young girls, some of them pregnant, had been eviscerated; babies were headless, old men and women had been blown apart.... I saw no young men, and certainly no soldiers among the bodies.[26]

Norris notes, 'it is important to know that the British government had given solemn assurances to the House of Commons that no bombing of the civilian population in Biafra was taking place.'[27] On his return to London, Norris showed the photos he had taken to Commonwealth Secretary General, Arnold Smith, who was making attempts to broker a peace deal. Smith requested a meeting with Foreign Secretary Michael Stewart, which Norris also attended:

> He looked at the pictures coldly. 'Biafran propaganda,' he said. 'But I took the pictures myself,' I protested ... 'It's just Biafran propaganda,' Stewart repeated, and tossed the photos back across his desk.[28]

The government continued to maintain its official line, echoing that of the Nigerian government, in the face of numerous accounts to the contrary, supported by a mostly compliant press, at least during the first year of the war.[29] An official memo, for instance, dismissed the Biafrans' 1968 United Nations petition, which had documented many civilian atrocities: 'This sort of propaganda is only to be expected and is the sort that will gain the most sympathy in Britain ...'[30]

Nevertheless, the constant drip of horrifying stories from Biafra put the government under increasing pressure to defend its position. As Young notes, 'Nigeria was on the agenda of nearly half the Cabinet meetings in May–December 1968 and concern was expressed about public attitudes, arms policy and famine'.[31] Earlier, the government had publically minimised economic interests, while stressing that a short war, with a decisive Federal victory, would ensure the least number of civilian deaths. However, as the quick kill became a slow death for hundreds of thousands of Biafrans in 1968 ... the Wilson government was faced with the rather difficult talk of explaining how its sordid role had nothing at all to do with oil interests[32]

Public Response

Throughout 1968, the government faced questions and concerns about its role as arms dealer, and its apparently perfunctory attempts to broker peace. Questions were asked in Parliament, and petitions and protests were organised. But the government had a decisive majority, and the protests were relatively small; a June 1968 march had only about 700 participants, while a petition calling for a halt to arms sales garnered only 2,000 signatures.[33]

At the same time, the Biafran claims of intentional genocide were starting to resonate, and in August of that year, the FMG announced that it was about to launch a 'final push' to defeat Biafra, and 'there was an uproar in the House of Commons, and a noisy demonstration outside', sparking a debate that was 'particularly uncomfortable' for the government.[34] By now, opposition spanned party lines; prominent Conservative and Liberal Members of Parliament pressed for the end of arms sales and stronger attempts to broker peace, while there was also growing opposition from Wilson's own Labour Party members. Labour peer Fenner Brockway became a major voice of the opposition, and formed the non-partisan Committee for Peace in Nigeria. The Archbishop of Canterbury, Michael Ramsey, seconded Brockway's House of Lords motion to end arms sales. A particularly notable spokesperson was the journalist Auberon Waugh, who after visiting Biafra, wrote widely about the issue, especially in the *Spectator*, and in 1969 co-wrote a polemical book, *Biafra, Britain's Shame*, sponsored by the Britain-Biafra Association, an active pressure group.[35] Much of the opposition rhetoric stressed the long relationship between the British and Igbo people, as well as the Igbos' modern and progressive accomplishments.[36]

There was fear that a vote would end in defeat for the government, and the FMG was urgently informed that unless a way could be found to prove that civilian deaths were being minimized, arms sales would have to be reconsidered. The result was an agreement to create an

International Observer Team to go into Nigeria and verify that no geno-cide was taking place. The FMG reluctantly agreed, and the team oper-ated between September 1968 and the end of the war, invariably con-cluding that no major civilian atrocities had happened. Much has been written about this initiative, with critics pointing out that the observer teams were always supervised by the FMG, that they never looked at events that had happened in 1966 and 1967, and that they were never briefed on what constituted 'genocide'. As Suzanne Cronje noted,

> at the very least the team should have included international jurists and professionals experienced in the investigation of crime and the record-ing of evidence, not to speak of social workers, medical men and people capable of telling an Ibo from a non-Ibo. [37]

However, the work of the observers undoubtedly gave the British government cover, and arguably may have helped avoid more civilian deaths, since their presence seems to have acted as an inhibiting factor on the Federal troops. [38]

Throughout 1968 and 1969, there remained a steady trickle of politi-cal protest, expressed in parliamentary motions and letters to news-papers and politicians. Typical is a group of letters published in *The Times*, 6 March 1969, written by MPs, officers of the Oxford Union, and others, called for Britain to intervene and broker peace. [39] A group of Royal Ballet Company members writes that 'Britain should redeem itself morally ... and make a constructive attempt to terminate this horrifying slaughter'. Labour MP Stanley Henig refers to a motion signed by over 100 MPs calling for an arms embargo and an attempt to negotiate a cease-fire. He argues that a public campaign is needed 'to impress upon the nation the shameful role we have been playing in this conflict'. The Oxford Union members, arguing that the atrocities against civilians are now proven, conclude that 'the time has come for an immediate ban on arms supply to Nigeria and a determined international peace initiative.' However, these attempts never translated into a major groundswell of opposition, and the Wilson government survived.

Perhaps ironically, one reason for this was that the mounting horror of what was happening in Biafra shifted the focus of activism in Britain away from political pressure and towards humanitarian aid. The press was now full of heart-breaking stories of famine, suffering, and death, made even more real by the fact that this was the first time television cameras were witnesses to such suffering. With Biafra now reframed as a humanitarian, rather than political disaster, the British public responded with an outpouring of support. All over the country, appeals were launched. One of the most famous was a campaign launched by the extremely popular BBC children's programme, *Blue Peter*. Each year, the programme had a Christmas campaign that asked viewers to send in some kind of recyclable (such as metal, wool, and so on), which was sold and used to finance initiatives like the refurbishment of housing for the homeless. On 5 December 1968, *Blue Peter's* lead presenter, Valerie Singleton, announced the appeal, striking in its sparse explanation and insistence on non-politicisation:

> There's been a war going on in West Africa for two years now. It's a civil war between the Biafrans and Nigerians ... We're not going to say which side is right and which side is wrong, except to say that all war is wrong. No matter whose fault it is that people are dying every day, it's not his fault [over photo of starving child] ... they don't know why people are fighting, they only know that their family and friends are dead ...[40]

Blue Peter requested that viewers send parcels of scrap fabric—wool and cotton only—which would be sold to buy a hospital truck for Biafra. Millions responded, like 'Matthew', who many years later wrote about it:

> I was born in 1961. And, like me, many people my age have two sets of black and white TV images in their heads. The first is of the US moon landing: 'One small step for a man' ... That was intensely exciting and impressive; I sat on the carpet in my pyjamas, eyes wide. The Americans are on the moon!
>
> The second is of black children with stick-thin legs and arms and swollen tummies. I had seen black children before—a black family had just moved into a house on my road in north Leeds. But the Biafran kids on the BBC news just did not look right, sat in the dirt, motionless, exaggerated skulls almost hairless. It was impossible not to stare, shocked.
>
> In 1968 I bundled up clothes for the *Blue Peter* appeal, to help buy a hospital truck for Nigeria-Biafra. Mum posted the brown paper parcel; so did a million other mums and dads.[41]

This appeal was only one of thousands that gathered momentum from mid-1968 until the end of the war and on into its aftermath—not only in Britain, but also around the world. Relief agencies, especially the International Committee of the Red Cross (ICRC) had been sending relief into war-stricken areas of mid-western Nigeria and Biafra since 1967, but this increased dramatically, and by the end of 1969, 250 metric tons of food and supplies was being flown into the re-purposed Uli airstrip every night.[42] Multiple NGOs joined the effort; in Britain these included Christian Aid, Oxfam, War on Want, and the Save the Children Fund. In November 1968, when it was clear that a coordinated initiative was needed, various international religious groups banded together to form Joint Church Aid (JCA), known to the pilots hired to fly relief supplies as 'Jesus Christ Airline'.[43] In the end Biafra became a watershed moment for NGOs and their role in humanitarian crises, establishing a model of international crises followed by massive fund-raising appeals. This cycle is so familiar today that it is easy to forget that Biafra was the first cause that mobilised this kind of response; it was also in this crisis that the now-famous Médecins Sans Frontières (MSF, or Doctors Without Borders) was born.

Fund drives for Biafra sprang up all over Britain throughout 1968 and 1969, as local people organised campaigns to collect money, food, clothing, and recyclables. Newspaper clippings that Rose Umelo kept in her collection of 'war junk' present a picture of a typical small town effort in her hometown of Frodsham, Cheshire. Mothers and children raise £23 in a jumble sale; a woman sets up a stall in a local market to raise cash; 'a car load of supplies was taken … to Liverpool'; 'Biafra relief aid ship due to dock at Runcorn'. While mirrored across the country, the efforts in the communities of Frodsham, Runcorn, and Helsby also had a deeply personal connection; the newspaper repeatedly mentioning Mrs Rhoda Martin and her daughter Rosina, 'whose baby was born in the Biafran bush five months ago'.[44] As well as the larger-scale contributions to shipments, local residents sent (at Rose's request) parcels of drugs and iron tablets to the small maternity hospital near where the Umelos lived. On 31 July, the *Runcorn Weekly News* passed on Rose's thanks for sending supplies, and shares her descriptions of starvation and the local relief work. In the same story, Rose points to the root causes of the situation she is describing:

> In Biafra, food is only a temporary relief to continual suffering. Humanitarian work can at best only reduce and never end the agony. The crisis is political, not natural, and needs a political solution.

But, as was typical in the British fund-raising efforts, this message was consistently muted; the local organiser in Frodsham, for example, wrote a letter of thanks to the community that stressed the importance of everyone contributing, 'whether the starving children are living under a Biafran, Nigerian, or any other flag'.

Thus the humanitarian, apolitical narrative prevailed in Rose's home town as in everywhere else: tons of aid continued to pour into Biafra. While people around the world responded to the Biafra crisis, 'In Britain, humanitarianism ... amounted, in essence to a benign reimagining of imperial compassion for a post-colonial world'.[45] Stripped of any political context, and intensely paternalistic, the appeals focused on the desperation and helplessness of the Igbo 'tribal' people, with little or no mention of the ingenious ways so many in Biafra were mobilising traditional networks and skills to survive. This aid undoubtedly saved lives, but may also have helped prolong the war, since the massive relief operations consumed public attention and served to remove the urgency from any potential British peace attempts. From the awakening of the public in June 1968, it took another eighteen months finally to bring Biafra to its knees.

Meanwhile, in Biafra itself, Britain was still seen as the best hope to lead a negotiation that would end the war. Rose notes that as the war progressed, the name of Prime Minister Wilson became almost a curse word; yet that hope persisted. N.U. Akpan, Secretary to the Cabinet in Ojukwu's government, wrote in his memoirs: 'incredibly, the rumours of a possible visit by the British Prime Minister to Umuahia in March 1969 were greeted with the keenest enthusiasm and expectation. Great receptions were prepared for him'.[46] The visit never happened and the Biafrans continued to be disillusioned:

> One of the things which badly disappointed even the greatest admirers of the British (including those who regretted the war) was the inaccurate statements which the British Government spokesmen frequently put out in the House of Commons. Many of us had come to regard the House of Commons as a place where nothing but truths were asserted. Those inaccurate statements undermined people's faith in the sincerity of the British ...[47]

This deep sense of disappointment was rooted in the history of Eastern Nigerians, and Igbo in particular, who 'tended to reflect characteristics that in colonial Nigeria suggested modernity. These included Western dress, Western education, use of English, Christianity ...'[48] Following secession, Biafran leaders had worked to present a model of their new nation as progressive, educated and modern—not subservient to former colonialists, but ready to deal with them on an equal footing. They expected Britain to respect them, and even when it was apparent that direct support would not be forthcoming, many continued to hope that Britain would be an 'honest broker' in negotiating peace. A confidential memo from an American relief worker, visiting Biafra in March 1968 noted, 'one was struck quite forcibly with the disillusion with Britain ... Yet in spite of this bitterness we were told that the UK was still in the strongest position to mediate.'[49] Ojukwu's Head of Civil Service believed right to the end that 'the British government ... could have found a way to end the war without compromising their policy ... if they had really wanted to'.[50] But it took no such action, and by June 1969, in his famous Ahiara Declaration, Ojukwu issued a vehement denunciation of Britain, 'a country whose history is replete with instances of genocide'.[51] Describing how the British stood by while thousands of Black Africans died, Ojukwu argued:

> Since in the thinking of many white powers a good, progressive and efficient government is good only for whites, our view was considered dangerous and pernicious ... we have learnt that the right to self-determination is inalienable, but only to the white man.[52]

Conclusion

Britain did not directly cause the civil war, nor did it create the blockade that starved so many innocent people. As Raph Uwechue, writing during the war, commented, 'Neither hatred for the Ibos nor a sacred attachment to the principle of preserving one Nigeria dictated Britain's ... position and commitment. Expediency did.'[53] As the war dragged on, both sides became even more deeply entrenched in their positions; for Nigeria, restoring political unity was the only option, while Biafrans believed almost to the last moment that surrender would result in annihilation. But once the horror of the famine was clear, there was a desperate need for some kind of outside mediation. Other nations, most notably the United States, were unwilling to intervene; Roger Morris, a senior State Department official at the time, described American policy as characterised by 'outer public compassion veiling its inner bureaucratic callousness',[54] driven by a commitment to the 'maintenance of the traditional Anglo-American patronage in Nigeria at almost any price'.[55] Britain had created Nigeria, and British institutions, language, and religion permeated its creation—in the East most of all. Michael Leapman, in 1968 the first print journalist to break the famine story in Britain, wrote years later how the release of formerly classified documents showed that there were several moments when Britain could have usefully intervened to broker peace, but failed to do so. Instead, British decision-making was driven by the need to maintain control over Nigeria's resources, and 'right and wrong were the last considerations on anyone's mind'.[56] According to Morris, Prime Minister Wilson informed US Ambassador-at-large Clyde Ferguson that 'casualties of the famine were no object. He would accept a half million dead Biafrans … if that was what it took to secure the old Nigeria'.[57]

Ultimately, the international transformation of 'Biafra' from a political claim to a humanitarian crisis effectively tolled the death knell to Ojukwu's ambitions, while muting the political opposition to Britain's policies.[58] The Igbo had begun the war with a reputation in Britain and elsewhere as the most resourceful people in Africa, ready to take on the world, and that theme was often emphasised in the political activism in Britain. But by the end, the agony of the 'Biafran babies' had drowned out that rhetoric, and Biafrans were perceived only as pitiful victims, fitting back into a familiar narrative of benevolent Westerners saving starving Africans. After all, 'Who, in the end, thinks a people symbolised by starving infants to be capable of creating a state?'[59] For most British people, the role of their own government in creating this crisis was not something they wished to explore.

From her village in Biafra, Rose Umelo did what she could to appeal to the long-standing ties between her native and adopted country. As well as seeking relief supplies, she wrote to politicians and public figures, hoping they would use their influence to encourage peace efforts. She still has the blue airmail letter sent by the Bishop of Chester, Gerald Ellison:

> I hope you will be in no doubt about the concern and sympathy which there is in this country in the tragic situation in Nigeria … You may rest

assured that everything that can be done has been done ... Only this week the Archbishop of Canterbury made a stirring appeal in the House of Lords for the cessation of the supply of arms to Nigeria ... you are all much in our thoughts and prayers.

This letter was written on 22 July 1968; Rose and her family were facing another eighteen months of war.

3

BECOMING A NIGERWIFE

Nigerian men have had relationships with, and occasionally married, foreign women since colonial times, but such marriages increased in the twentieth century, as more Nigerian men went abroad for higher education and employment.[1] Today there are thousands of such marriages; at one time the majority of foreign wives were British, but 'there are now numerous American (increasingly black American) and West Indian wives, as well as others of virtually all nationalities from Indian to Brazilian, Russian to Zimbabwean'.[2]

Exactly when the distinctive term 'Nigerwife' was coined is unclear, although it was certainly current during the Civil War. Today, it is a term officially used by the Nigerian Immigration Service for a non-Nigerian woman married to a Nigerian.[3] In 1979, a Nigerwives organisation was formed in Lagos, and now it has branches across Nigeria and abroad. The organisation's goal is to help foreign wives adjust to life in Nigeria, and many branches have taken on philanthropic as well as social roles. In 1987, a Nigerian-American married couple discussed some of the special challenges faced by Nigerwives:

> The roles of wife and mother are clear cut and different from those in the West. Men and women tend to live separate social lives, each with his or her own family and friends. The female network is important for the Nigerian woman, but the Nigerwife does not have her own family and old friends to support her.[4]

As Dominique Otigbah explains, the formal Nigerwives organisation sometimes

takes on the role of the extended family for occasions such as funerals, weddings or name ceremonies. This is significant since the Nigerwife is separated from her own extended family and for occasions like these in Nigeria it is expected that the wife's side is also well represented. So rather than the wife feeling left out or isolated since she does not have her own family there, the Nigerwives assume that role, enabling her to function like a Nigerian at these social events.[5]

From memoirs of life as a Nigerwife in the immediate postcolonial period, before the foundation of an organised body, it is apparent that foreign wives were quite well accepted in Nigeria, owing in part to the high status accorded generally to white people, a point Rose Umelo also makes.[6] A white skin brought innumerable privileges and many expatriates happily exploited this, living charmed lives that revolved around 'the club', supported by staffs of cooks, porters, stewards and drivers. Kenneth Ryeland, in a memoir of life in Enugu just before the war, noted wryly that although he was a relatively uneducated motor engineer, in Nigeria he was treated as a superior being, and he certainly took advantage of that fact.[7]

However, a Nigerwife had a more complicated life than that of someone living as a member of a white expatriate community. The transition could be difficult as husbands who seemed to have become very adapted to life outside Nigeria resumed their old lives easily and quickly:

when they come back to their home country, they return to their former values and behavior patterns. Pressure from family and friends encourages this. A common Nigerwife complaint is that she does not recognize the man whom she married, as he has changed so much since returning to Nigeria.[8]

As Rose Umelo commented, 'the Nigerian man who marries abroad has a double responsibility; he knows what he's taking her from and he knows what he's taking her to. She doesn't.' Some Nigerians, while not necessarily hostile to a white wife (and even possibly in awe of her), found it difficult to embrace her as one of their own, leaving many feeling isolated and lonely. Meanwhile, many in the expatriate community disapproved of such marriages altogether: 'it would seem that the main issue for these women was not the reactions from

Nigerians but the reactions from the British community.'[9] These nega-
tive reactions were mitigated if the husband was an educated member
of the Nigerian elite, which indeed most were; the complex interplay
of race and class was part of the day-to-day life of colonial and postcolonial Nigeria. In any event, Nigerwives often became friends, rely-
ing on each other for mutual support, even before the Nigerwives
group came into being. These connections became even more important during the war.

For Rose Umelo, the road to becoming a Nigerwife began in North
West England, where she was born in 1931, the daughter of Albert
Edward and Rhoda Martin. Her mother had been in domestic service
before marrying and becoming a full-time home-maker; her father was
a saddler. As she recalls,

> Horses were still important in war and on the farm, so he mended their
> tackle and had other leather work, bags and suitcases, all leather in
> those days, and of course, shoes … after a decline in that work pony
> clubs became fashionable with more such saddlery. He had a double
> workshop fully equipped with finishing machine, heavy duty treadle
> sewing machine, riveter, fist sized lump of beeswax for waxing the
> thread, and 1,001 other smaller items of his trade.

In contrast to her younger brother John, Rose was a bookish child:
'Give us a Meccano set; I'd be reading the instruction leaflet and he'd be
building the Forth Bridge.' Her studious nature stood her in good stead;
she was able to go to Grammar School in nearby Runcorn, and her exam
results won her a Cheshire County Scholarship that would enable her to
go to University. Accepted by Liverpool and Manchester Universities,
she decided to also apply to the all-female Bedford College, University
of London: 'London has always been the lure.' Rose, the first in her
extended family to go to university, was accepted by Bedford. She began
her studies in 1950, graduating in 1953 with a degree in Latin with
Greek subsidiary, winning a prize for her work on Latin poets along the
way. In 1954, she went on to a clerical position with the London County
Council, where she worked for the next ten years.

It was during that time that she met the man who eventually took
her life in such an unexpected direction. Rose Umelo's journey to
Nigeria began in the late 1950s, on that London tube station platform.
She recalls:

It was bitterly cold, it's above ground and the trains were throwing out sparks underneath as they did then, and this voice said, 'oh isn't it cold?' And I said, 'oh it is,' and that was the end of the conversation. But next morning, you know you go to the same bit in these stations where you get off the tube, and the voice said, 'good morning.' And I said, 'good morning,' and you know, things developed ...

Unlike many Nigerians in Britain, John was not a student or a professional; he worked in a warehouse in a blue-collar job. Rose acknowledges that their inter-cultural relationship was unconventional: 'it wasn't very popular I'll tell you.' She recalls that this was a time when racial tensions were high in London, following the murder of a young Antiguan immigrant, Kelso Cochrane, in Notting Hill. Cochrane was ambushed by several white youths and stabbed to death, in a killing that was widely thought to be racially motivated. At the time, Notting Hill was the base for far-right groups, such as the Union Movement (led by neo-Nazi Oswald Mosley), and the White Defence League, and the previous year had seen race riots in the area. The black community was outraged, and many marched in protest at police inability to make an arrest; the government established a public inquiry into race relations.[10] John and Rose coped in this highly-charged environment by, 'keeping a low profile':

there was a flea-pit cinema we could go to—audience 99 percent black. It was fine, and there was one pub we could go to just round the corner to have a drink, but otherwise, low profile.

The couple moved in together, and their first son, Ezenwa, known as Eze, was born in 1960.[11] Eighteen months later, they married. Life was not easy:

they used to say when I was in London in the 50s: if a woman goes with a black man, either she is a harlot or he is a prince. I got some abuse, not so much when I was with John because he was tall and hefty but when I was out with the baby—dirty bitch, and things like that.

Perhaps surprisingly, her own family did not object:

I won't say John was the son-in-law they'd dreamed of but it was a fait accompli and they could see we were happy. We went several times to Cheshire, once with Eze at 2 years old, and John got on well with those he met, especially my brother ... they liked him, they thought he was likeable.

But by 1964, the couple had begun to think about leaving London for a new life in John's home country:

> all Nigerians in London were thinking of getting back and making fortunes and the country was now independent and there'd be loads of money and opportunity ... John wanted to go back so I said, 'OK, you don't marry a foreigner and then say you're going to stay here ...'

In addition, Rose had become increasingly frustrated in her job:

> I went in as a General Clerical Officer and I took the exam which brought you onto the executive officer cadre which is more salary, and after 10 years, at three different departments, they promoted eight people. The two they left out were the women ... I was very stroppy in those days. I went to the head and said, why have I been left out? And he said, Well you've had two maternity leaves, and I said, What about Mrs. McPherson? She's got no children. No answer to that.

The couple learned that Nigeria was in need of teachers, and Rose decided to finally put her Classics training to good use, and applied, even though she had no formal training in education. She learned then that some Nigerians also disapproved of their unconventional relationship. Rose shared a reference letter written in support of her teaching application. A.E. Eronini, Chairman of the Eastern Nigeria Broadcasting Corporation, noted that her husband was from his home area: 'I was therefore interested in the affairs of the couple but did not hide my natural dislike for this "white-to-black" marriage.' He explained that his views had shifted after meeting Rose:

> I soon discovered, however, something most unusual in this particular case. Here was an extraordinary woman wrapped up in her interest and love for her husband and the African ... She longs to leave these shores for Nigeria, nurses her husband well, and makes the home a sweet one indeed. I think Mrs Umelo's colour is an accident ...[She] deserves a warm embrace and encouragement in Nigeria, and therefore recommend that her application for employment be given the most sympathetic consideration.

Rose was offered a contract to teach in Eastern Nigeria, and the family, now with three children, set out for Nigeria. Embarking on the sea voyage, Rose was truly taking a leap into the unknown; she had no idea where she would be posted. On board, she learned that she was being assigned to a school in the town of Aba:

The white principal was unfriendly (my having an Igbo husband must have made her think I was there for her job) and there was no available accommodation. If I could have hailed a passing magic carpet at that time I would have gone.

Struggling to manage her family in one room of the Government-sponsored Catering Rest House, she was delighted to suddenly hear that the Latin teacher at Queens School, Enugu, had left and she was being reposted there.

so we got into one of those big, you know, load carrying things with kids and loads and everything and we trundled up to Enugu. It was a nicer place to start with, we got to the school, were welcomed by the principal, and she showed me a house. So that was that.

Queens was an academically-focused school, typical of more elite schools in Nigeria, and was the only Government secondary school for girls in the Eastern Region, the others being run by missionaries or private entities. It taught a British-style curriculum, and Rose settled into teaching Latin and other subjects, usually English. Never a 'joiner', she did not become involved in the expatriate community, but enjoyed an idyllic life as her family grew by one more child. Unlike almost all other Nigerwives of the period, she was not married to a high status man; John worked as a licenced money-lender and took whatever opportunities arose, and the couple preferred to develop their own friendship networks rather than deal with the expatriate world of 'the club'.

By 1966, they were starting to hear about the horrific killings of Igbo in the North, and rumblings about secession were everywhere. Yet it seemed impossible that the country could be headed toward war:

It felt like when you see it in the newspaper, when somebody does something dreadful, maybe serial killing, and the person says, 'And why don't they stop me?' And we felt like that—why don't they stop them? It can't happen!

But happen it did, and soon the Umelos, like everyone in the new Biafra, was swept up in tumultuous events that ended normal life for the next three years. Rose's story, *A World of Our Own*, begins in Enugu.

PART II

A WORLD OF OUR OWN

4

BEFORE THE STORM

'*No-one had told me the East was beautiful*'

When encouraging me to come, they had told me all about the easy life—a car, government quarters, servants, no chores except those I cared to do, the social life. But I never liked that much in England and I felt I would be twice as diffident in a new country. As for the easy life, I had been brought up dourly to believe there was a price to be paid for everything in the end. But I resolved I would not be one of those who come to their husband's country, won't settle or adjust, and so go away again, adding another unfavourable detail to the composite picture of the foreign wife—expensive, unfriendly, infertile, and transient.

No-one had mentioned the beauty of the country, and as our lorry jolted into town, I thought Enugu a particularly beautiful place.[1] It wasn't just because we were at last out of Aba where we had spent six miserable weeks in the Rest House. These hotels are intended for civil servants on tour and businessmen in passage and not for the indefinite stay of a family with two lively young boys, a baby and daily heaps of washing. In contrast, Enugu was spectacular, with a burning orange-red earth, the undulating line of hills with strange rocky outcrops and towers looming by the road.

In our eagerness to get somewhere and begin something, we had travelled with our luggage in a school lorry, all shaking together in one

45

confused heap over the past hundred miles. While we were still staring over the tailboard, we were already running along wide streets. There were sprawling single-storey buildings with open fronted shops facing the roads, handsome upstairs houses bright with coloured paint and fretted concrete balconies ... and more shops. Then we saw a wide gate leading off the road. Two institutions shared the same hillside and a signboard pointed in towards Queens School.[2] Up the hill and round the corner we ground between a double line of trees; there was a glimpse of red and silver roofs along a side road and then the school—a confused first impression of purple flowering bushes, flowers like giant irises of yellow and scarlet, green washed walls, open doors, and the principal's welcoming smile.

We were taken to our house (wide wood-block floor, wide open windows). We unpacked at last. We had arrived. We had left London early in December 1964—my husband John, our two boys, Ezenwa, aged four and Uzoma, aged two, and our baby girl Nwaneze. We seemed to have been packing for months. Now it was February 1965. We could unpack our boxes, arrange our belongings, get our breath.

I had to adapt myself quickly to a new profession. I had worked in local government for ten years, where I had been part of a huge administrative machine. My duty was to move smoothly at the right time and not delay the wheels before and behind. Now I was on my own. Office work was all left behind at 5 p.m., but school work came home in the form of great heaps of exercises to be corrected and lessons to be prepared, so it could easily occupy all out-of-school time.

Queens School was the only Government Girls' Secondary School in the whole region, although there were three colleges for boys. Each year, several thousand girls took the common entrance examination. Between two and three hundred would be called for interview for the sixty places in Class I. When we arrived, the school had grown to over 300 students. It was double stream to Class IV with a single Class V, two classes of Lower VI, one Upper VI, and a Senior VI, made up of girls who were staying for a third year while taking special courses in subjects they needed before reading for Science degrees at university. It was a boarding school, as secondary schools all seemed to be, with students from all parts of the region, and a few from outside. There was a pair of two-storey classroom blocks with the Assembly Hall forming three sides of a square, and separate laboratories for General Science, Chemistry, Physics, Botany, Zoology, plus a Domestic Science block, a Geography room, Sewing room, and six large dormitories named after famous explorers.[3] There was a reference library of more than 5,000 books, as well as a smaller library. Everything seemed to be in a separate building; mixed with two different common rooms and a prefects' room, they straggled without much order across the hilltop, a time-consuming distance apart.

The buildings looked very bare at first sight, although Queens was outstandingly well-equipped compared to many other schools. 'Your laundry is a better room than most of our classrooms,' said a visitor to me one day rather crossly. The staff always wanted still more, particularly for their own subjects.

Everything was built of concrete blocks with zinc, asbestos, or tiled roofs. The floors were plain concrete, except in the Assembly Hall, which had a wood-block floor. Each classroom was equipped with a wall blackboard, bulletin board, teacher's table, and desks. Though they looked bare, they were not bleak. The fretted concrete that always looked such a dust trap under a grimy sky, in sunlight plays at changing the patterns of shadow across the floors. The windows were always open to any breeze from the brilliant sky.

The principal was an enthusiastic gardener who had transformed a bare hill by planting lovely trees. As the year progressed there were no words for their shades of colour. Pink, blue and yellow could only convey all the wrong impressions—too bright, too flat, and too unsubtle. Others were strange enough out of season, with eighteen-inch black seed pods, but at the due time the blossom flowed from branch to branch and the whole tree blazed. There were bougainvillea with flowers apparently cut from purple tissue paper, and frangipani, which looked like a moon-tree. It had a bare, grey stem and branches that dripped a thick milky sap, but when it put out long oval leaves and creamy perfumed flowers, it belonged for a while more to this earth.

Everything grew at a prodigious rate. The second house we had was only four years old, and the first tenant had planted trees and shrubs around it. In very short time, these were scraping along the roof, endangering the electricity supply line, tapping against the windows, cutting off the daylight. When we moved in, we had the bigger trees lopped and six smaller trees and shrubs removed altogether without leaving any noticeably wide spaces in the greenery. But at the beginning of the next rainy season the bare ground began to grow grass again, as it received some light and air.

Set about with the same lavish use of space, there were thirteen staff houses, far too few for the expanding school. As the working day began so early, it was convenient to live on the compound. The disadvantage was that you would be on duty at least every other term for one day each week as well as for one weekend in each term. This entailed handing out simple remedies to students who reported with their aches and pains and fevers. Anything more serious had to be taken to the emergency department of the General Hospital in the town. Most detested were those calls that came in the night, with a prolonged knocking at the front door and the murmur of many voices. There would be a group of girls wearing an odd assortment of head scarves, *lappas* (wrappers) and cardigans tied over their nightdresses, with a 'night-watch' in attendance carrying his bush-lamp. 'So and So,' they would chorus in reply to a grumpy question, 'is SERIOUSLY ILL!' This was said with an unquenchable air of triumph if you had earlier handed out basic medication and a brisk exhortation to snap out of it, and turned down a demand to be taken to the hospital. Then would come the walk along the dark paths across a compound that seemed twice as wide as during the day, full of night-time creaks and chirrups, littered with extra stones, ruts and hollows. 'Sorry!' the chorus would sympathise at every stumble. At last the dormitory would be reached, where everyone was gathered round one bed, already holding the wake. The mourners had to be removed and the patient surveyed. It was always difficult to know whether you were neglecting genuine emergencies or ferrying exhibitionists through the dark streets to waste everyone's time in hospital.

Senior Service[4] quarters were one topic on which our friends had waxed so eloquent in London, where most of us were living in crowded conditions in down-at-heel districts. They were furnished, down to mattresses, pillows, mosquito nets and cushions, so moving in and leaving needed a solemn ceremony with a clerk from the Public Works Department and the tenant gravely checking their duplicate lists—Tables (dining): one; Tables (drinks): four; Tables (card): one—before countersigning each other's copy of the treaty. The older houses at the school were small with only one bedroom, but were very attractive, with wood-block floors in the living room and usually a wide comfortable window seat along one wall. The newer houses had two or three bedrooms and were suitable for the married teachers with their families, who were replacing the single women who had come and gone on contract. There was a ceiling fan in the living room, a fridge and water filter in the kitchen. Nearly all the houses had a wood stove and the condition of the kitchen walls showed whether it was being used or not. Some tenants installed gas or electric cookers. Gas was delivered in cylinders; electricity was laid on but often cut off as the Energy Corporation of Nigeria (ECN) appeared to turn off our supply any time they wanted to shed the load. It was nothing unusual for our two institutions to be wrapped in gloom while below the town glowed and winked and the Enugu campus of the University[5] was lit up like a funfair. Every household had some form of lighting for these regular emergencies—kerosene bush lamps, Tilley or Aladdin lamps[6] with a clear white light ... or candles. On such evenings it was surprising how much heat came from a candle flame or a bush lamp when you had to bend your head near to get light enough to mark exercises. The ceiling fan seemed twice as motionless when you knew a touch of the switch could not set it humming to stir the heavy air.

Piped water was also laid on to the houses. Down in the town, those houses which didn't have their own tap in the yard had to send people to queue at the public stand pipe. We boiled and filtered all drinking water; from the tap it could vary between a smoky crystal and a rich brown soup. Sometimes in the rainy season we had to catch the torrents that teemed off the roof, since the taps had just run dry. Before our arrival there had been water shortages in the dry season but storage tanks had been installed behind all the dormitories. The staff houses had flush toilets but the older type of boys' quarters and many houses in the town had bucket latrines which were emptied by 'night-soil' men.

The only detail of life at the school which regularly irritated me was the telephone. As the newest on the staff, I had the most unpopular table in the staffroom. It was very small and the telephone took up most of the space. The phone itself was an extension from the school office and I came to dread it. Callers could seldom understand me, and I could hardly ever understand them. I was never sure whether any given name was that of the caller or of the person required. In one particular debacle, I thought the caller wanted Mrs Maiduguri, but actually he was calling from Maiduguri in Northern Nigeria. After that I gave up the telephone and basely found occupation at the notice board or outside the room whenever it began to ring.

I was no more successful in making calls. Most were to ministries where the switchboard invariably answered: 'Yes?' After you had established that you did have the right number: 'Could I speak to Mr So and So please?', the reply would be, 'He's not on seat.' Maybe it was the equivalent of the secretary's 'He's in conference,' or the London County Council's version: 'He's at a meeting.' At least these replies suggested the official might be back in a reasonable time. But in a society where senior civil servants went on study leave for courses lasting many months, 'not on seat' could mean his chair would go undusted for the next academic year.

You also had to be strong to stand the strain of attending hospital. All medical attention was obtained through outpatient departments and people began to come into the General Hospital long before dawn. By eight or nine o'clock there would be jostling crowds at each department without any apparent order and with some patients sitting or lying on the ground. You had to remember to bring enough bottles and jars with you or else you must go and buy some for twopence or threepence from the vendors outside the gates, who had all sizes for sale on their little stalls.

Conditions at Park Lane Nursing Home, a memorial of those colonial divisions, were quieter and far more comfortable, and the cheapest bottle at the gate cost fourpence. There were armchairs to sit in and a pleasant view of well-kept gardens. On entering the waiting room you took a number from a spike on the table, which was meant to ensure the order in which patients saw the doctor. It didn't always work. Sunk in a comfortable stupor, you could surface later to find those who had definitely arrived after you had somehow acquired a number before your own, or, arriving in a puff and a glow from the other side of town, you might see the waiting room totally empty in the early morning sun and the first number on the spike already 33. If you didn't count a doctor among your closest personal friends, the quickest way in a crisis was to go to the emergency department of an excellent private hospital. A £2 deposit had to be paid down and you were sure of seeing a doctor within minutes. Next day or so the settlement could be made, which would be either a refund of the balance or a payment of the bill, if it exceeded £2. It wasn't at all surprising that so many people preferred self-help. Enugu had so many chemists, pharmacies, and patent medicine stores, all doing good business.

People often spoke disparagingly of Enugu as a civil servants' town, claiming the real places for making money were Onitsha, Aba, and Port Harcourt, yet Enugu had plenty of stores and businesses. There was Kingsway department store, Chanrai's and Chellaram's—the same thing but smaller—and any number of specialist shops and showrooms for cars, books and expensive, imported clothes.[7] There were grocery self-service stores as well as roadside stalls selling good quality 'European' vegetables, such as cabbage, carrots, salad, and potatoes, as well as cheaper local produce like okro (okra), peppers and fruit.

My first shopping was done at Kingsway because the surroundings were more familiar. You just had to choose and pay; bargaining didn't come into it. Even then, there were oddities. There was no fresh milk and many households bought small tins of evaporated milk by the carton. There was sterilised milk in litre bottles and different sized tins of many types of dried milk powder. All the well-known baby formulas, cereals and little tins were there. Some familiar items appeared exotic when packed in tins and not packets—margarine, Farex,[8] Quaker Oats, Ryvita, baby rusks, chocolates, and some sweets. Most imported foods seemed to be twice or three times their English prices. Anyone determined to live on familiar 'European' foods could do so if he could afford it. But why did they stock rows of tins of Malayan pineapple? Fresh pineapple was sold outside the door. Who bought it? And who bought tinned potatoes and tinned fried onion rings? Maybe some of those people living in the bush slipped a few mighty tins in their enormous orders. Every time I saw someone stocking up for what seemed like months at a time, I remembered the book I had read before travelling. This advised keeping luggage to head-loads of 45 pounds, unless you were sure of travelling all the way by canoe. It was published in 1901 and included a suggested shopping list from Fortnum and Masons (of course).

But Ogbete Main Market came to be one of the pleasures of living in Enugu. Its approach road, full of potholes, jolted between piles of red planks ringing with the whine and squeal of circular saws, then led deep into the acres of sheds and continuous lines of corrugated iron stalls whose vendors sold everything at the top of their voices. At first I was apprehensive; it was so large and so noisy. But as I settled down, it soon became clear that while shopping in the stores was more comfortable and orderly, shopping in the market could be far cheaper. While stores prices were fixed, the market prices went up and down—and always well up at the sight of a European, who is always, as we well know, excessively rich. No-one, of course, was expected to agree to the price. Everyone loved bargaining, whether for a long length of expensive material or a handful of pepper. I never became much good at it but shopping at the stores gave me an idea of a price, and I would try to go lower. The real delight in the market was that there was so much of everything—sheds selling provisions, tinned foods and packets, fancy goods in a heaped-up confusion of pins, combs, pomade, talcum powder, handkerchiefs, clothes, shoes, and sandals. Not just a few of each kind but scores upon scores in a market area spreading over several acres. There must have been hundreds of sheds selling every type, quality and weight of fabric from woollen suiting to nylon laces and chiffons, through every type of cotton in between. Cloth sellers often specialised. Some stocked only nylon, others *akwete*, the heavy expensive hand-woven material, or George fabric, which could vary from plain checks and overchecks to lavishly embroidered lengths with brilliant silk and gold threads.

All the sheds had open fronts. Their stock seemed to ooze forward and out by their weight and volume onto the narrow walkway between each line so that progress was a matter of two steps up and one down, dodging this, round that, while the streams of people proceeded by little leaps like a cascade and the stall keepers joked and demanded trade with their shouts of 'Customer! Customer!' You could do rather well by going early, since vendors liked to make a sale to their first customer. It promised a good day for business, and because of 'morning market' they were willing to negotiate. But I left the cook to buy the okro, pepper, yams, different kinds of leafy vegetables, bananas, thick red palm oil, onions, plantains, guavas, limes, pineapples, oranges, grapefruit, and pawpaw. There were even more unfamiliar fruits in their season, such as *udara*, with big flat shiny seeds that the children used as counters.[9]

Further down the hill, the lines of corrugated iron sheds gave way to thatched wooden stalls and rows and rows of people selling from heaps of rice, beans and *garri*.[10] Empty tins were used as measuring cups and the salt, breadfruit, red pepper and so on was poured in and heaped up but not pressed down or shaken together. Foods could be sold by the cup, by the large or small heap, even by the basinful, so buying them required experience and skill with measuring by the eye as well as a sound knowledge of the state of the market. How on earth did everyone make a living? There was even a length of genuine ravine yawning in the middle of all the busy feet, which the developers had not had time to subdue, as well as a particular open space where all shapes and sizes of baskets could be bought—if only I were able to find the place two weeks together.

Before travelling I had read books a little later in date than 1901, and no longer expected to find everywhere alive with large animals. However, in our school there were plenty of snakes, and the girls used to set up a great shrieking at the sight of one, living or dead. Soon after our arrival I was hurrying up a little side path to the school when I had to stop to admire the sinuous wave of the grass as something long and unseen glided under its cover. In the grass there were small animals but they kept out of the way. We would usually only see them when the grass was burned off in the dry season and all the creatures fled before the fire.

The avenue of trees leading up the hill to the school was silently afluttter with bats in the late evening, little draculas swooping and gliding. In the house the wall geckos scurried up the walls and across the ceiling catching insects. They were faintly spotted and speckled lizards, the young ones almost transparent like lizard-ghosts. If you handled one it felt just like a joint of raw chicken from the fridge, chilly and goose-pimpled to the touch. All kinds of insects fluttered round the light. There were moths of all sizes, whirring things with long bodies like dragonflies, and a kind of termite that shed gauzy wings at one stage to become a crawling insect. Praying mantis, green or brown, whirled madly across the room banging into everything. The big ones were sinister but the smaller sizes were almost pleasant, with their triangular, goggle-eyed faces and little fringed mouths opening and closing on unimaginable swear words. Ants ran everywhere and we became used to them, both the tiny red brown creatures and the big black kind. But I never accepted the presence of cockroaches, big and brown, with their two inch long feelers and their speed. More dangerous were scorpions. The first time I encountered one, we were all sitting round chattering in our house at school when an insect ran across the floor under my chair. Tucking up my bare feet, I said innocently, 'Oh, that spider has a tail coiled over its back,' and was amazed at the sudden commotion this remark called forth. But a scorpion sting was nothing to joke about. Native medicine used the crushed body of the scorpion applied to the place to relieve the pain, but it was more reliable for the victim to have hospital treatment for the poison and for the shock. But we were obviously being favoured. I had only been in school for a few months and I had already seen my first snake and scorpion, while another English wife had been there three years without seeing either of the creatures alive.

The whole shape of the year was strange, not at all like the times I was used to, but the habit died slowly of calling the three terms after a far distant Spring, Summer, and Autumn. The school year began in January and the first term scorched through the driest months of the year, when the red hot paths burned their way across the bleached and shrivelled grass. The rainy season began in the second term and the whole earth leapt to life. There were fantastic thunder storms breaking in waves across the roofs, thunder rolling down the sky in some giant's game of bowls, colliding and crashing, while at night the lightning was so vivid that the prolonged flare brought back daytime colours to the flowers and grass. More silently theatrical were the rainy season sunsets when the whole sky glowed in improbable colours, with some hand flicking the lightning switch behind cardboard cutout clouds.

There was the same strangeness in the shape of the day. Classes began early at 8 a.m. and lessons were short, lasting thirty-five minutes. School ended soon after 1 p.m. and after lunch the school drowsed through the hottest time of the day. With the slow release of the sun, everyone grew lively again. The classrooms buzzed with the evening prep, then the noisy meetings of the different school societies.

The students came from all parts of the region and English was the common language. Many could speak other Nigerian languages besides their own, as well as the rapid, funny and confusing pidgin which scattered extra hazards in the way of grammar lessons for both teacher and pupil. Just try explaining the difference between questions that expect the answer 'Yes' and questions that expect the answer 'No' to any class first accustomed to the pattern in pidgin:

'You didn't write this, did you?'
'Yes.' That is, 'You are correct. I didn't write it.'

Even the youngest students seemed astonishingly self-reliant, well able to manage complicated journeys of more than 100 miles by launch, lorry, train, or taxi. All seemed to settle down without obvious homesickness problems and rapidly developed a social poise and confidence likely to be as great an asset in the future as their certificates and diplomas. There was an astonishing interdependence within the family. School fees were as often paid by guardians (uncles, aunts, older brothers and sisters, some married, some studying abroad, relatives-in-law and so on) as they were by the actual parents of the students. We also noticed some things outside our special little world of school, such as the way people dressed—or sometimes over-dressed. Men wore European clothes, shorts, or trousers with a short-sleeved shirt, often of bright cotton. For more special occasions there were suits, even with waistcoats, or the showy *agbada*, made in cotton, brocade or velvet with its extravagant folds and flowing sleeves. Women wore dresses or *lappas* in cotton for everyday, with something more expensive for church and social occasions. The *lappas* was generally made of two lengths of cloth some 48 inches wide and two yards or more long with a contrasting blouse or a top of the same material. The first length of cloth was wrapped round the body from waist to ankles and was knotted at the back. If you stand with your feet apart as you wrap and tie it, you have room to walk and you are not hobbled by the long skirt. The second length is wrapped over the first from waist to knee or slightly above, not tied but tucked in at the waist, with the surplus cloth flowing down in graceful folds at the left.

The second cloth had to be tightened now and again, but the first was safe enough. There had once been considerable scorn of foreigners who used safety pins, pyjama cords and their husband's old ties to provide extra security. But as thicker, more expensive cloth became fashionable, dressmakers had begun sewing wrapper skirts on a waistband to ensure less bulk at the hips. Some evening styles had long skirts with zips to fasten them and slits to allow walking. Many of these were made in brocade or nylon lace or the extravagantly beautiful versions of Akwete or George fabrics.[11] They were far more elegant than many European evening dresses.

Everyone doing manual work or trading seemed to work extremely hard, as did anyone in business for himself. Only civil servants had a reputation for slackness and disregard for the public. Easterners had spread over the whole federation, thoroughly enjoying the process of making money as traders or contractors, in property, hotels and transport. Though many of these businessmen and women were illiterate, there was a passion for education. Many schools were run by the Missions, for the East had known Christianity for many years. Education was not compulsory—not even free after Class III—and fees were a heavy burden on large families.

Even before we left the ship at Lagos, I had the sense of stepping into a different world. The luggage list to check for disembarkation contained space for portmanteaux, uniform cases, helmet cases, dispatch boxes and valises; no column for roped-up cardboard cartons.

Instead of being the most expensive item, one of the cheapest things you could buy was labour. Your house could be full of people—driver, cook, steward, baby-nurse. Particularly for the senior civil servants, this was a world of privilege. They obtained free medical services when others had to queue and pay. They often lived in furnished quarters with subsidised rents in pleasant parts of town. There were car advances to enable officers to buy their own cars and repay the loan over several years. There was the car basic allowance which was paid by the Government to senior officials who owned cars. Sometimes this was enough to cover the monthly repayment of the car advance and was in addition to the mileage allowance that was claimed if the car were used on official business out of town. Many of these advantages dated from colonial days. As the civil service was Nigerianised, the indigenous officials took over the extra benefits and privileges which the previous holders of office had enjoyed.

It was a closely knit world. People knew a great deal about each other—home town, family background, education, salary and prospects, as well as all the generally enjoyable gossip. Not much of this touched us as we lived sedately on our hilltop. I had another baby. The older children were starting school. It was a quiet and contented life with babies and books well mixed, assignments and sewing and writing. I seemed to be busier than ever, well out of that promised social stream and completely, gloriously happy.

5

NIGERIANS ALL?

Politics in England had always seemed an organised sport. The public were invited to join in every general election or, according to the luck of the game, in by-elections now and then. Otherwise the elected few had a free hand to play as they pleased. One could with effort learn the general rules of the game but visits to the House of Commons never impressed me with the dignity or authority of the players. I was not persuaded there was much sense of responsibility either among those who sat reading newspapers or slept on the comfortable benches while another, unheeded, dragged out a speech to talk out time; or among those who were stirred to some activity, banged papers and shouted down a speaker roaring with false indignation like unruly schoolboys. The politics of a foreign country seemed even more removed from real life. It was still a game but the rules were lost, played on an unfamiliar board with strange men, prizes and penalties.

Even so, no literate person could come to Nigeria without having a general idea. Nigeria became independent of British rule in 1960. The country was often called Africa's Giant. Certainly in its area, size of population, and potential as a market for the world's goods, Nigeria was a giant, although rather more like one of those creatures with many heads, not all on speaking terms with each other. The political slogan was 'Unity in Diversity' and the national anthem declared:

Though tribe and tongue may differ
In brotherhood we stand
Nigerians all ...

There were said to be 250 tribes, some bigger, some smaller, with 250 languages, some with linguistic affinities, cultures, and customs. There was considerable difference between the North and South of the country, despite their political amalgamation since 1914. To the unconcerned visitor there was something very romantic in the Muslim North. You could always find plenty on the library shelves about the walled city of Kano, where a blast of trumpets greeted the planes, modern successors to the camel trains arriving from the Sahara; about the power of Islam, the call to prayer from the mosques, the multitudes prostrate in the ritual observances, the mediaeval survivals of the emirs' courts. The South provided a far less glamorous scene, all politics, clerks and teachers—less heroic figures. Much depended on where the District Officer whose reminiscences you were reading had happened to serve. Generally these officials preferred 'their own tribes' to anyone else's, and saw a political agitator as more of a nuisance and less respectable than a dignified figure embodying indirect rule.

My own politics were true-blue apathy. I was inclined to disregard all the sweeping accusations of bribery and corruption as mere envy of those in a position to benefit by those who were not, but who would behave just as badly if they had the opportunity themselves. Much depended on point of view. If your own relative was in a position of power and helped you, that was no more than his duty towards his brothers. But if someone else was in authority and helped his own brothers similarly, that was nepotism. Still, it was impossible to remain unaware of a series of political scandals. First the census, then election crises where it seemed every rule was broken. Newspapers reported ballot boxes stuffed or stolen, candidates obstructed in filing nomination papers, arrested, beaten up, killed. But it all seemed a long way from where we were.

In mid-January 1966, I was tuning the local radio station at breakfast to hear the 6:30 a.m. news broadcast. Instead of the familiar routine, a hurried voice appeared to say 'Tune to Lagos. Tune to Lagos', and the station went off the air. I tuned instead to the BBC World Service and heard the announcer declare that communication between Nigeria and the rest of the world had been cut off. Just what had happened seemed obscure. Some said there had been an Army mutiny; some said the Northerners were marching against the East. Later it was said there had been an attempted military coup followed by a transfer of authority in Lagos from the Federal Government to the Commander in Chief of the Army, Major-General Aguiyi-Ironsi. Prominent politicians had been killed. Military governors were appointed to rule the regions. In the East it was Lt.-Col. Chukwuemeka Odumegwu Ojukwu.[1]

The military takeover was being greeted with apparent enthusiasm but all the old suspicions remained. Aguiyi-Ironsi was from the East and the army was mostly recruited from the North. Most of those politicians who had permanently left the field were Northerners or their political supporters and included the Sardauna of Sokoto, their most powerful religious leader. In his own first broadcast, Col. Ojukwu promised (or, considering the slow passion of his voice, one could as well say threatened) immediate reforms and denounced the years of conspicuous waste. A series of inquiries was begun at Lagos and elsewhere into the workings of various government corporations and undertakings—the railways, airlines, electricity corporation, Eastern Nigeria Development Corporation—as well as the bank accounts of highly placed officials accused of benefiting from bribery and corruption. There was an unpleasant move to denounce anyone who did not grant a request and to report the most trivial matters to the military governors. Apart from those trying to settle personal scores there were still more than enough scandals for investigation.

Before long, Col. Ojukwu came to our school. He was making a tour of government establishments and putting the fear of God into civil servants. There was a tense atmosphere heightened by a brisk search around the buildings before the governor arrived in a small convoy of police and military vehicles with flashing lights and siren. After a meeting with the principal, the Colonel came to the Assembly Hall to address the students and give us all a chance to look at him. He looked stern but so very young, of medium height, heavily built with broad shoulders. Perhaps he spoke so slowly to add authority to his youth but at the time he was alarming and gave an impression of tightly reined anger. After his short speech, he had the staff lined up and looked grimly at us ... then, unexpectedly, moved along the line shaking hands.

61

All over the country it seemed the movement for reform was continuing. Tribunals were sitting, decrees were issued. Not much of this interested me. I had been so short a time in the country and had no political interests, so I just kept on happily teaching. I remember being irritated by newspaper articles on the 'First 100 Days' and so on of the new regime. After years of what everyone now agreed was misrule it seemed unreasonable to expect instant success, instant reform, instant bliss.

At last something came nearer home. Decree 34 unified the country, abolished the Federation and substituted the Republic of Nigeria. There were to be no more regions; a man's place of birth and his ethnic origin were irrelevant in the unified civil service. Transfers could disrupt family life enough already. We discussed in the staff room whether this meant we could now be transferred anywhere in the country instead of within the region. Later we were told that others elsewhere were regarding this same decree as another move by the Igbos to extend their sphere of influence, since up until then only Northerners had served in the Northern civil service.

Rioting began in some Northern cities and was widely reported in foreign newspapers and journals as being against Easterners. Aguiyi-Ironsi, who had gone to Ibadan in the Western Region, disappeared with his host, Col. Fajuyi. The Eastern newspapers later reported that 286 other officers and men, mostly from the East, were also killed. Another Northerner took over the government, while Col. Ojukwu in a broadcast said he had agreed that the regions should draw further apart to prevent more bloodshed. It was painfully moving to listen to him and afterwards the national anthem sounded mournful: 'Nigerians all'.

There was more killing in what came to be called the 'pogroms' of July and September 1966. At first a few, then more and more of those Easterners who had been living in other parts of the country came hurrying home. By now there was a tense and frightened mood wherever people gathered to talk over the news. Many of our students came from families living in the North or had friends and relatives there. The first news of riot and massacre brought a crowd of students to the principal's house, weeping and imploring her to allow them to go back to look for their people or at least down to the railway station to see if they could see any of their families or hear any news of them. The principal did allow two of the senior girls to go to the station, although she would not allow anyone to leave school to go to some other place. They were only going to hear more rumours and little real news unless a train just happened to come in. At least they were safe enough in school. Many of the teachers were also under great strain, waiting for news. Sometimes one or other of them would be called to the telephone and from their behaviour the rest of us knew that someone else was safely home. But what of the others? No news.

Months later the Government put the total of those killed at 30,000, and this figure was generally believed to be correct although it could hardly have been more than a guess. Some two million were said to have come back, a few with their possessions. Banks had transferred accounts to the East but for most, part of their money was tied up in houses, shops, trading goods, loans, building land, vehicles, hotels and bars. Some came back nearly naked, many with only whatever they could carry. Charitable organisations met these refugees at the railway station and airport to give out clothing and food while hospital staff brought out the dead, cared for the injured, and vaccinated against smallpox. No-one knew when a train would arrive and there were torturing delays while crowds waited long hours. Food was prepared that could be kept without spoiling so that whenever the train did arrive the passengers could be fed. The reports of injured people mutilated with axe or matchet cuts, dumb or hysterical with shock, spread a shudder of revulsion. We heard of people hunted down like animals, beaten, burned, buried alive, of eyes torn out, hands cut off. A poster showed a headless corpse that had been brought off a train. They said the sick in hospitals had been dragged from their beds and killed; women in labour had been torn open and the unborn children cut to pieces. Girls, they said, had been given to lepers.

These reports and the return of so many refugees brought loss, suffering and grief to every part. 'There is no family that didn't lose someone,' I was told, and taking family in the Nigerian sense, with the closely woven fabric of relationships, it could well be true. In a way hard to imagine in European society where 'family' often meant only father, mother, children, blood relationship here is an unbreakable bond, and marriage imposes an immediate and genuine tie of obligation between all the 'in-laws'.

Before, I had only seen the extended family in action when unsuccessful members were asking for assistance. Now I saw it giving generously to the unfortunates who returned. Many had not been in their home villages for ten or twenty years.[2] Some did not know where to find their family land, and few had houses to go to. However the extended family took in its remotest members, fed and clothed them and found them space to lie down. There were no refugee camps in 1966. There were no beggars, and people took this achievement quite calmly in absorbing this tremendous rush of people. Newspapers outside enjoyed debate on whether or not persons moving from one part of the country to another part of the same country could be termed refugees. But it was beginning to seem already that this was no longer the same country.

Those who returned were not only businessmen who could have earned and deserved the hostility of those from whom they made their profits. All groups in society were represented—doctors, nurses, university professors and lecturers, graduate teachers, undergraduates from Nigerian universities, skilled workers and labourers, Federal employees of all grades. I went one day to the Public Works Department to collect a mechanic to repair the water heater in my quarters. On the way he told us how he had escaped in Zaria by hiding under a heap of dead until the Red Cross came to clear the bodies. A parent who came to school to see if his daughter could be admitted held the clerks silent with horror while he told them obsessively over and over how the other Igbo staff where he had been working had run to his office for protection, and the soldiers stood in the doorway and shot them down. Others did not talk, but their silence was eloquent. A young teacher who had come back from Jos sat huddled, staring out through the window in the middle of the staffroom chatter, and only gradually came out of her withdrawn oppression. Through and after all these stories came the fear that 'they' would not stop, that 'they' would come in and continue.

The number of students in school increased. Classes were so full that extra desks could no longer be fitted into the classrooms and the front row of children was right against the teacher's table. Classroom space was so short that I found myself teaching in the Library workroom, on the verandah, in a corner of the school hall, even once in the open air when there just seemed to be nowhere else to go. Yet despite everything, orderly life went on both in school and outside. Of course there were people from other regions living in the East. A flare of violence against resident Northerners in Enugu and Port Harcourt was brought under control by the police until non-Easterners could be sent out under police and army escort. But it seemed these instances of resentment and retaliation were reported elsewhere, even to the point that the 'disturbances' in the North were claimed to be in retaliation for the 'massacres' in the East.

There were many changes now in the town, particularly a great increase in traffic. Walking or driving had always had its moments, since there were no pavements for pedestrians and deep concrete storm water drains ran along the sides of the roadway. Things were worse when children were hurrying to and from school—hundreds of them in dark red, green or blue cotton dresses and shirts, scurrying across the roads. Level crossings complicated the pattern still further; people and vehicles would make a dangerous dash to get across under the pole instead of having to wait for ten or fifteen minutes broiling under the sun while a slow train rattled and thumped its way over the road. But now there was more traffic than ever—cars, lorries, buses, taxis, scooters, bicycles, pushcarts, pedestrians of all kinds and loads, with women carrying towering head-pans of produce, men balancing 20-foot planks on their heads, boys with a fluttering pole full of shirts or blouses for sale. There was one traffic hazard missing—the herds of bony, long-horned cattle which used to be brought down on the hoof from the North for slaughter.

There was also a great deal of building going on. Some houses which, since we arrived, had been left at ground floor window level were now being finished. There was such a housing shortage that buildings were let or leased before they were completed. Some better-off families, who failed to find a self-contained flat, took several rooms in houses which were being built as working-class single-room lettings. New businesses and factories were being set up. It seemed as if the East could benefit after all from the forced return of capital, skill and experience if only it could be left to do so and 'they' did not come.

In Lagos a debate was dragging on in Committee to try to decide on the future form of the country. Federation or Confederation were the words. There was also the question of the creation of states which would divide the regions into more pieces. But the meetings seemed to achieve nothing and were suspended without any decision being reached. Then, early in January 1967, we heard that the military governors had met on neutral ground at Aburi in Ghana. According to reports, first they put on record their belief in negotiation as the means of settling the country's problems and their rejection of force. Then they appeared to have worked out, quite amicably, a solution which would allow the Federation to continue but with the regions less closely attached to each other. There were other clauses concerned with the withdrawal of troops to their regions of origin. The tensions relaxed at the news of these agreements and also at the report that compensation was to be paid to those who had suffered in the events of 1966. However the situation grew anxious again when it became clear that none of the terms of the agreement were going to be put into effect. Young people started wearing T-shirts with the slogan 'On Aburi we stand'. The Government released a set of records said to contain the whole of the Aburi discussions.

One morning the last lesson was cancelled and the school was called to hear the choir give a dress rehearsal performance of two songs being prepared for the Festival of the Arts. It was usual for songs to be composed about things which had been happening, as we were to find in the villages later. That day, instead of the usual politely enthusiastic response, emotion swept the audience. Many, including teachers, were in tears as the choir sang:

> Still the dead in their quiet voices ask
> Oh God, what did we do?

The feeling of rejection that had come with the events of mid-1966 was being strengthened by the increasing isolation of the region. The governor announced that he would implement the Aburi agreement by the end of March 1967, but nothing happened. A series of 'survival decrees' followed; in particular, the payment of oil revenue to the Government was stopped. We heard that the Federal Government had cut off the salaries to Federal employees in the East, restricted postal communication, forbidden the export of food to the region. It was one of those unquestioned statements that the East could never manage to feed its large population from its own resources. A trite little song played over and over on the radio seemed to catch the prevailing mood:

> Close the door, light the light.
> We're staying home tonight,
> Far away from the bustle and bright city lights.
> Let them all fade away
> Just leave us alone.
> And we'll live in a world of our own.[3]

By the end of May the isolation was complete. It only remained to break the last link in name. With a mandate from the consultative assembly of chiefs and elders, the governor declared the former Eastern Region the independent Republic of Biafra. In an early morning broadcast we listened to his deep melancholy voice reading the proclamation of independence. It was the 30th of May. The suspense was over, whatever might be going to happen next. The new National Anthem was played, slow and sad for a new country without any of the usual polished ceremonial. No hauling down the former flag, no lavish exchange of greetings and compliments, no announcements of aid and agreements. Only a voice on a grey morning and the feeling that we had been driven back on ourselves and there we would stay, responsible for ourselves alone.

It seemed that the declaration of independence was greeted with relief. No public holiday had been announced but Enugu was full of processions and demonstrations. People greeted one another with a loud 'Hail, Biafra!' Cars and lorries were decorated with green branches and pictures of Col. Ojukwu torn from magazines and newspapers.

> We'll build a world of our own
> That no-one else can share.
> All our troubles we'll leave far behind us there.
> And I know you will find
> There'll be peace of mind
> When we live in a world of our own.

The school was jumping with excitement. I went to my Latin classes, wrote up the date, and '*Salve Biafra, patria nostra*'[4] on the blackboard, then tried to teach. It was no use. The stately dance of the syllables would not fit the day's drums. A false report that Biafra had been accorded diplomatic recognition by a number of other countries raised the excitement still higher until the principal gracefully cancelled the rest of morning school and allowed the students to take their own singing, branch-waving procession down to the town and back again.

Then we all went on with the preparations for the school Open Day and Prizegiving in early June. No-one could feel sure it would be held, but in the weeks of waiting that followed independence there was nothing else to do but carry on as normally as we could. And there it was. We had the usual programme—the school hymn and prayer, the principal's report, last year's examination successes. The staff in their newest and most fashionable attire were on the platform behind the distinguished guest—the wife of the governor. There were the heaps of glossy prize books, luckily obtained before the blockade; the speeches; the well practised routine. But some things were very new. As the audience took their places several men were wearing the traditional Eastern dress of *lappa* and European shirt, which was usually kept for leisure time. The showy *agbada*, which had originated elsewhere, had been the usual dress for such occasions. There was the new and poignant national anthem played from a tape recorder and heard in silence, since there were still no words written for it. And when the name of a prize winner was called—Dalila Mohammed, the daughter of an East African UNESCO official—there was a prolonged murmur and rustle among the audience, fading at last as the child came up quite normally to receive her book. After the Prize-giving in the hall the visitors spread out over the compound to see whatever they liked. As soon as the distinguished guest had been around the subject displays set out in the classrooms, the staff too were free to visit and compliment each other's efforts, watch the traditional dancing, or just slink home in exhaustion after the long-worked-for day. After all the excitement the school should have settled back into its routine, and the next big event should have been mid-year examinations.

War came first.

6

WE ARE AT WAR

The war began on 6 July. I happened to be in Ogbete Market when the radio broadcast the first details of fighting on the Northern border, and I stopped with the crowd to listen to a trader's radio blaring out. At the time John was in hospital for a long postponed minor operation and our visits to him, like everything else, became delayed and complicated by the road blocks and checkpoints that went up all over town.

The possibility of air raids was in everyone's mind. There was a tense meeting of staff who lived on the compound, in which we discussed what precautions to try to enforce in the over-crowded school and surveyed the place with new eyes alert to its dangers. Each two-storey classroom block had only one steep two-flight staircase to evacuate the three upper classrooms. The hall, full of light and air on the grassy slope above the games field, felt as fragile as an egg shell. The gas cylinders for the laboratories and kitchens were an obvious danger. I know I gave my opinions with a certain relish since I had heard of English-born wives being excluded from their neighbourhood civil defence meetings. Some of us had personal experience of air raids, after all. But the drills showed plainly that any actual air raid, even down at the town, would be a panicky experience while a crowded school was in session. We were all relieved when the Government closed schools late in July. It will just be for a few weeks, the principal told the buzzing Assembly: 'You are going on holiday earlier, that's all. I expect you will be called back earlier to begin next term.'

There was the general idea that this could not last long; world opinion must surely soon call a halt. In other quarters, the war was confidently expected to last 48 hours. The Biafran army was small, hastily recruited, mostly untrained, and the only weapons it was known to possess were a few hundred police rifles. The Nigerian army in contrast was supposed to be the best drilled and equipped in West Africa. It had been further strengthened by experience of actual fighting with the United Nations peace-keeping force in the Congo. As Quartermaster General in the Federal army, Col. Ojukwu must have been responsible for arms purchases, so he would be in the uncomfortable position of knowing the odds exactly. I was told of expatriate businessmen who said confidently that if war came it must be brief; after all it was only forty miles from the border to the capital, Enugu. And anyway the Igbo wouldn't fight; they'd compromise yet again. Another view, more perceptive, maintained that although logic must conclude Nigeria would win, since she had all the advantages in numbers, arms and experience, the one factor that could not be calculated in advance was the spirit of the Biafran people. The loss of life in the pogroms had touched every family and we constantly heard that ours was a fight for survival.

Indeed, with this surge of civilian emotion to sustain them, Biafran troops made such a good showing with pit traps, home-made hand grenades and petrol bombs that they extended the number of days before a grand parade and entrance into the capital. It was explained by the Federal government that Biafrans were delaying the advance by blowing up bridges along the road from Nsukka to Enugu on the northern edge of Biafra. But people who knew that particular road well said there were no bridges on the Nsukka road.

One expression of public opinion was a demand that Nigerian street names be changed, particularly those with painful memories of Northern towns like Kaduna, Zaria, or Jos. There was a demand for registration of cars that had come in from other regions and were still bearing their foreign plates. The order was made in September; all cars were to be re-registered—E for Enugu, P for Port Harcourt, W for Owerri, and so on, with white numbers and letters on red instead of white on black. A local bookshop opened an exchange section for numerals, since the effects of the blockade were already being felt, and everyone couldn't be sure of obtaining new numerals. Our Vauxhall changed from EE 9448 to E 380, and friends' well-known and familiar cars suddenly became unfamiliar. The only cars which didn't change were those recently re-registered with the VIG (be VIGilant) number plates for important people. Other registrations that came later were BA (Biafran Army) and GRB (Government of the Republic of Biafra).

Another demand aired in the newspapers was that companies with Nigeria or Eastern Nigeria as part of their corporate name should drop the outdated country of origin or replace it with Biafra. Government concerns had of course made the change at once. The newspaper *Nigerian Outlook* became the *Biafra Sun*. The Electricity Corporation of Nigeria (ECN) became the ECB. The local broadcasting station changed from the Eastern Nigeria Broadcasting Company to the BCB—not BBC, since someone was already in occupation there. The University of Nigeria, Nsukka, became the University of Biafra on all its vehicles. When stocks of postage stamps were exhausted, the post offices began collecting the fees and rubber-stamping envelopes 'Biafra, postage 4d paid', and so on. Some town postmarks still included Nigeria, but gradually all removed this part of the rubber stamp or blurred it into an inky indecipherable smear.

Like many other schools left empty by the premature ending of the second term, our school was used as a militia training centre. Some 2,000 men arrived in goods lorries one black Sunday, when the news from the Nsukka front was particularly bad and the BCB was inexplicably repeating a brief panicky announcement: 'We have been betrayed ….' The lorries were bringing men to Enugu apparently in the belief that an attack on the capital was imminent. When the situation became calmer, around 600 militia were moved into the school dormitories for regular training, and a checkpoint was mounted on the road up to the school offices. Our staff houses lay in part of the compound outside this barrier, so we had to pass through, constantly explaining our foreign faces to new sentries on duty. To save time there, as well as at the main gate to the compound and in the town, the school office prepared brief identification papers for us on official letterhead. My own read: 'To whom it may concern: Mrs R. Umelo is the wife of a Biafran citizen. She is an Education Officer and a tutor at Queens School, Enugu. She lives in the school compound.' This simple document proved invaluable as it answered the regular checkpoint questions, at least when I was returning to school. 'Who are you? Where from? Where are you going? Why?' An English wife who had produced an older identity card once issued by the Ministry of Education, and headed Government of Eastern Nigeria, had been briskly told off by a police officer. He had seemed quite unaware that his cap-badge, shoulder flash, belt buckle and all read, bright and shining: 'Nigeria Police, Nigeria Police'. She had really not liked to point it out to him.

On our way up and down from the office we used to see something of the militia's rigorous training at the hands of regular soldiers. If they didn't move quickly enough or get down flat enough, a stout stick made the meaning of the command plainer. Drill was practised on the level space outside the school offices, advances from cover across wide open space beside the road, mock assaults on various buildings. Recruits went for training marches and runs round the large compound. And they sang. All the children learned these first militia songs and sang them around the house, but their piping voices could not hint at the shattering effectiveness of the men's deep voices rolling across the early morning or weaving complicated harmonies through the moonless dark. Banal though the words, or the translation, might be, these songs were transformed by the singers' inborn feeling for harmony and rhythm, even more by their emotion, into something very moving:

> We are Biafrans, marching to the war,
> By the name of Jesus, we shall conquer.
> We are marching to defend Biafra (Biafra)
> We are marching to defend Biafra (Biafra)
> We are marching to defend Biafra (Biafra)
>
> Oh, Biafra, Biafra my home.
> No more Hassan, no more Gowon,
> There will be no more Nigeria when the war is over.
> Ojukwu, give us arms.
> One by one we shall finish Nigeria.

A simple journey to the library, market or Kingsway was complicated since, if something had happened to arouse suspicions, it entailed passing through many checkpoints. A permanent post was mounted at the main gate. At each checkpoint the car would stop at the barrier, usually a pole laid across empty oil or paint drums. The militia, police or, at really important road blocks, the Army would come up and take a look at the car's occupants. Often everyone would be told to get out of the car, which was quickly searched—bonnet, boot and glove compartments. Any briefcases, handbags, shopping bags were inspected, the driver and passengers questioned: 'Who are you? Where are you going? Where have you come from?' And after that, usually, 'You can go,' even if it was only on to the next check, just along the road, perhaps within sight of the last. It was certainly wearing but not at all intimidating and I never found anything seriously to resent in the search and questioning. Sometimes the initial approach was brusque but calm answers always improved matters. Our driver was far quicker to resent things than I was and I lectured him frequently on how necessary it was to keep cool while being questioned. No doubt we looked very funny when I was wagging a reproving finger at him, since he is 6'3" and I am 5'1". If we kept calm and replied quietly, a quarrel could hardly develop. I felt in a way that wanting an explanation of the foreigner in the back seat was justified. Many doubts were being expressed about British officials and the conduct of the British Government, so anyone on guard duty naturally asked, 'Who is this white woman?' Of course to those who had previously enjoyed a certain prestige in working for a European it was galling now to be treated with more than usual suspicion.

One afternoon I went down to the Club. I had never been a member, as there was always so much to do. There had been a radio appeal for all women who could knit. A surprising number had assembled and a table tennis table was piled high with wools of many colours, weights and qualities. We were lectured on the need for warm clothes for the soldiers fighting on the chilly heights around Nsukka and asked to make sleeveless V-necked pullovers as quickly as possible. Some of the women were commercial knitters with knitting machines, and a contract agreement was made with them at a lower-than-usual price. The rest of us were amateur hand knitters. We were given out eight ounces of wool; we signed and went away clutching our skeins of emerald, turquoise, scarlet and orange. It appeared that for the moment only thinner, poor quality wools were available in appropriately drab hues of brown, grey/olive and maroon. So we left these for the machines and chose the better, thicker, brilliant wools. 'Very gay coloured army we shall have,' said someone dubiously, looking at her heap of geranium puff balls. 'I mean, you could hardly call this a camouflage colour, could you? Whoever gets this will feel warm just to look at it.' Over the next few weeks I passed the time in an approved way, knitting in all my spare moments—green, blue, brown, red, olive, yellow and lilac, dutifully changing the pattern from V-necked sleeveless to V-necked with sleeves, to high rolled collars with sleeves...

An office was opened in Enugu by the Biafran Council of Women's Societies, where completed work could be handed in and more wool collected. All kinds of voluntary work were coordinated there, making use of surplus energy and the desire to do something useful and officially approved. It was carried on through three small cluttered rooms into various out-buildings and a quickly-erected plywood and zinc workshop. Here was the collection centre for food donations, empty tins, bottles and jars, clothing and blankets, and just moving from one room to another meant dodging around and over a well-organised confusion of cardboard cartons, filing cabinets, bundles of books, heaps of sweaters, bulging polythene bags, and unravelling balls of twine. Toilet kits were made from plastic sheeting and packed with soap, razor blades, chewing sticks and so on. Women worked on day and night shifts sewing buttons on uniforms. Ordinary tee-shirts were dyed dark green for army use including, suitably enough, some of those which read, 'On Aburi we stand'. These dank-smelling clothes had to be washed, rinsed and dried to prevent skin irritations. Later, uniforms began to be made from cloth of any suitable weight, and had to be dyed dark green also. These were much heavier to wash and handle. This went on day after day with the numbers increasing. Often a car would come in packed with bundles of washed uniforms on the back seat and floor, and the boot so full it had to be tied with rope. The first weeks of suspicion had passed and nobody now queried a foreigner's car being loaded with anonymous army uniforms. Another English wife recalled as she chatted with a militiaman that she still had a bagful of Rising Sun shoulder flashes on her lap.

Anyway there were fewer foreign faces to be seen around town. Members of the Peace Corps and Voluntary Service Overseas had not been free to decide for themselves whether to leave or not; those I knew had gone very unwillingly. The VSO girls left soon after the beginning of the fighting, while the men left later when there was a mass departure of Europeans. People were upset by this evacuation since there seemed at the time no need for panic. As usual many assumed that those who left had some secret information that something bad was on the way. It looked uncomfortably as if the British Government were removing material witnesses, and few foreign wives of Biafrans responded then to the urgent advice to get out while there was chance.

Other towns had had their first experience of air raids by now, although nothing yet had happened at Enugu. I heard a story that in England the BBC had shown pictures of bomb damage in the capital with the Hotel Presidential in ruins. But the war seemed to be going well, with Biafran forces in control of the Midwest Region, well into the Western Region and threatening the power supplies of the federal capital. In mid-August the Government announced the date for re-opening schools, and a great rush began. Class I and Class VI interviews had to be held before the school reassembled for admissions in January 1968, since candidates came from such distances that many had to stay at least overnight. Fortunately nothing happened during the days the small children were in the compound. But while the Class VI candidates were there, Enugu had its first air raid. By English World War II standards it wasn't much. I was on duty in the Hall helping to invigilate the exam when we heard a first dull explosion, then the sound of a plane, then, answering our silent questions, the tak-tak-tak of machine gun fire. The candidates fled outside though not far enough from the building for safety. A few wanted to lie sobbing, but the rest were eagerly looking up to see the plane. I sat under cover of a flowering tree with the head of the French department, setting a display of traditional British phlegm that pleased us both.

These first air raids were hit-and-run affairs by one or two planes, usually dropping a few bombs from a great height. Even so they were alarming if only because there could be no warning. Blowing hooters or train whistles only confirmed that the plane was there already, not that it was on its way. The school compound was usually so quiet that you could hear the drone of a plane's engines even before you could see it against the bright sky, and now that there were no more commercial flights, every plane must be suspect. Down in the noise of the town a plane would just be suddenly seen and there would be immediate panic. Some people wanted to run and hide but anyone with a gun used to come out and fire at the planes. The streets resounded with the noise of police rifles, automatics, double-barrelled shotguns, pistols, even locally made hunters' guns loaded with gunpowder. It did no real good but it helped morale. I didn't agree with many of the official instructions on what to do in air raids; to close all windows seemed to invite trouble from flying glass. To look for the plane and then go the opposite way produced more injuries at first from falling into and over obstacles than from the raids. So I instructed the household to leave windows open, not to run about outside but to take cover under the solid wooden table. When I was home I used to take the children into one of the big built-in wardrobes and sit on the floor with them. Some people were digging trenches to serve as hiding places but these seemed particularly dangerous to me since they were without timber supports for the sides. Every time I passed those dug at Ogbete Market they looked more and more like open graves with a dismal detritus of rubbish and mud collecting at the bottom.

Indeed, visits to the market were becoming less of a pleasure, although the attitude of the people was still generally very friendly. Prices of some imported tinned foods were beginning to rise slowly though there was plenty of fresh food everywhere (except for meat, of course) at normal prices. Salt was the first commodity to become noticeably scarce and more expensive.[1] Sacks, bags and tins of salt vanished from the stores overnight. Loose salt, sold by the cigarette cupful, was up from one penny to one shilling. Sugar then became harder to find. Small tins of evaporated milk went up by pennies from sixpence to a shilling each, while a 5-pound tin of dried milk went from 18 shillings to £2, and baby formula was double prewar prices. A 5-pound bag of flour rose in price from three shillings and ninepence to 10 shillings and sixpence, and bread was sold out within minutes of being delivered to the stores. Most people were blaming the increases more on the greed of traders than on the effects of the blockade. The department store, Kingsway, sold all its goods at normal pre-war prices until its once well-stocked shelves were bare.

The increased air raids prevented schools from reopening. Primary schools were open for a day or so, then closed again. The war was now not going so well. The Nigerian tactics of shelling until Biafran forces retreated and then advancing were having some effect. They claimed to be coming steadily towards Enugu, but they had been claiming this for so long that commentators suggested Enugu must be a kind of mirage city that moved away at the same rate. They even announced the capture of Asata and Ogbete, districts in the town.

> 'And how do you go to the market now that the enemy have captured Ogbete?'
> 'I am learning to say, "Please let me pass" in Hausa.'

The citizens were derisive, but no-one knew how real and near the danger was becoming. There was a sudden, apparently purposeless withdrawal from the Western Region and the Republic of Benin.[2] Rumours were spreading, everyone seemed nervous, and more than ever we were listening for strange sounds. A friend whose house had the best view of the town and the hills beyond told me ruefully: 'I keep looking, expecting the Hausas to come over the skyline like the Indians on the warpath in a cowboy film.' We heard the occasional roll and boom reverberating across the slopes but they were dismissed vaguely as 'testing'. In our house we were more often alarmed by the bathroom door, which closed with a dull thud like a distant explosion, or by heavy lorries grinding up the hill.

There was enough trouble about without inventing more. But halfway through September news spread of a serious plot against the Government. Arrests were made but suspicions spread wider and no-one could tell how far the conspiracy had reached and who might be involved. People were leaving town or sending their families and luggage to their villages. Just when everyone was hoping that after all we had escaped a great if vague danger, we began to hear heavy guns firing at some distance away, the sound re-echoed and magnified by the surrounding hills. Now some said it was more testing and some said they were our own guns where some of the enemy had been cut off in a valley, and some said … But it was several days before most people said that after all the tense weeks of waiting and listening, it must be that Biafran guns were being used by saboteurs on the outskirts of the town, even though the supposed ringleaders had been executed.[3] We spent so much time listening and wondering that when something was really wrong, we couldn't believe it.

On Tuesday, 26 September, I happened to be up at the school talking worriedly to others when we heard a noise worse than anything so far, a sound like the slam of hell's gates. Everyone ran to stare across the bright valley, then scattered. I hurried to my house and agreed with John that we should take the children to his village until the situation was clearer. There was no chance of packing our possessions. The car was going to carry ten people instead of its normal load of five or six. There would be no space for best clothes, no space for books, no space for any luxuries, but we believed it was only for a week or so. We packed a suitcase with everyday clothes, gathered up all the tinned food we had in the house along with a small box of medicines. We put in some bedding, blankets and pillows. Odd items were picked up by chance and added—the family photograph album, the scissors, a bag full of reels of cotton. We made futile careful gestures—drawing curtains, locking doors, discussing whether to leave the kitchen window open for Sootypuss and his relatives—while all the time the compound seemed to grow more dangerous. One way out, one road, one gate. We filled the car—our driver, John and I, our four children, our nephew Evarist, Angelina and Apollonia who helped me with the children, and we drove away. The bright morning had changed to soaking rain and we moved heavily through the sodden, half-empty compound. There was a last-minute visit to tell friends where we were going, a telephone call to the principal, and then we went away. The children, excited by all the rush, were singing:

> We are young Biafrans, we are young Biafrans,
> Come along and join the army. Oh come along,
> Come along Gowon, come along Gowon,
> Come along and fight the battle.

Silent though the adults were, we knew the extent of our loss. Enugu was being captured, and much of the cheerful self-confidence of the country was being undermined by this first suspicion of sabotage. From now on the 'sabo' would be the bogey man to explain every setback or problem. In personal terms, the house keys I was so carefully carrying would still be in my purse a year later, pocked with rust. The singing gradually stopped as the children grew tired of the crowded car and the windows blurred with rain. Except for the necessary explanations at checkpoints on the road the rest of the journey passed in dreary silence.

7

RUNNING FOR HOME

We arrived in my husband's village in Ogbaku, at the end of the long unhappy day.[1] The direct road from Owerri had been closed (no one knew why), and we had to go round by a longer route. The last few miles were along a bush road in places axle deep in rainwater. We swished through a long succession of deep wide puddles as the last grey light was fading and turned at last into the family compound. The sound of the car brought the rest of the family flocking out into the drizzle and there was a rush of people from nearby houses. Everyone had heard there was trouble in Enugu and had been waiting for relatives to come home. We brought out our tired, cross children from their packing of blankets, pillows and boxes and carried our few loads inside. The tiny house was already overcrowded with the furniture and belongings of a sister-in-law, herself a refugee from Lagos where she had been a wealthy trader. With her were her own son and three of her brother's children. We sent someone to peel and fry yam slices for the children, another to make tea, and sat down wearily to answer questions. What was happening at Enugu? Everyone wanted to know, but we could only say what we had heard, and why we had decided to leave. When the children had eaten and were asleep, we talked it all over again. But everyone was sure it would only be a few days before saboteurs were cleared and we could go back.

At the end of the week, John decided to return at least to pick up some more clothes as he only had what he was wearing. The car left at first light and returned after dark with a load of odds and ends but no better news. More and more people had left town, and many areas seemed almost deserted. The periods of shelling seemed heavier and nearer, and the anxiety and uncertainty were even worse.

I soon learned it was no use thinking about Enugu before going to bed or the result would be long hours of sleepless tossing and worrying. Still, I never doubted we would be going back. The only question was when. At the end of three weeks? By Christmas? I had not previously spent nearly as much time at Ogbaku as I should have done if John had been in the country all the time instead of spending fifteen months away in England. During his absence I stayed in Enugu, and even when he returned I seldom travelled down with him when family affairs called him home at inconvenient times. As a result I was not used to village life nor were the people used to me; John was the first of their sons to marry a European and bring her home.

Of course everyone knew all about the problems of having a white wife. The expenses of maintaining her, feeding and clothing her far outweighed the initial saving in not having to pay a dowry. A foreign wife was a fragile ice flower who had to be kept for most of the time in a specially cooled atmosphere. She could not walk, except from a big shop to her car, nor could she do any hard physical work or carry anything except an expensive oddment or two in a paper bag for a very short distance. To have one of these exotic creatures in their midst caused some of the older people an enjoyable mixture of excitement and apprehension. I found it very wearing to have everything I did become the subject of comment and speculation.

For the next few weeks I felt very ill at ease. After so many years of being efficient and hard-working, I resented my enforced idleness. There was little housework to be done in our two cluttered rooms. No one liked to see me sweeping with a broom made from a bunch of palm fibres. Things could not be unpacked or arranged, but only stowed away in suitcases or cardboard cartons under the bed or in corners. No-one would allow me to carry water from the well, and to tell the truth, my two-handed heaving or my one-pail-in-hand staggering looked far harder work than when the girls walked without apparent effort, carrying with a brimming pail or even a full pail inside a full bowl balanced on their level heads. I could not cook. The acrid smoke from the open fire made me sneeze and my eyes water. No-one would allow me to chop firewood. An indefinite future spent sitting, being looked at and talked about had no attraction. To remind myself there were things I could do and that I was even good at doing, I marked a long-neglected set of exam papers that had somehow been put in the car, finished the last of the army sweaters, and then with nothing left at all, I had a mild attack of fever for some days. After that, I stopped fretting and settled down to wait for the end of the war.

From our hill top at Enugu we had been able to look so far across grassland, roads, roofs and tree tops that the view at Ogbaku seemed even more restricted by contrast. This was forest, and on every side the bright sky was frayed by the branches of trees, every kind of useful tree. There were palms of all kinds, and fruit trees—orange, grape-fruit, pawpaw. There was the oil bean with its tiny evergreen leaves, and the timber trees of the bush—mahogany, silk cotton whose slender trunk fans out at the base into natural buttresses—and most magnificent, the massive *iroko* that soared above the village meeting place and the well.[2] It seemed a smaller, safer, hidden world.

It was also a great deal more crowded than our earlier spacious life. Home was now a small, zinc-roofed house standing well back from the bush road. It had four rooms, each about 10 feet by 10 feet, built in a row with a small store-room at one end. In front was a covered verandah about four feet wide. Behind the house was a dusty yard with two pepper cola trees and a couple of raffia palms. There was also a place for bathing—an enclosure made of a thick fence of palm branches but with no roof. Behind the boundary fence there was some farmland planted with cocoyam and more trees, stretching away to tangled bush. In front of the house was another, bigger yard. On one side were more mud-built kitchens, one for the grandmother and the other for John's late brother's wife. Opposite was another kitchen which our sister-in-law, Happiness, used. This was bigger, lighter and cooler, just a palm-thatched roof supported on tree branches and lengths of wood. This was also used as a sitting out room for visitors when the verandah was too hot or the sand flies were biting. Behind this place to the edge of the compound there was an untidy tangle of growing things—cocoyams, cotton bushes, pepper plants, orange and pawpaw trees, coconut and raffia palms and several *oha* trees, whose slightly bitter young leaves were used as a vegetable in soup.

Our arrival overcrowded the compound. There were ten of us and thirteen people were already living there—John's mother, our relative Akoma and her six children, a teenage nephew, our sister-in-law and four children, not to mention chickens and a round young goat. But at least that was our full complement. Other compounds continued to increase as members of the family kept returning, from the North and West, Ibadan, Lagos, Nsukka, and now Enugu. You could easily tell those who had left a disturbed area; they jumped and started at the sound of hunters' guns or funeral shots in the darkness of the night.

There were other night noises—the whirring, chirping, rasping, ringing sounds from the bush. But among the thick sheltering trees, one familiar sound was always missing—the small persistent sound of the wind whispering across long grass. As night fell and people were in their compounds it was time for announcements. Clang-clang, clang-clang. Someone unseen was passing along the road stopping at each compound to shout and bang the *ugele* (bell) to attract attention. At times a woman was enquiring about a missing goat or chicken, or a borrowed iron pot that had not been returned. Or men could be summoned to do some communal work next day or to comb the bush looking for strangers, camping places, hidden food or arms. For matters requiring discussion the men were called to meetings under the *iroko* tree by the *ekwe*, a drum sounding several notes and made from a hollowed log.

John was immediately reabsorbed into the village life he had left long ago. With other men of his age, he was called for communal duties, particularly for cleaning the paths leading to the market on the morning of market day. He was also called on for contributions to this and that activity, to provide palm wine for the night guards and kerosene for the bush lamps at the check points outside the village and to take his turn on duty if he couldn't arrange for a substitute.

One result of the events at Enugu was a surge of suspicion throughout the country. There were checkpoints everywhere on all the tarred roads, on junctions where bush roads joined the tarred roads, and around villages where they were mounted night and day. Everybody had to account for themselves and their movements and submit to being searched if required. Militia groups were in training everywhere, drilling with wooden guns. Any announcement of recruiting for the army brought a rush of hundreds of young men to join up. Requirements were still very high, including a minimum educational standard of a pass in the elementary school leaving certificate. Many young men were rejected for some slight physical defect and had to present themselves several times before they met some less exacting recruiting officer and were accepted. Because of the general suspicion of strangers, John asked me not to go far from his compound where people knew me and could account for me to any questioning police or soldiers. This restriction was another source of frustration. There seemed nothing to do except sit and look on, although even from a chair on the verandah there was plenty to see. There was local traffic along the bush road at the end of the compound. Traders carried immense heavy loads on bicycles—sacks of *garri*, yam or cassava tubers. Women passed with loads of produce in heavy enamel bowls balanced on their heads, or with big knobbly bundles of firewood.

Everyone seemed astonishingly strong. People politely assisted each other getting a burden up and down, but once it was balanced on their heads they could carry it on the cushion of their hair, supplemented by a piece of cloth coiled into a pad or even leaves swirled into a round. Goats tiptoed about the yard, chickens scolded and scratched, swarms of naked children stopped to stare. To the Igbos children are wealth. A man without children has nothing, however rich he may be in other respects. The more they had, the better, although some were already maintaining that a family should not boast of the number of its children but of the number that had been educated. An English woman might be unwilling to sell her pram and cot or give away baby clothes, in case it meant she might unexpectedly need them again. An Igbo woman would not part with any of them in case it meant she would not be needing them again. Children also worked hard. They collected firewood, following their mother to work in the farm, or went to the well, tapping out a tune on the pails they were carrying. They came with a piece of broken pot or the outer shell of a coconut to collect glowing embers to start their own cooking fire.

Towards evening I would call someone to take a walk with me along one bush path to the market and back by another way to enjoy the evening air and look about at the flowers. There was a creeping plant like a purple convolvulus and a yellow daisy-like flower. The children

83

used to pluck off the petals from the lower edge and call it Biafra Sun. Very occasionally there would be something breathtaking, when a little further from the path spectacular flowers would suddenly appear in bloom with blossoms as wide as my outspread hand—orange-red or creamy white. I had seen something similar at Enugu once when a kind of lily blossomed in a tangled hedge, seemingly made of hundreds of tiny flowers massed in a compact ball. A black line of palms seemed painted on an apricot and lemon sky. As the light faded, all colour in the bush was lost and the roads looked exactly like the illustrations in nineteenth-century tales of exploration, painstakingly drawn with a fine pen in varying shades of grey.

After a week or so I heard that a register had been opened in the office of the Administrator of the province where displaced civil servants and others who had left Enugu could enter their names. We hurried to Owerri to get ourselves on record, found the place and wrote our names in a hall full of anguished chatter. There again we heard that the Ministry of Education had established a temporary headquarters at the Government College, Umuahia. At the end of the second week in October we drove to Umuahia to notify the Ministry where we were living. It was not a happy or comfortable journey. After several weeks of a very sheltered life I was back in the world of violent alarms. The road, particularly between Owerri and Umuahia, was busy with road blocks and at each we had to explain who we were, where we came from and where we were going and why. The little pass I had used in Enugu was very useful in supporting our identity and story. We were constantly having to get out of the car while it was thoroughly searched. At last we reached the Government College, met several members of staff on the same errand, and heard news of others. The principal was also there, en route for England. She told us how she and her husband had been the last to leave when shells were already landing in the deserted school grounds. The journey back again was easier since the militia and soldiers on duty generally remembered us, but at one checkpoint outside Owerri, while we were answering the routine questions, a suspect was being thoroughly beaten up by the militia a few yards away. A relative who passed by sometime later told us that in the end the man was killed.

It was very difficult while we stayed in the village to know anything of what was happening outside. Our radio, which had worked well enough in Enugu where we were right underneath the transmitter, had always been temperamental once it was brought into the bush. Just when it was most urgent to hear what was going on, it simply refused to work at all. We carried it, turned it this way and that, balanced it on the car roof. All useless. Until our batteries faded we borrowed a neighbour's radio, but when the batteries were finished it was impossible for a while to get more.

For some time we placed a disproportionate value on the radio call sign: 'This is the BCB, Enugu.' 'Our radio is still talking,' everyone said, until they realised that wherever the radio station was, certainly no-one was talking from Enugu. Keeping the call sign unchanged had a certain defiance about it, a kind of 'next year in Jerusalem' hope and promise, a refusal to admit that the capital was lost forever. Some of the announcers timed the pronouncement particularly well: 'This is the BCB ... (pause) ENUGU!' In one way or another we managed to hear something of the attacks on Onitsha and Calabar in October.

Every week or so we travelled into Owerri, our nearest town, seven miles away, to visit the bank where salary was paid, post internal letters, or see what we could buy there that we couldn't get in the village. Surely it wasn't just in comparison with Enugu that Owerri seemed a poor neglected place with a dirt approach road beside the market, deep in pools of mud and water. There was generally something to buy in the market, although not the profusion we left behind in Ogbete. Prices were slowly rising because of the influx of civil servants, which prompted traders to ask 'senior service' prices. We bought tinned food mostly, such as corned beef, tomato puree, or milk, all at inflated prices. We bought candles, matches, tea, coffee, simple medicines such as aspirin, antiseptic ointment, or Freedom Balm, a popular cure-all. We were able to buy bread sometimes, and a hunt along the stalls occasionally produced other surprises. We could get newspapers, although because of the shortage of newsprint these had a strange appearance. The Government paper, *Biafra Sun*, was still published at a reduced size on normal paper, but a number of new papers had appeared, and we liked the *Mirror* best. These new papers used lined foolscap paper, then blue and red lined ledger sheets, and ended up after many months on ordinary lined exercise book sheets. For several weeks the *Mirror* did very well using brown wrapping paper, not quite dark enough to be illegible. As for our purchases, they were wrapped in cocoyam leaves, rather like a large rhubarb leaf.

Now we had started to move around a little, we met more of our friends. One was writing from her husband's village outside Onitsha, having moved from one sound of shelling to another. An English wife, last seen on the morning we left Enugu, recognised our car outside the market and left her address tucked into the windscreen wiper. We also met some of the traders we'd known at Ogbete, but their greeting of 'Customer! Customer!' was no longer so cheerful. One who had kept a well-stocked haberdashery and clothing store told me he had brought out nothing at all, either from his house or his shop. Others said they had made their escape on foot and walked over twenty miles carrying a small suitcase until they were able to find transport home to their villages. Although we enjoyed getting out and meeting people, there was little in the journey to leave anyone happy for long.

Locally produced food was all cheaper in the village markets, though I seldom went to buy any. Besides all other restrictions on my movements, my arrival always had a disastrous effect on the prices, and Angelina or Apollonia usually went instead. As well as the foods I had been used to eating, we could now eat bush meat—small animals caught by hunters in the bush. Squirrels cost sevenpence. They were very small but made a strong and well-flavoured broth, even if there was little meat in it. 'What a pity to eat the little things,' we said, sucking their fragile bones. A 'rabbit' cost four shillings and sixpence, but this was no bob-tailed, flop-eared bunny but a giant rat with small pricked ears and a long bare tail. Its diet of roots, leaves and bark was rabbity enough and we ate it. Less often we were able to buy porcupine, which really did taste like pork, and grasscutter, another large rodent with plenty of tender meat and probably the most delicious of them all.

Soon after our arrival John went on a trip to Ahoada in search of cheaper salt and there he bought a crocodile. It was not too big and was still alive; the hunter killed it before handing it over. It cost £1 and he bought it almost as a joke, certainly as an experiment, though he had been assured it was very good meat. On the way back, at every checkpoint, when the searchers opened the car boot and saw the crocodile they offered to buy it at steadily increasing prices. A hunter came and skinned it, then the meat was cut up and cooked in a big black iron pot.

And so I was served my first crocodile steak, a thick slice through the tail, bone surrounded by meat. I expected it would taste like old mud bank but it was very good, a white meat like rather dry chicken in flavour, but dense in texture like pork.

Doves and guinea fowl were shot sometimes. Ordinary poultry cost eight shillings and sixpence for a local fowl, more for a huge 'agriculture' or English bird. There was no longer any beef but still plenty of goat meat. If you happened to have a fridge (and electricity) it was cheaper to buy one on the hoof for £4–£6 than to buy it by the joint. But without any good way of preserving the meat, the small expensive piece was the one we could afford. Goat and rabbit were prepared in the same way, by being singed over the fire with a penetrating smell of burnt hair. The animal was then washed and cut into pieces. The meat was part boiled then hung in the smoke of the fire. It would stay good for several days. Others could eat meat that was really high but my sensitive nose twitched at the least suspicion of taint. Storing food was a problem. I could see now why there had been such a ready market for empty tins and containers in the household. A tin with a really close lid was the only way to keep ants out of everything, not to mention rats. These were mouse-sized, not giants, but still I disliked hearing them under my bed, gnawing on the cardboard cartons or polishing their teeth on the stock of tins.

With so much time to spare I watched the business of cooking. The most important item was the mortar. It seemed as if nothing could be prepared without being pounded. The mortar was hollowed out of a solid block of wood with sides and base inches thick in the larger sizes used for household cooking and preparing palm oil. Every compound had an old mortar or two thrown into a corner with a great hole worn in the base from years of pounding and thumping. The pestle was three or four feet long and was also made of heavy wood. There were small sizes of mortar used for crushing salt and pepper together. Fresh tomato and onion were crushed before being added to the soup.

Groundnut oil reached six shillings a pint bottle before we stopped buying it and relied on palm oil, thick and red as tomato ketchup. Once people had used plenty of tins of tomato puree costing fourpence or fivepence and every market was piled high with the small shiny tins. Now these cost two shillings if you could find any, and so had to be used with miserly care. I liked the various kinds of stew they made for me and ate them with rice or yam. I was not so fond of cassava, the cheaper food. This was prepared as *garri*. The tubers were peeled, washed, grated and put into a sack to be squeezed and pressed for several days while the compound was full of the sour pungent smell. Then the dry flakes were fried golden with a little palm oil. Or the tubers could be prepared as something called (they said) 'decayed cassava'; the smell of that was exactly what anyone might expect.

The local product to drink with all this food was of course palm wine. It cost a shilling a gallon and with its natural yeast was a good food. Early in the morning when just brought down from the tree it was generally mild and sweet. As the day progressed it became a tougher drink altogether as the sweetness grew less and the alcohol increased. When we arrived, our own raffia palm was being tapped twice a day and the household was awash with free palm wine. Women generally preferred the sweet raffia wine to the harder product of the oil palm. Igbos of course had a separate word for each variety of palm tree, but in English the one overworked word had to manage for three trees. There was the raffia palm which produced sweet wine and was killed by being tapped. Its fronds were lighter in weight; rope and string were twisted from its bark. The coconut palm produced the big nuts only. The oil palm was the most useful. When tapped, it produced a strong, un-sweet wine. If it were left to fruit it bore clumps of orange red palm fruit from which palm oil was prepared. Then the stones inside the fibrous flesh were cracked and the kernels extracted and chewed as a rock hard nut. Before the blockade, kernels were bought by dealers and exported for the manufacture of margarine. This kind of palm tree had heavier fronds; the centre rib was called 'bamboo' and was used in fencing and making seats. We often watched someone climbing a palm tree to hack off a few branches. The fronds sailed down as gracefully as ostrich plumes until they landed with a heavy crash among the undergrowth. The dark green strips of leaves were also used. Palm thatch fastened to a base of split palm rib was called an 'attached roof' (or a thatched roof) and used to cover mud built houses, kitchens and so on. Or the thin strong fibre down the middle of each strip of leaf was cleaned, tied in bundles and used without a handle as a broom.

One day was so like another that without a radio or regular news-papers it began to be difficult to know what day of the week or even what time it was. Without a radio to make a time check, the clocks gained and gained and were often as much as an hour ahead of the right time before we could set them right again. Sundays were recognisable because most people dressed up and went to Mass, but in between it was really hard to know the day of the week, and for me this became disproportionately important. I took to crossing the days off on the calendar printed on the back of the exercise books I was using, and when the next one had no calendar I wrote one out. Some of the exercise books had calendars for 1968; looking at the next 12 months neatly printed ahead of us we wondered how many I would have to cross off before we returned to Enugu.

Like everyone we seemed to be living from hope to hope, deadline to deadline. First the war was going to be over within 48 hours. That had passed. Then people spoke of a 'Kinshasa special', supposed to be planned to coincide with a September meeting of the Organisation of African Unity (OAU) in Kinshasa.[3] Afterwards they said this had failed not only because of the drive on Enugu but also the plot against the Government. That had passed, but Enugu was lost. Now we heard there was to be a 'Christmas special'—an attack by Nigeria on impor-tant centres with poison gas. When this did not happen we heard it was because the pilots who would have flown on the raids refused to take part. Who was to know what was true?

And now Christmas itself was near, the most anticipated Christian festival. Children expected something new to wear and for many these always used to be their only new clothes in the year. I brought out my last pieces of material to give the other small children dresses. To my own I explained that we would not have any new clothes while we stayed in the village until the war was over. They cheerfully agreed since they had a few better clothes than everyone else, which they could put on to celebrate the holiday. We killed a goat, but even a whole goat doesn't go far among 18 people. We were rather fewer now, since our sister-in-law had gone to live in Owerri with her family.

Then Christmas was over, the once impossible limit of our stay. It was time to start marking off the days of a new year.

8

IN THE VILLAGE

After three months the local people were getting more accustomed to our being among them. The children were learning Igbo fast. Eze had been able to speak the language before we left Enugu but Uzoma and Nwaneze had always said it was too difficult. Now everyone was talking and it looked as if the youngest girl, Iheoma, was going to speak Igbo as her first language and not even a mixture of Igbo and English. As well as learning the language, the children were also learning the games, stories, proverbs and songs. These were usually short and satirical and many were composed by a neighbour's son about local gossip, scandal and adventures. Quite often, I was told, the subject of such a song would hear about it and go and bribe the composer to suppress it before its publication. When it had been sung once, everyone would soon be singing it.

> Owerri, I am looking for my brothers.
> Owerri, Owerri, I am looking for my brothers,
> One girl has ruined two sons of the same mother,
> But that one won't spoil me.

And again,

Apollonia said:

> Don't talk, don't open your mouth.
> Amula is going to marry me.

Now, Apollonia, you talk
Has he married you? And will he?

My children learned these songs as fast as anyone and were always singing about Chaser and her vain remorse, or Felicia's trouble.

We all went to visit Felicia.
Felicia was lying on her mat.
We all went to visit Felicia.
Felicia on her bed lay flat.
'I have some trouble inside,' she said.
When we asked her 'How do you do?'
Later we remembered every word she said.
Big trouble was inside. True, true!

But I still tried to keep up the habit of putting the children to bed around 8 p.m. since they were always up by 6 a.m. So they missed playing out on moonlight nights when all the village children seemed to be awake, playing games and singing. Some of the more serious-minded adults would go out to hush them or send them out of their own compounds. But playing in the bright moonshine was too old a tradition to end so quickly.

For myself, I was still speechless, although even my slower ear could now pick out words and the flow of sounds had stopped being as alien and incomprehensible as birdsong. I suppose my love of formal language made it harder for me to learn just by repeating sounds. Besides that, Igbo is a tone language. One word can have seven quite different meanings according to the pitch of the voice, compounding the opportunities for ludicrous mistakes. For example, a slight difference in pitch turns 'Our father who art in heaven' to 'Our father on a bicycle'.

My speechlessness did not stop people talking to me. Everyone talked and usually a third person would be at hand to translate. Complicated three-cornered conversations took place, but these were nothing to the palaver over writing letters. I often used to write for other people since I could compose more quickly and fluently, particularly when a piece of elegant English was required. First the visitor told me what he wanted to say, then the interpreter translated. I asked enough questions to make sure I understood the details. Then I composed the letter and read it to the interpreter, who translated it to the visitor to see if I had said what he wanted to say.

I was also always in demand for medicines. I had brought some from Enugu and as items finished I tried to replace them from the new expensive remnants still on sale in Owerri. I wished many times that I had more medical experience and knowledge, as I was called on to advise on illnesses I knew nothing about. I tried to find a balance between being timid and doing nothing and being cheerful and doing the wrong thing. The mystery patients were advised to betake themselves quickly to hospital, while fever, diarrhoea, dysentery, coughs and colds, small injuries, aches and pains were treated. Some more obscure ailments were also dealt with. 'My stomach is turning me', yielded to Milk of Magnesia, as did 'My stomach is giving me headache'. 'Heat in the belly' and 'Pins in the waist' were cured by aspirin.

I tried to stop people from taking the strong purges which were the favourite ways to cure almost everything. The more violent the action, the more effective the treatment was thought to be. Patients with malaria used to purge themselves to exhaustion. Even more dangerous, people with diarrhoea or dysentery would take purges and this could result in dehydration, collapse and death. The purges given in native medicine were alarmingly violent and most people took an overdose of patent medicine and store-bought laxatives, as a matter of course, to get the same effect. They also liked injections and thought them better than capsules and pills. As well as wanting injections any time they went to hospital, many people patronised the unqualified who gave injections, and would go to them whenever they had an infection or slow-healing injury, or just felt out of sorts. They seldom took a full course of treatment as it would have been given in a dispensary, but just had one or two injections, usually with an unsterilised, communal needle. After all the strict control of drugs in England I found this very alarming.

I found out very little about native medicine. There were potions made from roots, herbs, bark or leaves to treat fevers. These seemed to work well, with their incredible bitterness. The native doctor was more than a doctor. He was also a priest, a soothsayer—one who could look into the causes of illness and advise who or what was the reason for the sickness. There was magic as well as medicine in his mysterious bag and my ignorance of the language was far from being the only barrier to my curiosity. One day a relative was being treated for a persistent fever. While doctor and patient chatted, I watched him place a thin twig on top of an egg half buried on end in the sand. The twig began to vibrate and twist like an uneasy compass needle. When it jerked itself off the egg, it was casually replaced to continue its writhing. I thought with admiration of those anthropologists who have only to arrive in a society to have the whole structure explained to them, most secret thoughts and all, and then they write a book about it.

Ogbaku was in a very dry district without any surface streams or ponds. The water supply came from a deep well, constructed with four concrete cisterns, so you could finish drawing up the water before beginning the equally laborious task of carrying it away to the compound. The well was covered at night, opened early in the morning and closed at 5 p.m. There were penalties for opening it without authority, and no quarrelling was allowed. Any woman who was drawing water wearing a head tie had it removed and had to pay five shillings to get it back again. If anyone dropped a head tie or anything else into the well, they had to pay a fine of £1. Many people still used water from an *umi*. These were pits dug where they could catch the rainwater that runs off the road. At first, seeing them dug in a line at the entrance to compounds, I thought they were tapping some underground source of water, but they were only collecting surface water. John insisted that up to his generation everyone had been brought up on *umi* water without taking any harm. I was not convinced. I used to boil and filter the well water and forbid the use of *umi* water except for watering the garden; for that fertilising purpose it seemed to be particularly suitable.

Mosquitoes were no problem since the district was so dry. This was a blessing since we no longer had mosquito nets. There were sand-flies—nearly invisible black specks with an itching bite that was potentially dangerous, since I had read somewhere they could carry dengue fever.[1] The bites easily became infected but would heal slowly if they could be kept clean. For weeks at a time one child or another would be wearing bandages from knee to ankle. Sticky plaster dressings would have been smaller and neater but it was no longer possible to find them, and bandages could be washed and used many times. In the dry season there were jiggers—sand fleas that showed themselves too late in itchy swelling around the toes. A little skilful excavation with a needle or a porcupine quill would extract a small wriggly grub from under the skin. This was disposed of by being dropped into the fire. Sizzle-pop! Sandals were some protection, but I still had three or four during their season, caught when the sand sifted through. Usually the place from where the jigger was extracted would heal quickly, but again, it was necessary to keep the place clean somehow. No-one liked wearing socks at the hottest time of the year, but that seemed to work at least as well as dabbing the place with kerosene.

Only a few houses had a latrine and people used to go into the bush. One area was for women, another for men. We soon decided to dig a latrine—a pit that was about four feet across and more than 20 feet deep, and cost 15 shillings to dig. Then a 'little house' was constructed over it of palm thatch, both roof and sides, with the angled entrance usual in toilets. Stout branches of trees were buried in the floor and a piece of wood made a lid to keep out flies. The result was simple but effective. In peace time the little house would have been built of concrete blocks with a zinc roof or of mud with a thatched roof. As it was, the building made all of palm was cool, with a fresh sharp smell of leaves. Soon after this a village dispute closed access to one of the traditional pieces of bush, and soon many compounds were digging their own latrines. I was becoming more than usually fussy about water and sanitation; I found myself pregnant again.

About this time, the great money change began. The Nigerian Government announced that they were to change their currency notes. Since Biafra was still using Nigerian currency, this would leave her with obsolete notes that could not be used outside her own borders. In particular they could not be used for arms purchases. Everyone was instructed to pay all Nigerian banknotes into banks, post offices, and local treasury offices. Only a few days were given for the exercise, so that it could be completed well before the expiry of the period Nigeria had given for the same purpose. The banks were jammed and surrounded by immense queues stretching hundreds of yards, and the whole process was very slow. Many depositors had no bank accounts and had to open savings accounts, and we knew many people who stayed in line for days. We went to Owerri three times but couldn't face the queues, even though we had an account with Barclays Bank. We thought it would be easier to withdraw money from the bank when the time came than from anywhere else, but as time was running out, we paid what we had into the local County Council offices and went away with our receipt.

For the next few weeks there were no banknotes in circulation, only Nigerian coins. In the markets, prices came down since few people had much money with which to buy, and in Owerri, traders gave credit to their established customers. There was speculation on whether the new currency, when at last it was issued, would be pounds or perhaps francs (since there were so many rumours about French support of the country), or even something entirely new. When new notes appeared they were £1 and five shilling values and had a very handsome design with the palm tree and the rising sun. The five shilling note had four smiling Biafran girls (known widely as 'Biafran babes') on the reverse and was much admired. As time proved, the paper was not really strong enough to stand up to hard use and the five shilling notes particularly became rubbed and worn.

Biafran postage stamps were also issued for the first time. Up to now we had still been managing with rubber stamp franking. The fourpence stamp was a darkish grey-green, inscribed 'Republic of Biafra, May 30, 1967', with the coat of arms above in black and white and the flag below in colour. The twopence stamp bore the map of Biafra in the national colours, with a small map of Africa in the bottom left corner, and was inscribed 'Republic of Biafra Independence 30 May, 1967'.

Since postal communication had been cut off, one of my problems had been how to let my family know we were safe and well. In Enugu I used to give letters to anyone I found who was going on leave; I could take letters to the British Council, who always knew of people who were going out. The problem became more pressing when we had to leave Enugu and everyone who was likely to leave had already gone. When I met the principal at Umuahia she took my family address so she could write to them and say she had seen us. After that, there seemed to be no way of sending word until I thought of asking the Reverend Fathers at the College along the road.[2] Their school was a technical college with an ambitious programme for expansion all approved and ready to begin, although no building had been started before the war began. The Fathers kindly agreed to pass along letters now and then, and I was able to give them a letter telling all our no-news. For a while I was also able to hand in air letters at the post office, so I did all I could to let the family know we were all right. Early in March a letter arrived from friends in Canada, the first word from outside since the post had been suspended in May 1967. Within ten days, two air letters arrived from my mother and we were in touch again. Gradually a tenuous line of communication was built up. Letters could take anything from five days to two months to arrive. They leap-frogged each other and arrived out of sequence but many came, and I was no longer conducting a one-sided conversation.

At about the same time, the visit of the Papal delegation to Biafra brought very important visitors to see the country for themselves. This ended what had been aptly called the 'information blockade', since it seemed that mostly Nigerian-based reports were being circulated outside, together with the idea that the war would be over by 31 March. As well as helping with letters, the Fathers gave us all kinds of assistance with news, as the College had its own generator and the radio and television were working.

It was strange to go back into a household with electricity. The light seemed harsh after the muted glow of bush lamps and candles, while the ceiling fan was something to watch with astonishment. Iced water numbed the mouth after so many months of tepid water, made cooler from a clay pot. Soon we were being invited to film shows. Whenever they could get hold of a film and projector there was a programme, and it was very pleasant to sit out in the cool darkness while the film was projected onto a sheet hung against the back wall of the house. Other Reverend Fathers used to come in from other Missions and after the show there would be exotic things to eat—cheese sandwiches and cakes—and then talk, talk, talk about the war.

One evening, as well as the main feature, we had an added attraction, the commercial film made for Daimler's advertising of the Ferret, Saracen and Saladin armoured cars. The audience watched with rather strained attention as the film showed the things concealed in bush, or fording rivers seven feet deep, moving undeterred by deep mud, or riding tilted at an angle of 45 degrees along narrow sunken tracks or dried up watercourses. The smooth voice of the commentator enthusiastically listed their qualities, the advantages of six wheeled vehicles over those with caterpillar tracks, their armament, their rate of fire, 'now proving their efficiency in all parts of the world'. 'Including Biafra,' said a voice from the back.

It was at one of these film shows that we first heard about the air raid on Awgu Market that was to set such a grim pattern for the future. The Vatican delegation had been almost on the spot and people who had been there photographed the scene. Seventy-eight civilians, according to this report, died in the raid, too many for the small local hospital to take in its mortuary. Rolled in mats, the bodies were stacked in rows outside. Children's feet protruded from the shapeless bundles. More of the 150 injured died later.[3]

A market provided the most defenceless target. There was no chance of retaliation, little chance of escape, and for attacking planes, little chance of mistake. Every village had its market place, a clean swept area of sandy earth, wide and deserted except on market day when it was filled with a dense crowd of people, wandering, gossiping, bargaining, while the muted roar could be heard far enough away, just like a waterfall. Most of the traders were women, from housewives selling the spare produce of their farms and gardens or pettytrading in salt, pepper and dried fish bought for resale, to market women who would normally be dealing in goods worth hundreds of pounds. There were people to do repairs to bicycles or shoes and sandals, while tinkers mended pots and pans. Tailors were there with their sewing machines making new clothes and mending old ones. Most women sat out with their basket, tray or head-pan in front of them, chatting and suckling their babies. The repairers and bigger traders might have a shed of palm thatch to keep off the sun. But when a plane swept in over the trees there was no shelter from bullets and no escape for the densely-packed people before bombs exploded. The terror caused by reports of market raids carried by the BCB and the newspapers was so great that afterwards the faintest suspicion of a plane would empty a market square in seconds. Even the mistaken sounds of a lorry or the sight of a circling hawk menacing against the bright sky could cause a panic-driven flight into the bush, careless of scattered food and goods and anxious only for life. Markets were a clear and conspicuous target both in the countryside and in the towns, where the bright zinc roofs were added to the crowds of people as an attraction. For some months township markets opened only for a few hours in the morning and evening; closing time in Owerri was strictly enforced. In any case few people had any inclination to linger; there was less and less to buy and crowded places felt too dangerous. The banks also changed their times. For one period they opened only in the early mornings, for another in the evenings.

In the village it was hard to see a plane until it was almost overhead, as our horizon was so much restricted by trees. After the attack (pictures were in an overseas paper) on a family compound in Orlu, no one could feel safe even in their own yard. As soon as we heard the sound of a plane, I used to gather all the children together and lead them into the bush behind the house. If the plane was passing over we went just a short way. If it was circling, or we heard any sound of explosions, we went farther from the buildings and crouched down in the undergrowth. Even though Owerri was seven miles away, the noise of any raid there seemed to be just down the road. Worst was the sound of what they said were fragmentation bombs—anti-personnel bombs that split into razor-jagged shrapnel to lop off heads and limbs. It was hard not to believe the raid was in the next village just beyond the trees. Sometimes the planes just buzzed across the sky; the sounds of a jet seemed to leap from all quarters of the clouds, lagging behind the plane, unsuccessfully pursuing it.

People said the British pilots would attack from low altitudes, while the Egyptians[4] preferred to drop their bombs from high up, out of reach of anti-aircraft fire. In any case, how many guns were there to defend the townships? There was nothing to protect the villages. The only other thing that could be done against the fear of air raids was to cover the zinc roofs of houses with palm fronds to try to camouflage them. There was no way of knowing whether this was effective; friends had told me they had been able to see every mud house quite distinctly when flying between Enugu and Lagos on commercial flights. It certainly dimmed the bright white shine under the moonlight, but then the aircraft did not seem to fly at night. The palm fronds bleached under the sun to a dull pewter grey and gradually slipped down the angle of the roof, so that as you looked out through the door, instead of the straight edge there was a jagged border black against the light. Much later I saw military buildings where the fronds had been placed on end standing against the walls as well as across the roof. This looked altogether more effective.

I was still looking for ways to pass the time usefully. I borrowed books—any books—from the Reverend Fathers and read everything:

theology and church history, biography, all kinds of fiction, school text books. I happened to have a small Latin dictionary with me. I borrowed Latin texts from schools, bought exercise books and studied whatever I could find as exhaustively as if we were to have an examination on them. I marked off the passing days on the back cover of the exercise books and on the front cover I noted significant quotations and relevant aphorisms.

> Multa quae impedita natura sunt, consilio expediuntur (Livy XXV)[5]
> In rebus asperis et tenui spe, fortissimo quaeque consilia tutissima sunt[6] (Livy XXV)
> Veritatem laborare saepe aiunt, exstingui nunquam[7] (Livy XXII)
> Nihil usquam nobis relictum est nisi quod armis vindicarimus[8] (Livy XXI)

Reading Latin generally puts the present day into perspective.

I was also becoming very good at patch-patch and that was taking up more of my time. Patch-patch consisted of taking something beyond repair and somehow making it wearable again. Village people had always worn their clothes for a longer time than ever seemed likely. I saw someone wearing a cloth whose design commemorated the coronation of Queen Elizabeth II in 1953. But as the supply of new clothes, new material and even second-hand clothes grew less, and at last stopped, everyone had to wear clothes they would in ordinary times have given up and thrown away. It was so difficult to find material with which to patch and cotton with which to sew. Anything was used to mend everything else and if it didn't match, never mind. I was lucky enough to have a supply of sewing thread most of the time and I worked away energetically. Gradually a system evolved for the worst things—making a kind of lining and sewing the shreds and tatters onto it. Some of my better efforts really deserved preservation for some future display of wartime arts and crafts and the desire for survival. Without sewing cotton, of course, the most enthusiastic patch-patcher is lost. I sent regular appeals home to my family for cotton; as a three-pence, 100-yard spool was costing five shillings and ninepence, a 500-yard spool was at least a pound. I discovered what you did when you had no cotton when a young relative came to stay; the seat of his pants was mended with fine raffia.

More and more items were beginning to wear out. Either there was no replacement or it was prohibitively dear. For lack of maintenance, the house was looking very shabby, with crumbling concrete steps and dirty paintwork. The ceiling boards were being eaten away around the edges by ants and one by one they began to sag and fall, leaving a large, square, cobwebby space under the zinc roof. Now it was possible to lie on the bed and watch the rats along the rafters instead of just listening to them. When we had petrol and were still going to Owerri occasionally for shopping, the car would not start unless it was pushed. If we kept going, our dark green Vauxhall would purr along, glossy bright and splendidly Senior Service. But once the engine stopped, we had to implore passing strong men to give it a good push. We pushed it in the car park, in the market, and if the engine stopped, at checkpoints. But of course we were not alone. Hardly any car seemed able to start without help and it was nothing unusual to see a crowd running a bus or lorry to get it underway.

Anyway, my visits to Owerri were now ending. The bank and market were open at inconvenient times and the car insurance was running out. Petrol had been rationed for some months but luckily we had a full tank and a full reserve jerrycan, even at eight shillings and sixpence a gallon. As I was not engaged in anything essential, I was not eligible for petrol coupons, and we could not pay the black market prices of £2–£3 per gallon. We decided to keep the little we had to warm the engine now and then. After the end of February I hardly stirred from the village. Indeed, more and more civil servants were laying up their cars and using bicycles or walking to work. A sound, second-hand Raleigh bicycle that once cost £8 was bringing £30 or more, while a foreign newspaper quoted £100 for a new bicycle. It could have been true.

Tyres were the biggest problem. Some civil servants were able to buy a bicycle tyre and tube for £1 10s, but on the open market a new tyre cost £10 and a tube 10 shillings. We had an old bicycle and spent as little time as possible regretting the good one left behind in Enugu with so many other things. Any time John wanted to go to Owerri, he had to set off at first light and return about 10:30 a.m., travelling before the sun was high and before the usual time for raids. All the men preferred to wear coloured shirts because anything white was thought to attract attention. At the first sound of a plane, everyone would leave the road and hide in the bush. But there was more to occupy us in the village for a while, for as the end of the dry season approached it was time for clearing the bush ready for planting, the beginning of the busiest time of the year.

9

LEARNING TO MAKE DO

The latest deadline for the end of the war was 31 March 1968, but it passed and the war went on. Onitsha was captured, first by the BBC, they said, and later by the Nigerians.[1]

In our village everyone was busy preparing to clear the bush ready for planting. As Ogbaku had plenty of land, it was customary to clear and plant land in rotation and after being used, an area was left for five years fallow to recover its fertility. At the end of that period, it would be covered with a dense tangle of bush up to 10 feet high, with some few bigger trees which had been spared last time the land had been cleared. The first task was to cut down this younger growth in the hot and dusty weeks at the end of the dry season. This was communal work. The men went all together to the areas to be cleared and each man was allotted his share of the work to be done by the oldest man in the family-community. Clearing the bush with heavy matchets was very hard work.[2] Everyone developed painful blisters and those who were unaccustomed to the work, since they had been living and working in towns, had hands that were rubbed raw and bleeding. Only trees and bushes that could be used to stake the yams were left. Everything else was cut down and the roots were grubbed out with matchet and hoe. A few days under the hot sun made the bush tinder dry. It was then piled in heaps and burned so that the last days of the dry season smelled of wood smoke and the evenings were full of little fires. People were cleaning their own compounds also for planting, and one late evening our neighbours set fire to their own rubbish. From our side of the fence it was incredibly theatrical, as raffia palm fronds curled down into sight out of the blackness and were illuminated from underneath by the leap of the flames.

When the cleaning had been finished the land had to be allotted for planting. After some lengthy palavers this was done. The oldest received most and the youngest least. The area allocated to each man was smaller than usual because there were now so many men at home in the village who would otherwise have been living busy lives elsewhere. Also some of the land which should have been available this year had been pledged a long time ago and never redeemed. Some sharp questions were asked. Land could not be sold, but it could be pledged to pay a debtor or to raise some money to meet an emergency. The man who held the other's land could not sell it or pledge it to anyone else. When asked, he was bound to return it and receive the amount of money he had advanced to the owner of the land. But if it were the year when the piece of land was due to be farmed, he was entitled to receive double the amount he had given for it. Some land was owned by the family-community and some by individual families personally, but the same rules applied. The whole system seemed so complicated, and relied so much on boundary marks and the fragile memories of old men, that I was no longer surprised that there were so many disputes and lawsuits over land. Even the mildest men were ready to go to extravagant lengths over such cases in their passionate attachment to the land. But I did wonder how these land disputes were ever settled in a court some distance away. They seemed so intensely local, concerned with this very stone and that very tree and with what the other old man had been heard to declare his father had once said ... Such fundamentals hardly seemed to have a place in the elegant legal edifice of enactments and precedents.

As the working parties moved into the bush to clear it, the sound of voices and the ringing smash of matchets prompted all the wild life to begin moving away from the disturbance. This season was the time for hunting—one of the few times when larger animals could be seen, including a kind of antelope the size of a large dog and another as big as a European deer. When rat burrows were found, the animals were dug out. Tortoises were sometimes picked up but generally the bush seemed disappointingly bare of animals and birds; the district was too densely populated and thoroughly hunted. John had stories to tell from his boyhood of the troops of monkeys, scurry of many squirrels and flights of birds to be hunted with bows and arrows, as well as larger animals that made the bush paths dangerous in the dusk and early morning. But now most of the wildlife was small and wary and there had been more snakes seen in the school compound than in the forest.

Still, the time for clearing the farmland was when whatever animals there were would be on the move. We often used to watch a group of hunters assemble, wearing their tough old clothes, greyish brownish green like the scrub, with several dogs scratching fleas and swearing among themselves. Most men carried a matchet and some kind of knife and all except the very youngest had guns—generally the very long single-barelled, locally-made guns. Some of these fired large cartridges, while others needed to be loaded with a charge of black powder from a powder horn and pellets made by a blacksmith. All the guns looked as dangerous to the hunters as to the game, but the men understood their weapons and any accidents were usually caused by a twig catching a trigger as the hunters struggled through dense undergrowth and not really by any weakness in the guns. Even for the experts, reloading took time and so there was only one chance and one shot if something burst out towards the line of men. An animal might be hit by several men but it belonged to the one who actually seized it, but who may possibly not have hit it at all.

The weather in the last few weeks was exhausting, very hot and humid. Everyone went to work very early so they could return when the sun became too strong. I suggested to the technical expert at the college that he might produce a table fan that could be wound up like the old fashioned gramophone for use in households without electricity. In the meantime I made do with a big hand fan beautifully woven from palm leaf. Nearly every evening, great clouds would tower into the sky with the uneasy flicker and flash of lightning twitching like a restless nerve. Sometimes there was thunder muttering and growling to mingle with the test explosions from the direction of Owerri, making everyone anxious. Then at last it would rain, drenching down on millions of leaves, roaring across the forest nearer and nearer while we hoped it would reach us and not pass by. The first drops slammed against the roof, then the full storm burst. The thick dust of the yard turned to grey mud. The bush road was awash with a passing car wallowing through. Gradually the rain roared away and the air was cooled and shaken for a few hours until the heat and humidity could build up again into the next violent storm.

These first storms reminded everyone if their houses needed repair. It was the time to patch roofs and replace frayed thatch. Palm thatch was made in lengths; a strip of palm leaf was folded in half over a length of palm rib and secured with palm rib splinters. This process was repeated until the whole length of palm rib was full. The completed lengths were fastened onto a split palm rib frame, each overlapping the length below. The resulting roof was waterproof except when the leaves dried and crumbled, often from the heat and smoke of the cooking fire beneath. It was fairly easy to replace a decayed length of thatch but too often, just when the worn out sections had been removed and there was a stretch of sky instead of a white star of daylight, it would rain. A drip became a downpour. There would be shouts from inside the house and loud complaints from the unfortunate outside, still trying to slide new lengths of wet thatch into place under the rain.

Cracked and flaking walls in mud houses and kitchens were also repaired or repainted with a coat of bright red laterite and often finished off with a curlicue design in black paint made from charcoal and water. Properly maintained, the mud houses lasted for years, but if the rain penetrated cracks and soaked the heavy walls enough, they could collapse.

But the main work was still on the land. As the heavy rains softened the ground it was time for planting. First the yam heaps—squareish mounds in which the seed yams were planted—had to be prepared. After the yams, corn was planted four or five grains together. Melon would grow in the spaces. The fruits weren't eaten as such, but the seeds were called *egwusi*, the essential ingredient in the favourite *egwusi* soup. By the time the yam was beginning to show, cassava would be planted, and then everyone could draw breath for a short while and give their painful hands time to heal. The tools for this work were very simple. The short handled hoe, with its blade set at an angle of 45 degrees, was surely one of the most awkward implements ever made. Deep digging was impossible; it could only scratch the surface and scrape the topsoil together to make yam heaps and ridges. A good deal of practice was needed before you would know how high to make these heaps, beds and ridges, and just how to construct them to prevent deep gullies being sliced into them by the force of the rains. Some people had ordinary rakes and spades, but these seemed to be used in tidying compounds and so on, and the hoe was the tool for serious farm work. To make the holes for fence poles or yam-sticks, a length of special wood was used, very heavy and close textured. A suitable piece would simply be carefully peeled of its bark, then pointed and smoothed with the all-purpose matchet.

Around their houses people planted cocoyam and some little patches of vegetables. Angelina and Apollonia, who both came from districts where vegetables were more valued, thought the local efforts rather feeble and planted more My mother-in-law allowed me to use a piece of land in the compound that she usually planted with cocoyam.[3] We cleared out some cotton bushes and a do-no-good banana stem and fenced it rather lightly. It was impossible to lay out beds and ridges properly because people had scattered seeds here and there, and leafy green vegetables, pumpkin, pepper and tomato plants were soon coming up in odd places. So the ground had to be prepared where nothing happened to be growing and scattered plants were transferred as soon as they were big enough to handle, so that the vacated patch of land could then be made into a proper ridge or bed. As a result the beds were all sizes and the paths wandered drunkenly this way and that. I was no good at this work, but as soon as the basic job had been done I had more time and patience for cultivating seedlings, planting out, watering, putting in stick supports and tying up plants as they grew. Against the back fence were the nursery boxes—two old mortars with holes in the base, a bottomless bucket, two bottomless enamel bowls, all rescued from the bush and pressed into use. As everything that can possibly be mended is always mended over and over again, anything that has been finally discarded was sure to be as thoroughly finished with as anyone could imagine. We remade the bases with sticks, plantain or cocoyam leaves torn to allow drainage, and filled them with rich black soil. They were safe enough unless they were lifted, when everything would fall out and you had to start again. I planted most of the seeds in these containers, since it was less wasteful than scattering them under the bruising rain.

Local vegetables grew very easily. Waterleaf would grow like a weed if the bare leafless rootless stems were just pushed into the ground after the leaves had been stripped off for soup.[4] There were two kinds of pumpkin. One had round fruits streaked green and yellow, which I was told had always been rather despised as 'poor man's food', although the leaves were regularly used in soup. I preferred the very dark green, iron-rich leaves of the fluted pumpkin, but I never had a chance to taste its improbable fruit, which looked like a big dusty green Chinese lantern. These pumpkins needed some sort of framework for support and a little protection against goats if they were planted outside the fence. Even the goats wouldn't eat snake tomato plants, a vine with a peculiar musty smell on the leaves and snow crystal flowers that produced another improbable fruit—long and cucumber-like, but soft to the touch and easily bruised. If nothing was in the way these might grow straight down but if there was any obstacle, they grew in sinuous shapes. People said that pre-war it had been little valued, but now the soft red pulp round the bean-sized seeds was being used as a substitute for tomato in cooking. Finally there were all different kinds of leafy green vegetables, oddly named 'white green' and 'red green', various kinds of peppers—the small familiar chili-type peppers that grew on a bush and were often used when still green, and the big sweet 'agriculture' peppers on their small, slow-growing plants. But 'English' vegetables needed more care, and I preferred not to plant them out until they were strong little plants. We grew beds of ordinary tomatoes, trying to keep some coming into production as others finished.

Before long the garden was breaking down the fence. Something had happened to the okro, which was eight feet high, and the clumps of maize were even taller. Pumpkin and sweet potato vines leapt everywhere. There was Indian spinach growing all over the inside of the fence and snake tomatoes on the outside, and something edible with shiny green leaves in all the corners. Four bean plants snatched at everything with their tendrils. Before the whole garden could burst out, John came to our help and made us a stronger fence enclosing a rather bigger area of land. To make a fence, you go to the bush and cut plenty of sticks about six or seven feet long. Using the digging pole, make the holes and plant the sticks. Take strips of split palm rib and tie them before and behind the sticks. Lastly, fill in all the spaces with palm fronds driven in as thickly as possible between the strips of palm rib. I added to this by spending several days pushing thin sticks into the ground to make the fence chicken-proof. Many of the fence sticks took root and began to bud like Joseph's staff in the rich earth.

The fence was to keep out goats, fowl and children. After that there were smaller pests to contend with. Crickets would bite off succulent young tomato plants and leave them withering on the ground. We traced them by their holes and dug them up; then the young children in the compound roasted and ate them. Nematode worms bored the root of more mature tomato plants, withering and stunting them. I wanted to try planting marigolds to get rid of the nematodes as described in *Silent Spring*, but never had a chance to try.[5] As all the plants began to produce every morning, we went around picking tomatoes, okro and caterpillars. Tomatoes were removed before opening or the heavy rains could split the skins. Okro left too long became coarse and woody. We stocked three main kinds of caterpillar. One was small, brown and hairy and ate okro and *ofe* leaves. The second was huge with thick legs and a tail, like one of the more curious creatures from the coloured pages of Natural History in the *Children's Encyclopedia*. This giant, together with the green caterpillars, used to clump over the tomato plants and could eat a branch bare of leaves in the course of a night.

Every day we ate large quantities of fresh vegetables, with so many varieties growing next to the kitchen. The incredibly fertile soil continued to produce so lavishly that even though our diet was getting more restricted, it was hard to imagine a shortage of something to eat among such rich profusion. However, some items were now in very short supply. I heard that hospitals were running low on drugs and equipment, and it was getting more hazardous to have a baby, since the drugs were not available to meet complications, even those that can happen fairly often. Late in March, Caritas International, the Catholic relief organisation, had begun to airlift milk, baby food and drugs through Port Harcourt from the island of São Tomé for refugee relief.

Then, in mid-April, Tanzania was the first country to afford Biafra diplomatic recognition. People coming from Owerri brought the news, and some came to ask whether I had heard anything of it. Fortunately I had received a note from the College, as they knew the radio wasn't working at the time. John, who had been to another village, heard of it on his way home and rode through pouring rain to reach the house more quickly and find out whether it was true. So we drank to the future in cocoa, for the want of anything more festive. That same evening, I was lent a small collection of cuttings from overseas newspapers, and they seemed at the time exquisitely funny in their testy annoyance with Biafra for continuing to fight, for continuing to exist at all after such well-informed opinion had declared further existence impossible.

Later, as I received more regular supplies of cuttings, such reporting wasn't so amusing. One way to reduce the standing of any Africans is to refer to them as tribesmen. So the Consultative Assembly, in which all ethnic groups were represented and which had mandated the governor to declare independence was regularly described as a 'group of Igbo tribesmen'. Like 'jungle', 'tribe' is a word with well-defined connotations. The tribe is primitive; it is small in size and narrow in outlook; it is cruel in its customs; hostile to strangers; quarrelsome towards neighbours; swayed by irrational urges and superstitious fears. Every African, however highly educated and Europeanised, is born into a particular tribe; to be so born is not a permanent certificate of barbarism. But the use of the word is a quick and effective method of reducing articulate, responsible Africans, who ought to be heard with respect, to the level of spear-waving, shouting savages who are rightly disregarded.

I had been telling my children that they would have to manage with their old clothes while we were in the village. I would make new clothes when the war was over. Soon I found myself mending and re-mending until I seemed to be expending more sewing cotton than the rags and tatters were worth. When I did manage to get a small piece of new material I decided to make the two little girls a dress each in a simple style. Great excitement attended the cutting out and the trying on. I didn't at first understand the reason. At last Nwaneze (Anne), smoothing the skirt of her new dress, looked at me hopefully: 'Is the war over then?'

For a little while we felt the war might be ending. Gabon, Zambia, and Ivory Coast had also recognised Biafra. There were even peace talks, at Kampala in Uganda. But while they were talking of peace, in a pattern that was to be repeated several times, the Nigerian Government pressed harder for a military solution and nothing came of the talks.

Port Harcourt was captured and a fresh wave of refugees came to the village.[6] The attack on Port Harcourt had come during the day when people were going about their work or were in the market. Many had no chance to reach their homes to pick up the smallest piece of their property, but fled just as they were. Many of those who returned to Ogbaku had been working and earning something to help support their dependents at home, so even more hardship was caused. The forty-mile walk to Owerri took a sad toll on the sick, the elderly and pregnant women. After the shock of the attack, the pain of the flight and the physical hardship of the long trek, many women miscarried or gave birth prematurely. Among other personal stories I heard, the following are typical. A nurse, herself pregnant, safely delivered a woman in labour at the side of the road. A husband and wife were escaping together when the woman's labour began. The husband carried the premature infant to the nearest hospital; when he returned for his wife, she was dead.

There were ugly rumours of sabotage again, of money being demanded by the drivers of lorries sent by the Government to help in the evacuation. They said one driver was later shot for this But for most people there was no transport at all and the refugees who poured into Owerri reached there on foot. A friend who was going early to buy food saw a newborn baby being washed in the gutter in the entrance to the market. Food prices went up quickly with the capture of Port Harcourt. Some fish had been coming from there, some salt prepared from sea water, and some petrol and kerosene had been produced there. The relief flights had been coming to Port Harcourt airfield which had been the chief link with the outside world, but now the Government was using the emergency airstrip at Uli, near Ihiala. We heard something of this from a visitor who told us: 'We have an airstrip made from a straight stretch of road. It is twice as wide as a road and half a mile long. The Nigerians have dropped 40 bombs and hit it four times. Thanks be to God.' Now, as darkness fell, we used to listen if there would be any plane passing over the village. During the day it was something to be dreaded but at night we longed to hear it. A good deal was being written in the world press about the poor condition of the aeroplanes being used, and each night we used to listen for the sound of the old engines grinding in across the sky. Our helicopters used to

111

fly over very often and it was hard to tell at first whether the noise was helicopter or aeroplane. All the children used to stand poised for flight into the backyard and bush beyond, until it was clear a helicopter was coming and all could relax. The helicopters used to fly low, generally following the road and in daylight. One particularly dark wet night, we heard an engine noise. Helicopters did not usually fly by night and it was not only dark but raining hard. The noise passed overhead, receded, then grew louder again. As we looked at each other in alarm we heard a heavy thud very near, then nothing but the rain drumming on the roof.

'Oh God, my father,' said someone. 'The helicopter fell down!' As the rain died away the militia were out looking for the wreckage, sending messages to the nearest Air-force base, keeping guard, while the villagers plodded unhappily through the mud and puddles speculating on what could have happened. The first idea was that, flying low and blind, it might have crashed in the darkness into one of the huge *iroko* towering high above the other trees. But it wasn't so. The bodies were taken away, the wreckage cleared and the incident remained one of those unexplained sad grey events.

The increase in the black market cost of petrol didn't trouble us much since we were still managing with what we had when rationing began. Every other day or so the car was started, driven round a few corners and brought back. We had constructed a lean-to garage roofed with palm thatch both to camouflage it and to protect it from the weather. Kerosene, which we used in the bush lamp, increased in price within the space of a few days from seven or eight pence a pint bottle to five shillings. This affected us far more because the lamp was our only lighting, as I had stopped buying candles once they increased in price beyond six shillings a packet.

'What shall we do when there is no more kerosene?' I asked. 'Use palm oil,' said John. Indeed, it seemed in every shortage we had to turn back to the palm tree. No wonder they depicted it on the currency. Before many weeks 'Biafra lamps' were on sale in all the markets. They were made of thick baked clay, with a cotton wick, and burned palm oil. 'It looks like something dug up near the Pyramids,' said someone, producing her own newly bought lamp with disgust. Still, it worked, and that was all that mattered once you learned how to keep it burning, to keep it filled with oil with the wick pulled up high enough. Otherwise you had to keep dropping oil in the wick with a fizz and splutter of sudden flame or it would go out. I always expected the coils of wick in the bowl to give a sluggish heave beneath the prodding stick. For walking about at night you could use thin branches of a resinous wood which burned brightly once it had been well beaten and frayed. Or you could use 'Biafra torch', made of the squeezed pith of the palm fruit which was left after palm oil had been prepared. The pith was plastered round a thin strong twig and then well dried over the cooking fire for several days. These torches also made good firelighters if the wood was damp and wouldn't burn well.

As soap became more and more expensive people began to make the black soap that had been discarded in favour of more 'civilised' perfumed tablets of toilet soap, or long bars of laundry soap. The black soap was made from palm oil boiled together with the lye made by washing the ashes left after burning the fibrous base on which the palmfruit is produced. The whole process took several days and the soap looked very home-made—strong smelling in shapeless, hand-sized lumps. But it made some lather, washed quite well and had the reputation for being good for skin troubles. While palm oil remained cheap and plentiful, black soap was better value than the scarce imported soap that now cost five or six times as much. The base of the palm fruit stem could also be cut in pieces and left to soak for several days. The softer parts would decay leaving the tougher fibres to be used as a sponge or loofah to scrub the skin while bathing. After their bath most people liked to use something on their skin to keep it smooth. There were no more skin creams and lotions, and so 'Biafra pomade' was widely used again. Palm kernels were cracked and the inside nuts were roasted in a pot until they yielded a great deal of smoke and a thin dark brown oil. This was also prized for health, for reducing fever and headaches and driving away evil spirits, particularly those that plague sick children by shouting 'Hooo' at them as they are falling asleep, making them wake and cry.

But for some things there was no substitute. Just when everyone was most anxious to know what was happening, fewer radios were working, as batteries faded and few people could afford 15 shillings each for replacements. Most listened instead to the 'radio without battery'—

rumours. Anyone who could tune his radio at news time to the BCB would find a little crowd had gathered by the time the drum signal and fanfare had ended. Before the news, listeners were exhorted 'The price of liberty is eternal vigilance. Biafra, be vigilant!' and afterwards, 'Biafra, fight for victory, fight for survival, fight for freedom!' When we found some batteries again we used to listen to news broadcasts in the early morning, watching the children sweeping the yard with a dry palm branch, making wave-like patterns in the damp earth as they changed the direction of each line of strokes. We listened again in the evening as the thick dusk enveloped the trees and the dark figures sitting beneath or the whole scene sprang to life and colour when the kitchen door was opened and firelight poured out. Listening to the radio, listening to those who had run from Port Harcourt, we could see no end after all.

The first anniversary of independence had passed. The first anniversary of the beginning of the war was soon approaching.

Figure 1. Rose and John Umelo's wedding day, London, November, 1961.

Figure 2. John, Rose, and Ezenwa, Islington, London, 1964.

Figure 3. Visiting John's family in Ogbaku before the war, January 1967. Rose's mother-in-law, Ukwuaru, is in the centre.

Figure 4. Street scene showing Kingsway Store, Enugu, before the war. Photo by Simon Ottenberg, c. 1959–1960. Simon Ottenberg Collection, EEPA 2000–007–0895, Eliot Elisofon Photographic Archives, National Museum of African Art, Smithsonian Institution.

Biafra
GOVERNMENT OF ~~EASTERN NIGERIA~~

Telegrams : COLLEGE ENUGU

Telephone : ENUGU 2231

Your ref ....

Our ref ....
(*All replies to be addressed to the Principal.*)

QUEEN'S SCHOOL

ENUGU

19th. August ...., 19 67.

TO WHOM IT MAY CONCERN.

Mrs. Rose Umelo joined the Queen's School Staff in February 1965. She is an Education Officer on Contract. Her contract expires in 1968.

Mrs. Umelo is an Honours Graduate in Latin of London University. Her subsidiary subject is Greek. She obtained her Degree in 1953.

When Mrs. Umelo came here she had not taught before. For 10¼ years she had worked in administration for the London County Council, serving in several branches. She worked in the Architect's branch for three months, when she was transferred to the Public Control Section. There she remained for two years, finally being transferred to the Valuation Department, where she worked for eight years. On her arrival in Enugu she was asked to teach Latin and English, and this she has been doing most successfully since she came. I was surprised how easily and skilfully she adapted herself to the situation here, and there is no doubt that she has a gift for teaching. In the three years she has been here there is a marked increase in interest in Latin throughout the School. Mrs. Umelo has been equally successful in her teaching of English. She has been in charge of Sixth Form General Studies, and to help other members of Staff has drawn up a Syllabus to cover the contents of this somewhat undefined course for Sixth Forms. In this respect she took part in a recent Seminar on the teaching of English, and I have been told that her contribution was most valuable.

Mrs. Umelo has a quiet unobtrusive personality and is a woman of excellent character. She is very efficient, reliable and trustworthy, always willing to do extra work outside School hours. Her relationships with other people are very good.

She has many undoubted gifts. These include the production of plays and the writing of short stories, one of which was used by the B.B.C. While she has been here she has taken on the extra duty of Secretary to the Principal, and her experience in administration has made a marked difference in the running of the Principal's office.

I have found it pleasant and easy to work with Mrs. Umelo, and her contribution to the entire life of Queen's School has been most valuable. I recommend her without hesitation or reserve.

Signed:- *Mary Kirkpatrick*

(Mrs.) Mary I. Kirkpatrick, M.B.E., M.A.,
Principal.   H.Dip-Ed.

Figure 5. Letter of recommendation for Rose from the Principal of Queens School, Enugu, 1967.

Figure 6. Rose and senior students of Mungo Park House, where she was Housemistress, Queens School, Enugu, before the war.

Figure 7. Rose presents a prize to a pupil, Queens School, Enugu, before the war.

Figure 8. Rose and her new baby Osondu Elizabeth, born in the bush in 1968. Photo by John R. Sullivan, who used it in a booklet, *Breadless Biafra* (Dayton, OH: Pflaum, 1969), and sent Rose a copy after the war.

Figure 9. Rose and her five children in 1968, while they lived as refugees in a family compound in Ogwa.

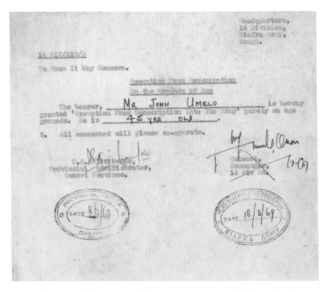

Figure 10. John was able to avoid being conscripted through the use of this official pass, declaring him too old (although his exact age is actually not totally clear).

GOVERNMENT OF THE REPUBLIC OF BIAFRA

Ministry of Education,
Administration Division,
c/o St. Clement's School,
Omukwu, Onicha-Ezinihitte P.A.,
Via Umuahia.

Our ref:P.25/Vol.II/500.   10th December, 1969.

Mrs. R. Umelo,
c/o Rev. F. U. Nwaorie,
St. Peter's Parsonage,
Alaeyi Ogwa, Ogwa P.A.,
Via Owerri.

Madam,

Renewal of Contract

I am directed to refer to your letter
dated 14th January, 1969 and to inform you that
the Public Service Commission has approved,
provisionally, the renewal of your contract
appointment as an Education Officer for one tour
only with effect from 6th November, 1969.

2.   Will you please report at this office as
soon as possible for the execution of your new
contract. You will bring along with you a single
one shilling postage stamp.

I am, Madam,
Your obedient servant,

(C. J. U. Oti)
for Ag: Permanent Secretary,
Ministry of Education.

EEE/RNE:

Figure 11. Throughout the war, the Biafran bureaucracy continued to function, even when supplies of all kinds dried up. Rose was issued a new teaching contract in 1969, neatly typed on a page torn from an old exercise book.

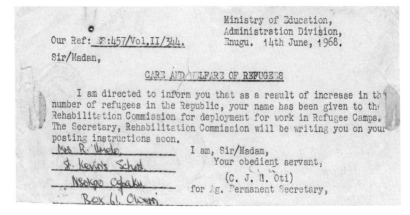

```
                                     Ministry of Education,
          o                          Administration Division,
    Our Ref: F:457/Vol.II/344.       Enugu. 14th June, 1968.
    Sir/Madam,

                    CARE AND WELFARE OF REFUGEES

         I am directed to inform you that as a result of increase in the
    number of refugees in the Republic, your name has been given to the
    Rehabilitation Commission for deployment for work in Refugee Camps.
    The Secretary, Rehabilitation Commission will be writing you on your
    posting instructions soon.

    Mrs R. Umelo                     I am, Sir/Madam,
       St. Kevin's School               Your obedient servant,
       Nsokpo Ogbaku                        (C. J. N. Oti)
       Box 61 Owerri                 for Ag. Permanent Secretary,
```

Figure 12. Another official document, authorising Rose to work in one of the many refugee camps that were operational by 1968.

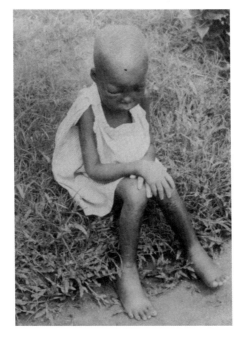

Figure 13. A child with the typical symptoms of severe protein deficiency (*kwashiorkor*)—swollen legs, feet and face, with no energy to move or respond. Photo taken at Emekuku, about fifteen miles east of Ogbaku, by Brad and Jean Abernethy, courtesy of American Friends Service Committee Archives.

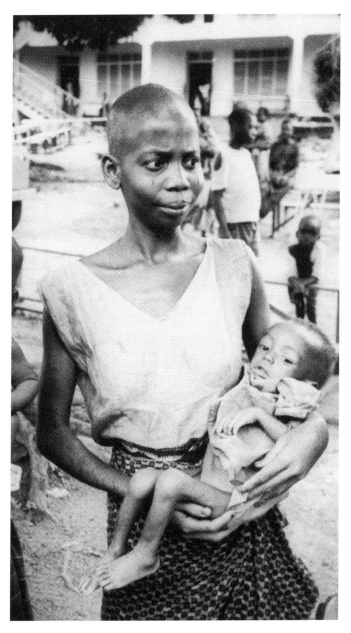

Figure 14. A mother holds her child, who shows the symptoms of extreme malnutrition (marasmus) caused by starvation. Emekuku, photo by Brad and Jean Abernethy, courtesy of American Friends Service Committee.

Figure 15. Front and reverse of a Biafran 5 shilling note, issued in 1967. Source: http://www.africafederation.net/Biafra_Notes.htm

Figure 16. Refugees on the move in Biafra. Photo by Al Venter, used with his permission.

Figure 17. Rose, her mother-in-law, and six children, together with a cousin, Alice, after the war.

18. Rose, pictured in March 2017, photo by Elizabeth Bird.

Figure 19. John in later life.

Figure 20. Rose and her children in London, 2017. Back row: Elizabeth, Nkechi, Ifeoma, and Anne; front row: Uzoma and Eze.

10

THE HUNGER

Food prices were much higher in the townships than in the villages, and anyone living in the town used to go outside to local markets if they could find transport. My three friends in Owerri, all English wives, began to visit Ogbaku regularly on our local market day to buy, then sit with me until it was time for them to leave. We discussed the war, prices, the war, recipes, the war, alternatives to whatever was the latest thing unobtainable, the war ... I enjoyed these afternoons of talk in my fairly silent week.

The Igbo week has four days: Orie, Afor, Nkwo, Eke. We had two markets locally, one rather small one held every other Afor, the other quite large, held every other Orie. As Orie Ogbaku was held every eight days, one week my visitors came on Monday, the following week on Tuesday, and so on. Sometimes by the day of Orie Ogbaku the corner of the living room was piled up with heads of plantain, green bananas, a bowl of breadfruit, a basket of palm fruit, local beans, guavas or whatever was in season, heaps of corncobs. At one time *garri* cost twice as much in Owerri as it did in our local market.

In their turn, my friends brought us news, soap, tinned goods if anything came into the market, and carried away commissions, took letters, brought and exchanged library books, carried away shopping lists to add to their own.

By now there was plenty of corn. The first heads were boiled and roasted and eaten with roasted pears and crunched sweet as nuts. These purple-black oval pears were more like a vegetable than a fruit, with a thin layer of buttery green flesh, and more like a plum than a pear with a very big but softish 'stone' inside. Maybe they were some kind of avocado—which were themselves called 'English pears'. Perhaps 'English' was equivalent to 'foreign'. Ducks were called 'English hens'. As corn became plentiful and cheap, we began to make *akamu*, a favourite breakfast dish, instead of buying it (looking like creamy coloured putty) ready-made from the market. The usual method of making it was to take a heap of corncobs, strip off the outside layers and take off the grains. These were left to soak overnight in cold water, particularly if the corn was old and well dried. In the morning the corn was taken out, put in the mortar and pounded. Then the paste was rubbed through a fine metal sieve. The wet residue would be thrown away. Cold water was poured over the sieved corn starch and it was left to settle into a thick layer at the bottom of the bowl. Then the surplus water was carefully poured off. The thick paste was prepared for breakfast very quickly. It would be softened with enough cold water, then boiling water was poured onto it and it was well stirred. It could be eaten with *akara* (fried bean flour cakes), if anyone could find any beans, or fried sweet plantain slices. This *akamu* or pap was the traditional weaning food for babies and since the usual baby cereals were scarce and very expensive, many mothers were using it who would in peacetime have been buying Farex, Cerelac, or other products. They could prepare it with some milk to add more food value or use it to make any infant food they had managed to find last longer and go further.

I also learned the theory of how to make flour from yam, plantain, banana and cassava, but the rainy season didn't allow much practice, since everything had to be well dried for days in the sun. Sometimes my friends brought me some ordinary flour which I generally used to make a kind of drop scones … flour, sugar, baking powder, an egg, mixed with milk and fried in spoonfuls. When supplies became scarcer, I made the scones without egg, without sugar, with less milk, even without baking powder by beating the mixture well and cooking it before the air could bubble out. A kind of fritter made by beating several well mashed bananas into the mixture at its plainest was delicious and the children ate them as fast as they cooled from the pan. Children from the surrounding compounds seemed to know by instinct when I was preparing banana fritters and if I turned to blink the smoke out of my eyes I would find a row of small children perched on the bench, watching and waiting.

By now I was beginning to take more notice of any way of overcoming shortages of baby food and clothes. Impossible as it had seemed five months before, it was now quite certain that we would still be in the village when the time came for the baby to be born. White cotton poplin was costing £1 per yard. All the baby-size dresses had been left behind in Enugu as well as the collection of pretty odds and end of material. I decided to make baby clothes from an old well-washed bed sheet that had become very thin.

Of course, I was lucky to have a bed sheet I could manage to spare. This single sheet provided enough for seven dresses in the simplest style. I made them less plain by binding the armholes and necks with strips of bright, left-over cotton from the girls' new dresses. If the result was hardly up to Kingsway standards, at least it was neat and cheerful. One sheet of polythene made four pairs of rather crackly plastic pants. A large, soft plastic picnic tablecloth went into the suit-case against the day a larger size would have to be made. Iheoma had still been using nappies at night when we left Enugu and I had sixteen towelling nappies in all conditions from rags to tatters. When a cotton bed cover wore out, I cut more squares from the stronger pieces and machined the edges until, for once, my sewing cotton was nearly finished. Then, I had to save the last few yards for vital repairs, sewing on buttons until I could get more.

The miscellaneous items John had seized on his final trip to Enugu included a shawl, a vest, a matinee coat, two pairs of bootees and two maternity dresses. 'What on earth possessed you to bring those?' I had asked rather crossly, marking the absence of much-needed items. Obviously he had known what he was doing. With other odds and ends—a jar of zinc and castor oil cream, a tin of Vaseline, a rubber draw sheet—I was really quite well equipped. There was no point in remembering the two cots, the big English pram, the high chair, the play pen, all the clothes and everything else left behind. We were getting back to the essentials.

It still remained to decide where I could get antenatal care and go for the delivery. Owerri had a General Hospital, but it was seven miles away. There was a fine Mission Hospital at Awo-Omamma, seven or eight miles in the opposite direction towards the airstrip and another at Ihiala beyond the airstrip. The problem was that we had no transport, since there was now no petrol for the car. I was not used to travelling by bicycle carrier and this was not the time to learn how to balance behind a rider, when balancing on one's own two feet could be difficult enough. There was a small, privately-owned Maternity in the village and that would have to do. I presented myself there for the usual examination. My blood iron test was only 60 percent—a surprise to me as I'd thought myself rather healthy. My friends brought me iron tablets in Owerri market. They were discoloured but otherwise seemed all right. I began taking them more dutifully than I had done before and asked Angelina and Apollonia to put plenty of fluted pumpkin in my soup.

The bicycle carrier was becoming more and more important as petrol grew scarcer and the number of cars on the road grew less. His rates went up of course. A year before, the fare from Ogbaku to Owerri was one shilling. Now it was one shilling per mile and more. Many people walked rather than pay such an increase. A patch of tyre or inner tube once cost threepence, but now it was already costing a shilling. Most people's tyres and tubes were held together with patches, since a new tyre was £10. If trade was slack in other businesses, the bicycle repairers at least were busy. The bicycle was the general beast of burden. It could carry huge loads of *garri* or corn, shallow baskets of cassava, or passengers. If it were a man's bicycle, the passenger balanced uncomfortably on the cross bar. Most had a carrier fixed behind the saddle and there the passenger could sit more gracefully. The carrier seat was often extended with two sticks and so could be used to carry even bulkier loads. Everyone seemed to know how to ride; even the smallest children used adult bicycles by standing on the pedals, since the seat was out of reach. Many bicycles had no brakes; at the unusual sound of a car behind them, the less confident riders often tipped the bicycle sideways into the bush. It was polite for pedestrians to move onto the sandy patches at the side of the road at the sound of a bicycle and leave the rider the hard bare strip. In the dry season dense clouds of red dust billowing behind a car would engulf pedestrians and cyclists alike. In the rainy season the deep stretches of rain water and the ruts torn by the storms were another hazard. I was glad to be able to walk to the Maternity Home, which was along the main tarred road.

John mentioned one day that a friend's child had died. I asked what had been the matter.

'He had this swollen foot disease,' was the reply. A few weeks later the local Red Cross came into the compound to look at all the children and make a note of their physical condition. I asked the one in charge what in particular they were looking for. 'Kwashiorkor,' he replied, and the swollen foot disease was named. So far, he told me, over 100 children had been listed and only six were in really good condition.

Cordelia, one of the other children in the compound, was painfully thin and the Red Cross told me she was showing the first signs of the disease, though her other sisters were in fair condition. Later I found this was quite usual. The rest of the family would be in reasonable health, while the weakest on the same diet was developing kwashiorkor. What did I know about this? Whatever knowledge I had all came from books. I could remember I had seen it described as preventable, a protein deficiency disease caused by inadequate diet. I suppose I should have seen it coming since so many of the population didn't value green vegetables and were managing on *garri* and yam with less and less meat and fish. There had been no milk to speak of for months. I wished I knew more about nutrition since it looked as if it was literally going to be a matter of life and death.

Our meetings on Orie Ogbaku day discussed first and second class protein. If there was no animal protein, what about vegetable protein? If meat, fish, eggs, cheese, and milk were unobtainable, what were the local equivalents of the textbook peas, beans and lentils? There were Biafra beans, of course. We had four plants growing in the garden, or rather growing out of it like Jack's beanstalk, their tendrils grabbing the hair of anyone who passed, leaning over tipsily, propped up by a stout sapling, cutting off the light from two beds of tomatoes. Altogether not a garden plant. We could use breadfruit, they told me. That seemed to be the seeds of a fruit like a tough green football. When the inside had well rotted, the sticky seeds were picked out of the earthy interior and cleaned of their slime with sand. Its beginning was not promising but we soon liked breadfruit. I found it heavy and hard to digest, but cooked with yam it was a little better. But when the girls began to prepare it with fresh pepper, with pumpkin or green pawpaw, the dish was far lighter, golden and delicious. We ate platefuls and recommended it to parents anxious about their children. Green pawpaw it was said, also contained some protein. But many people still refused to try it because it was something they had not eaten before.

I began to try to increase the protein Cordelia was taking but it was difficult. I had very little protein food and she, like all the rest of the family, was very suspicious of anything new to eat. I had several times been cross when they tried to persuade my own children not to eat something or other we had prepared by assuring them that it was 'not an Igbo thing'. I managed to get some precious tins of Heinz beef and liver soup for babies and tried to get her to take a four ounce tin every day, but her usual reaction to anything different was to heave it up as soon as it had been reluctantly swallowed. After some wasteful experiments I found that if I mixed the hot soup with some peppery cooked rice to give it a familiar taste and texture, she would eat it. We also tried a little diplomacy; a young man industriously scraped out the empty tin and loudly wished for more in an attempt to make her think she was being given something worthwhile. It all helped, but there were few tins and all were soon finished.

One of my friends from Owerri was helping in a clinic and had some harrowing tales about the cases she saw there. In the village I saw few of them since the children who were developing kwashiorkor were mostly hidden from sight in their family compounds, lying on their mats, unable to walk on their swollen feet. When kwashiorkor was still an unfamiliar word, people called the condition 'diddly-pom-pom'. Later they exercised that wry sense of humour I had admired before when noting that the flamboyant flowing *agbada* was called 'let me speak' and the town girl's tight skirt was 'cross no gutter'. Now they were calling the brown skin swollen tight from toes to knee 'Gowon's rain-boot'. Some people thought the sickness was caused by lack of salt and many of those families who suffered from it were cooking almost all the time without salt as well as without fish or meat. A goat cost £20–£30, according to size. A bush rat was between £1 and £1 and 5 shillings and was now being sold by the 'joint' and snakes by the piece. Even tiny squirrels cost two shillings and sixpence. Lizards were on sale in the market from sixpence, up to one shilling and sixpence for the bigger, fatter ones. When a mouse fell from the eaves of the house into the water barrel, the shout of 'meat, meat' at once arose. The young boys who trapped small rats on the farm land offered me one rather hesitantly. After all, it only differed in size from the giant bush rats we had been eating before under their courtesy title of rabbits. My only complaint was that it was so small. From the point of view of flavour, it was fine.

There were many factors creating this food situation. Overriding all was the blockade, which had prevented imports for well over a year. The East had always imported large amounts of meat and there was no local source of milk. I never heard of anyone making use of goat milk. The occupation of the coastal areas cut off the main supply of fish, though those places near rivers and lakes could still obtain some. Many people were too conservative in their diet to try other foods when they could still get the usual starchy *garri* and so on. Because of a shortage of currency, first of cash then of notes, the banks were restricting the amount clients could withdraw. Lastly, the particular season of the year, just before the harvest, had always been a time when even yam and *garri* went up in price. Prewar, it had been usual for children to be breast-fed for 12–14 months, or even longer. There were sometimes signs of malnutrition when the baby was weaned onto a restricted diet. I remembered reading that people called kwashiorkor 'the disease that kills the first child while the mother is making the second', because there was nothing to replace breast milk satisfactorily and cheaply enough. Starchy food was everywhere easy to grow and cheaper to fill the stomach. Before the new yam could be harvested, there were traditional ceremonies, which helped distract our minds from everyday hardships. First we went to Ihe, a nearby village, to watch their dancing which was locally well known. Everyone said it was far from being as good as usual since so many young men who would have taken part were away in the army.

Then it was time for the *juju* to run through the villages.[1] Of course we had seen *juju* before, and heard their falsetto voices calling to each other once when we visited Ubomiri. Now for days together it could be very difficult for a woman or an uninitiated male to move about the village, to go to the well, farm or market, when the *juju* in blanket and painted mask would appear at any time, stalking out of the bush. The boys seemed to like being chased as if they were taking part in a dangerous, alarming, but enjoyable game. Women experienced a genuine

121

terror. They had to do their best to avoid meeting the *juju* and would rush panic-stricken to hide in someone's compound or kitchen if it appeared on their path. Sometimes it would let them alone if they hurriedly removed themselves from the way. Other times it was more violent and would pursue them into the compound sending everyone screaming into the house or the kitchen while it beat on the door or tried to jump on the roof. If a woman had to go along the road it was safest to ask an initiate to escort her. Then if the *juju* appeared, he could intercede for her while she hid her face. Sometimes women spent several hours hiding in the farmland while the *juju* paraded and pranced to and fro on the road and kept them cowering. On some particular nights we were told we must not show any light outdoors or leave the house. In the dead of night the voice of the *juju* would be heard, an unearthly hooting and wailing out of the darkness now near, now far away in the trees. Even on ordinary days as dusk was deepening it was strangely chilling to hear men shouting: 'A woman is coming, a woman is coming!' to avoid such a meeting, while the *juju* wailed and shrieked somewhere in the distance. There were heavy penalties prescribed for breaking the old rules wilfully. Towards the end of the time, *juju* from other villages used to pay more ceremonial visits with their mortal followers to greet us and get gifts, usually a few pennies. Even after the *juju* had flown away for that year, a further traditional duty remained to be performed. The head of each compound would sacrifice a fowl before new yam could be brought home, prepared and eaten openly.

Meanwhile, another English wife had come to stay with her children in the empty principal's house in the College grounds. Our friends the Reverend Fathers had moved some miles north to Awo-Omamma to conserve their supplies with another Seminary. I often used to go along there with my children. While they all played together, we talked once more about the war, prices, the war, recipes, the war—and now how peculiarly depressing it was to have your radio station jammed into incomprehensibility. It seemed unpleasantly like a foretaste of annihilation. Too soon the College buildings were taken over as a military hospital and our new acquaintances stayed only long enough for us to miss them when they had gone.

Every week now I was attending the little Maternity Home near the Mission. On one of my visits there, I found quite a crowd of women gathered. They greeted me cheerfully and said 'You're too late. The work is all done.' I found that a feeding centre was in the process of being established amid the usual amount of controversy. It seemed no-one had liked to ask me, but if I wanted to come, they said they would be pleased. The centre was being organised by the local branch of the Biafra Red Cross. The food was coming from the Caritas office in Owerri. There was powdered milk in polythene and paper sacks, dried egg, wheat flour, and Ovaltine. It was too small a quantity to allow for any distribution. Instead a gruel was being prepared on the premises and a cupful given out to each child as they were paraded at the Mission primary school office. Next day I arrived with my kitchen stool and large spoons and spent a couple of hours blending and stirring.

When the supplies for that morning had been made up, I was invited to go and see the distribution. A crowd of several hundred was already waiting outside the office. Parents and children were lined up with their tin basins and mugs. As the scheme became better known there were more and more children, but at first it was fairly easy to keep everything under control. 'Come and meet the nurses': I was invited through into an office where a young nurse, a refugee from Aba hospital, was sitting with a few envelopes of pills in front of the barred but open windows. As it happened we had met several times before, so she asked me to help her by logging records of the children treated and the medicines each received.

'What are you giving?'

'Today there are iron tablets, vitamins and Piperazine.[2] There isn't enough. I had to choose the worst cases.'

These were the children who had been brought into sight from where they were hidden in their family compounds. She called to the Red Cross members near the window to begin. A young man picked up the first child and held him high enough for us to see the swollen feet. The taut stretched skin had split wide open and was oozing something watery. I copied his name into the exercise book from his card and wrote the dose. One iron pill. One multivite.

The second child: the same tortured feet.

The third child: All bones and eyes, the child stared in at us.

The fourth child: a tall boy. He wept as they lifted him, shaking his painful limbs.

The fifth: She unwrapped the cloth that covered her from neck to ankles just enough to let us see that she was blotched with pale raised lumps and bumps all over her skin.

The sixth: But some trouble had arisen over the sixth. Under cover of the confusion I asked the nurse why they were disturbing the children by lifting them up for us to see again. She explained that as there was so little medicine it could only be given to the worst cases, which she had picked out herself. She was just making sure that no children had been pushed into the line by their anxious parents who would take the dose needed by another still worse. 'Though they all need medicine, God knows,' she added. The sixth child was now ready. He was about six years old and swollen from head to foot as if he had been beaten. He peered at me through slitted eyes in his puffy face.

Most children received one or two tablets. It seemed a pathetic amount but it was still better than nothing, said the nurse. I wrote their names as fast as I could. The stream of suffering children seemed as if it would never end. The supply of medicines ended first and we all went home. I walked with the careful steps of late pregnancy along the sandy road, patterned with the prints of bare feet and bicycle tyres, past the College—now a military hospital with bandaged soldiers sitting by the roadside or hobbling to buy from the women who had brought food to sell—past the principal's house where we had once enjoyed the film shows, past the hedge that always looked like the creator's first attempt at making flowers, circles of petal stuff snipped here and there, smelling of blackcurrants, out of the sun at last and into the trees.

Old people were now dying faster, as well as the children. The traditional burial with its night-long 'waking', with singing, dancing, eating, drinking was still carried on but with more and more difficulty. A man is buried in his own compound but a dead woman is taken away by her own family community, who come hurrying with songs to collect the corpse after her immediate relations have settled what is to be given. Everything cost so much more that it was harder than ever to give to the dead what was due to their dignity in goats, dogs, chickens, as one death followed another. The children died and were buried with less ceremony but the full measure of grief. A family I had visited at Nsukka just before the war lost four children, two of them within three days, and had two of their six children left. Another family of refugees, returned from Lagos, lost eight of their nine children.

It was not surprising that more children attended each day at the feeding centre, as their parents heard of it. Many were more interested in the medicine than in the gruel since they did not see how such a small amount could do any good. I did my best to explain, as well as assuring them that the committee had not to my knowledge 'chopped' all the best themselves. Others again would not risk sending their children in case, as they said, they might catch kwashiorkor from those already ill. Some put their faith in native medicine. One of these, a pretty girl of about eleven called Eunice, liked to spend her days lying on the bench in our thatched kitchen watching the other children playing. Her face and limbs were streaked with the medicinal black dye called *uri*.

I was going every day to the feeding centre to do whatever I could.

John, Stephen, Matthias, Barnabas: I wrote down their names in the exercise book and saw the parents take the couple of pills, their hope that, after all, these children would live.

Ignatius, Alexander, Marcellinus, Peter: What they needed was good and regular food.

Felicity, Perpetua, Agatha, Lucy: What could two pills do for them?

Agnes, Cecilia, Anastasia: The only choice was between two pills or nothing.

Donatus was a sudden heap of rags crumpled on the floor of the office. The Red Cross boys lifted him outside where there was more air in the larger room. The crowd rustled and sighed round the windows but he was not dead yet. The nurse trickled milk into his mouth. He swallowed. There was only milk left to give him and not much of that.

'Who is with him? Tell his people to take him to Owerri.'

'But he may not live until tomorrow. The tall boy who was weeping yesterday died on his way home.'

Over and over: 'Take her to Owerri.' 'How? There is no transport, no money. The mother is sick herself.' 'Take them to Owerri. Take them to the hospital.'

There is nothing on the table, nothing in these few envelopes to treat those whose bones stand out like an anatomical specimen or those shrivelled babies whose inhuman faces peer out from their mother's cloth.

The nurse stayed cheerful, assuring me that all but the very worst cases would live if only they could have the proper food. I felt despair at the sight of so much suffering day after day, and guilt too. It was a British politician who had promised that policy would be reviewed if there were 'unnecessary civilian deaths'. Presumably these children all round me did not come into that category. Shifty politicians, why couldn't they be here to admire the results of their policies? If they felt some dull stirrings of remorse as they looked at Maria Assumpta and her grandmother, both dying by inches of malnutrition, they could hand the iron tablet and the multivite themselves and tell the old woman and the two-year-old how deeply they regretted the necessity.

When a plane was heard there was a surge of panic through the crowd. Luckily the chief was there that morning and roared, 'Sit down! Sit down!' After a long moment of hesitation, all sat down in the shadow of the Church in the shade of the trees and listened to the plane droning across the sky. At least the crowd was not as conspicuous as it would have been streaming away over the wide green field.

The supplies of food kept coming. One morning there was a tiny extra allowance of Nido, whole milk for babies under twelve months. A line formed. The babies slurped up their measure and looked round yelling for more but there had only been two tins and that was soon finished. 'It's like Lactogen,' we explained to the mothers. Everyone remembered that name. The last 16 oz. tins of Lactogen at Owerri were sold long ago for £6 each. The supply was never enough, but it kept coming. Then the news went round that next week we would be cooking stockfish. Stockfish hadn't been seen for over a year. These big, ugly dried fish, up to three feet in length, used to be one of the cheapest sources of protein before the war. They were imported from Scandinavia and looked like pieces of wood. Some jaws could chew them but most people used to chop the fish into suitable pieces and soak them before using them. The Red Cross officials had their work cut out trying to convince people that the workers weren't eating and wouldn't eat all the fish before the day came for cooking it. Suddenly the feeding centre became a very popular place to work.

I armed myself with a tray, chopping block and vegetable knife and spent most of the morning picking and chopping pumpkin leaf. We worked our way through mounds of the vegetable. Others were picking and pounding *egusi*[3] and pepper. Two men took their matchets and began to chop the stockfish into pieces. Of course it should have been started hours ago. I suggested that in future the stockfish should be cut up the evening before, but this would not do. It had to be brought out of the Reverend Fathers' store under everyone's eyes and cut up in public, otherwise some would accuse the others of helping themselves. Children peeped round the corner of the building and edged themselves forward. When the men rested, they rushed out to gather up the chips and flakes of dry fish that had fallen on the ground. Half-heartedly they were chased away, then allowed to come and scavenge. The kitchen was full of smoke and heat and gossip. I sat on my stool in the fresh air by the angle of the door and remembered the lines of sheds at Ogbete market, all selling dried, smoked and salted fish, all humming with flies and fishy smells … while I picked my way through the heap of pumpkin leaves. With suspicion and anticipation to sharpen their appetite, the crowds on the field would have to wait longer than ever.

When at last I came to the end of my leaves to be chopped, I went over to meet the nurse. There seemed to be twice as many people as ever before and three times as many were very sick. We had more medicines: Thalazole (for diarrhoea), Camoquin (for malaria), as well as the iron, vitamins and Piperazine. I could hardly write down the names quickly enough; as well as the usual record, we were now keeping a special list of the worst cases in the hope that a doctor might miraculously appear with iron injections and special treatment. When someone tried to get a second turn in the medicine queue she was driven away with abuse.

The day's allowance of medicine was finished and still the people waited. It was late afternoon before the soup was served but it was a great success. Two days later, when everyone had gained a little strength, the whole performance was repeated for the remaining villages.

The next week we were back making gruel but this time with a new and sinister accompaniment. As we worked there was the sound of distant shelling, a shudder in the bright air. Overnight there were new parties of refugees in the school buildings and along the road.

11

THE WAR CLOSES IN

As the situation was becoming steadily worse, we had already talked over what we ought to do if the fighting reached our town. There was so little petrol in the car that there was no point in driving until it gave out somewhere along the road. Besides, the war was now all round us. If we went to Awo-Omamma, that was on the line of advance towards Uli airport. There was fighting at Oguta. Orlu and Umuahia would be objectives as soon as Owerri was captured. There seemed to be no alternative but to go to the bush, where at least we would be near the farms if nothing worse had happened to us by then. Surely, we thought, the soldiers would not stay at Ogbaku but continue their advance along the tarred road to Uli; this would give us more chance to harvest yams and cassava and hide it against whatever might happen.

There had been refugees passing on the roads before, after Port Harcourt and Aba had fallen. Some were going to their home villages or to stay with in-laws and friends whose homes were not disturbed. Now the roads were filled again with the silent people. They were coming with bicycles loaded with everything, even with Vono beds[1] and rolled up mattresses, baskets of chickens, goats bellowing with their legs tied together. There were family groups, father with bicycle, mother with the baby on her back and a head-pan piled high, children carrying whatever they could and each other. They were obviously moving ahead of trouble, probably from the approaching sound of the guns, since they had had time to pack up their loads. There was a difference between those who had moved at their own pace and those who really had to run. But whether they were moving at their own speed or not, the trouble was drawing nearer. The question asked all the time was 'Where from?' One by one the villages on the other side of Owerri were moving. One morning a woman passed on the main road with a labourer pushing a handcart loaded high. When she was asked in the usual way, she replied, 'Owerri.' The others abused her almost hysterically as a 'sabo': 'Your husband is one of them. He told you to run before he kills us all. That's what they did at Enugu and Port Harcourt ...'

The refugees continued to pass. At the Maternity, while we prepared the food for the feeding centre, we watched them passing on the main road. At home we watched them passing along the bush road at the end of the compound. We worked and talked, listening to the guns and the sound getting closer, no longer a vague thundery rumble. There had been no defence of Aba. It looked as if there would be no defence of Owerri. Over the weekend of 15–16 September, Nigeria radio claimed that Owerri had been captured and that 'life there was returning to normal'. Some men who tried to go to the town were turned back by a road block before they could enter. BCB denied the claim and said 'the town is firmly in the hands of gallant Biafran forces'. So no-one knew.

On the afternoon of 17 September, I was sitting as usual on the verandah. I had sent Angelina and Apollonia to a market at some distance to buy cassava to make into *garri*. They returned with a story of gunfire nearby, which had scattered the market in panic. I carried on sewing a skirt for my niece, since there seemed so little one could do but wait. We had so few possessions that the car could be loaded in a very few minutes, and packing had been no problem. And perhaps after all they would not come.

Towards evening the crackle of gunfire sounded on the outskirts of the village, somewhere on the tarred road. We waited no longer. The car was loaded with cooking pots and children. All round us Ogbaku, like thousands of other communities, picked up its load and ran for the bush.

We spent that night under the misty stars outside the village, in farmland planted that year with cassava. There was no shelter and very little cover among the young plants. We had carried with us two large plasterboards from the ceiling, and rigged a roof with these. Someone was better provided with a large tarpaulin, but most people lay under the open sky and watched the faint lights of planes passing overhead to the airport. Towards dawn it began to rain a little but cleared away with the light. Again we discussed what to do. Our present position had no advantages, as we were far from water and quite unprotected. A single plane could wipe out everyone; we could not stay where we were, and some were deciding to move further away into thick bush. We made up our minds with some others to go back nearer the village into farmland that would have been cleared the following year. It would be closer to the Nigerians if they came off the main road—but then they might not. It would certainly be nearer to food and water. And so we moved back, meeting on the path other groups still moving away. No-one knew what to do for the best. No-one believed the advance would stay long at Ogbaku, but would continue along the wide tarred road and be stopped (if at all) at the bridge over a river near Awo-Omamma. So we went back along the path and turned off into the dense tangle of undergrowth and young trees. When I arrived, John and our driver with two other young men had already constructed a shelter made of a large piece of thatched roof supported on the branches of trees in a small clearing.

Over the next week we set up quite a comfortable camp. A space about ten by twelve feet was covered by the first two pieces of roof. Then we added another piece about three by five feet at one end, over the cooking fire. The suitcases and boxes were piled at one side, raised on logs to keep them from the damp earth. At night we hung blankets and *lappas* over the open sides of the hut, to shut out the night and give us the illusion of security. We covered the roof with light branches as camouflage against the passing planes, but left many of the larger trees standing undisturbed for general cover. Even so these trees were not very tall, since this was farmland. The biggest were those which had been left last time the area was cleared and planted because they were suitable for supporting the yams. Everything else was light growth of the past five years, at the most ten to twelve feet, but very tangled and overgrown, with narrow paths the width of a hunter's shoulders winding through. To keep our immediate area sanitary we dug a latrine pit some distance away. Our two ceiling boards now became part of the floor and at night we spread out the plastic tablecloth I had bought to make into plastic pants and used it for a groundsheet to keep out the

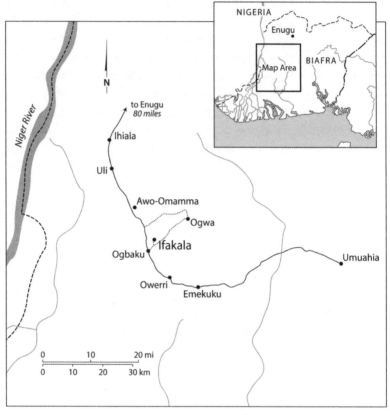

Map 4: The Umelo family moved to various locations within the shrinking Biafra enclave. Map shows the villages where they stayed, and nearby towns. Cartography by Bill Nelson.

damp. On all sides other groups were setting up similar camps in nearby spaces.

Our children accepted the whole incredible situation quite easily. The only event that seemed real to me was the approaching birth, which could be at the most only a couple of weeks away. Some people were very disturbed 'to think of a person of my age sleeping in the bush like a madman'. The driver, with his sister Apollonia, left us and went away. The big problem every day was a shortage of water, since there was none nearer than the village. No-one dared to go and draw up slow clanking pailfuls from the deep well. Instead, if everything was quiet, people would steal down to the nearest houses, take water from their *umi* and creep away. I put Milton (a disinfectant) into the pails of brownish water, boiled it and hoped for the best. Every time it rained, the edges of the thatched roof were fringed with basins, bowls, pails, even empty tins to collect as much water as possible, while we regretted the water that dropped from the trees and ran to waste where we couldn't collect it. Even so, many times we were very short of water when no one dared to go to draw it, and the clouds sailed on over our hide-out. In the middle of the equatorial rain forest, an address that always sounds perpetually dank and dripping, there would be a desert situation, offering the choice between washing in two cups of water or drinking the same amount of tea.

For some days there was more food than there had been for months and it was comparatively cheap again. Some villagers had fled with their animals, but when the goats began to bleat the owners would be visited by men camping nearby, imploring them to slaughter the animals before they could betray the hiding place. A price would be agreed, then the beast would be killed and divided. A large goat was sold for £7–£8, a small one for £2–£3, while a chicken cost three shillings. There was plenty of yams and cassava from nearby farms. Snuff and palm wine could be bought. There was much stealthy coming and going along the hunters' paths between the encampments and the next village, Ifakala.

Of course there was shooting, and sometimes it sounded very near. Often at first light the guns would begin—cok-cok-cok—and no-one could be sure who was shooting or where, since the sound travelled across the silent forest. But once a relative in the Commandos visited us in our camp and obligingly identified the bangs, slams, and crumps that were making up the dawn chorus that day. As anyone will, we soon established a daily routine. We would wake at first light to the sound of shooting echoing across the cold, damp trees. It was often drizzling with a chilly rain. Someone would feed the glowing embers of yesterday's fire with dry twigs and blow it into life, then put on the kettle for tea. While breakfast was being prepared—usually boiled or roasted yam—I would tour round the radio for news, listening to the BCB at 6.30 a.m., Voice of America (VOA) at 7 a.m., BBC at 8 a.m. After

eating, I would try to tidy the house and the little space that surrounded it. As the day grew brighter and the bush became dry, we
would spread out the blankets to air them. Then the others would
creep out to try to get yam or cassava, to gather firewood or, if the
firing had stopped, to go down quietly to scoop more water from the
nearest pit. I was unable to do very much now. I sat on our plaster
board floor with the sewing machine on a stool before me and sewed
shirts for the boys. This prosaic occupation was very calming both for
me and for those who were watching me anxiously. There was no
chance now of delivery in the local Maternity Home and no-one was
sure where the midwife had gone. My mother-in-law consulted the
'native midwife'—the wise woman who delivered village women in
their homes if they were old-fashioned enough not to want to go to
hospital or if their mother-in-law was determined not to allow them to
attend there. A brisk woman in late middle age, she came to examine
me. And so we waited.

September 26 was the anniversary of our flight from Enugu. We
came under fire for the first time and spent much of the afternoon
lying on the floor listening to the whine of stray bullets and a loud
alarming bang-pow-wow-wow, which someone said was a rocket.
Many children from other encampments crowded into our hut while
the shooting lasted. Perhaps they felt safer near to the white woman
who can (we all know) do anything, even perhaps turn aside bullets.
The next day, shooting began in the late afternoon and continued hour
after hour without ceasing. The continuous din was shattering, with the
clatter and slam blasting across the bush. Bullets whined overhead,
clipping and smashing the branches of those taller trees. Those people
who had tried to move further away found they were still within range.
Darkness came and the firing went on and on. We cowered behind our
screen of branches and blankets, damped down the fire and talked in
whispers until the exhausted younger ones slept. As night passed, I lay
wakeful, heavily and restlessly shifting my position from side to side,
unable to believe that something was happening to me at last. My husband was also awake, listening to the hellish noise, watching the slow
drift of mist or smoke through the boughs.

> 'Don't you think we ought to try to move?'
> 'I can't. The baby's coming.'

At the worst possible time, in the dark, under fire, the baby was indeed coming. In an atmosphere of controlled consternation, the wise woman was called. She came, examined me and confirmed that labour had started. 'Call me when something is happening,' she said, with all the unfeeling efficiency of any staff nurse in the labour ward, and returned to her own camp. I lay this way and that, got up and lay down again, tried quick, light breathing, tried to roll along the surging contractions. I tried deep breathing … then suddenly, unmistakable something was happening, strong and sure.

'Quick, call the midwife!' Someone had already run, bent double, along the path. By the time they returned, it was clear the baby was coming very quickly. There was no time to wake and send out the teenage boys, still soundly sleeping in the hut. John knelt beside me translating instructions. In former days I had threatened to compel him to attend a delivery some time—now he had no choice. There was no trouble, anyway—just the unromantic, hard work reaching its climax. A delay of a few moments while the midwife slipped the cord to a better position, and then the child was born into the glow of the firelight and the yellow light of the bush lamp, the pattern of thatch coming and going above me more real than the noise outside, the spiteful whine of bullets, the clip and smash in the branches.

'What is it?'

'A girl.'

'It ought to have been a boy in all this battle.'

'Never mind.'

'Make her cry. Is she all right?'

'Listen, she's crying now. Everything's all right.'

The rest of the people in the hut were still sleeping.

There were more women here than I had realised before. While some attended to the baby, two helped me outside to bathe and shiver with reaction in the cold night air. Inside again, I lay in that luxurious peace that comes after all the effort. Singing a little song of welcome just above a whisper, they brought me the baby washed and wrapped in her shawl. She lay on the mat beside me sleeping again, with shooting and whispering for her first lullaby. In the crook of my arm she was there at last, surprisingly big, strong and healthy. Whatever happens now, at least I have seen you.

The firing seemed to increase with the dawn and for the first (and only) time we agreed to separate. John took the older children, with Angelina and the rest into another part of the bush. His mother and I lay in a corner of the hut with the baby between us; we listened, prayed and slept. Then one of my nieces came back and they insisted on cooking some food for me, regarding it as the worst detail in the whole sorry business that I had not yet been given anything to eat since my delivery.

Meanwhile, in another part of the forest, John and his party met a Biafran soldier who demanded to know what they were doing there, and how many more civilians were still in the bush. Towards 10 a.m. the firing at last stopped. I was sleeping again in my corner when a Biafran soldier appeared in the hut: 'Madam, what are you doing here with these people?' 'They are my family,' I said crossly, feeling at a disadvantage lying down half asleep while he was standing up and wide awake. Convinced at last by the sight of the baby if nothing else, he went away and soon John came back to tell us he had arranged with the soldiers to move us out with the remaining civilians. I would be brought on the carrier of a bicycle if I could just manage to hold on. People came to pick up the boxes, and Angelina carried the baby. I climbed unsteadily onto the bicycle, put an arm round the shoulder of the young man who was helping John get the bicycle along the narrow path. And so we came out.

We stayed in the village of Ifakala for two weeks in the house of an in-law of one of John's friends. Although his compound was full of refugees, he managed to give us one room and those who couldn't fit in it at night had to manage in the kitchen. Ifakala was barely two miles from Ogbaku, and we were far from out of trouble. The noise of shooting seemed just as loud but only once did the ground shake as something heavier exploded on the edge of the village. It reminded us that we were within range if they started using mortars. Discussing the last day we had spent in the bush, it seemed clear that there had been no casualties among the people hidden there because small arms were used. But who had they been shooting at? All those hours nothing seemed to have replied. It seemed likely there had been no Biafran soldiers in the bush to shoot back.

But now we were seeing Biafran troops all the time—not the well-pressed and starched officers at their ease in the back of commandeered cars, or the stoical wounded, but the fighting men. They wore uniform shirts and *lappas*, or khaki green trousers with cotton shirts, captured steel helmets ornamented with leaves or streamers of green baize, heavy cartridge belts, daggers, knives, or matchets. An automatic rifle was slung over one shoulder while rosary beads were worn round the neck or looped over one shoulder. They always seemed to punish breaches of discipline in the open space outside the house where we were living, and the children would rush to watch, then tell me some-one was rolling to and fro on the dusty, stony ground, or frog-hopping with his hands clasped behind his head, urged on with a stout stick if he moved too slowly. I paraphrased the Duke of Wellington: 'I don't know if they frighten the enemy but by God, they frighten me!' But in fact they were always friendly and polite to me, and many of the toughest looking came several times to see the baby as the story spread around. Some of the villagers complained that the soldiers were less interested in the fighting than in enemy two-legs (chicken), enemy four-legs (goat) and in four-oh-four, that speeding vehicle (dog), even in enemy no-legs (snake).

Of course, in a society where pregnant women worked hard up until the last moment, this was far from the first baby to be delivered in the bush. The birthplace of the child was generally remembered in the child's name. 'Uzo' was born by the wayside, while 'Nwaohia' would have been born in the bush. The thing that made this baby's birth memorable was that one of those exotic, fragile and increasingly rare foreign wives had shared this fundamental experience with her village sisters. Some people were already calling her 'Bush-girl' and 'War-baby'. As I looked at her wide eyes, for reasons of my own I rather liked 'Bush-baby'. Names are generally chosen carefully and proposed by relatives to commemorate something that was in the mind of the family at the time. Many names are religious, even the non-Christian: Uchechukwu (the thought of God), Ikechukwu (the power of God), Uchenna (thought of the father), or Ifeanyichukwu (nothing is impos-sible to God). When we remembered all the circumstances of this baby's birth and her deliverance from all possible dangers, there would have been added significance in Chinedum (God leads me), Ngozichukwu (God's blessing), Chidilim (God protects me). Ogueri (war shall not finish us) was a popular name at the time too. But John chose Osondu, part of an Igbo proverb: 'When you run for life you don't get tired.'

The birth of a baby is one of the most important events in any family. The other women would announce the arrival to the rest of the village by a shrilling shout repeated three times for a girl, four times for a boy. If a child has been born in a hospital, mother and child are escorted home by all the women of the family, singing, often dancing on the way while grandmother, prouder than anyone else, usually carries the baby. Visitors pour into the compound to welcome the child and thank the mother for her efforts, saying, 'Thank God. You did well. You have tried,' with even more enthusiasm if the baby were a boy. The mother has lumps of local chalk on hand for women who visit her to smear on their cheeks and forehead, or, more up to date, a big tin of cheap scented talcum powder for them to dredge on lavishly so anyone who sees them will know they have been visiting a new baby. Boys are circumcised in the first week or so, but female circumcision was already old-fashioned and the custom was dying out. The old prejudice against twins was also generally a thing of the past. But a baby was still expected to utter its first cry before it is picked up and tended. An infant that does not cry at all was regarded with horror, and if born in a remote place could be quietly made away with.

Three ceremonies for the mother form the ritual of 'coming out' on the fourth, eighth, and twenty-eighth day after the birth. Friends and relations come in with gifts, gallon jars of palm wine and food to sing, dance, drink, and enjoy the feasting the happy parents have arranged. The mother does not have to stay literally inside the house all the time until those days are completed, but she does keep within her compound with the baby, doesn't go visiting or to work on the farm or to market. My mother-in-law remembered the count of the days even though little of this was possible for me and said wistfully to my husband one morning, 'Rose ought to be coming out for the third time today.' In the same way everyone could tell you at once when Orie Ogbaku market day would be, even though market had not been held for weeks or months. The old fabric of life was too strong to tear.

Children are passionately loved and wanted. The idea still is the more the better, although people are increasingly taking the view that it is not enough to have plenty of children and leave them illiterate and untrained, and so the expenses of education would tend to limit numbers. But boys are still the first consideration and a man without a son is in a wretched situation. Even if he does not blame his wife, his family certainly will do so and will try to persuade the man to marry another wife. If the family still only produced girls, then rather than allow their compound to close, since there would be no male to inherit, it used to be the custom for one or two of the girls not to marry, since children always belong to the husband and his family. These girls would have children for the benefit of their own family, in the hope that sons might be born to save the family from dying out. In a 'rags to riches' story I heard in London, the narrator, describing the good fortune of his hero, declared: 'Every time his wife delivered, she delivered male. Every time his goats delivered, they delivered female.'

The refugee family from Lagos had lost their ninth, their last child.

More than anything we wanted to go home. Home was a scant two miles away through the trees, along those sandy paths where the guns were still firing at first light or chattering in sudden challenge and answer in the small hours. I heard them night after night as I sat feeding the baby and everyone else was sleeping, arranged in rows on the floor. During the day, day after day, there was nothing to do but listen to the guns, carry the baby, listen to the news bulletin, talk and long to go home.

Eunice died. Her family carried her back in the darkness and buried her somewhere on the edge of the farms so she could lie in her homeland. My mother-in-law, who had endured our life in the bush without murmuring, now spread her mat on the verandah and lay waiting to go home. Home was the direction from which the fighting men came back. After all, the Nigerians had not hurried through on their way to Uli, and the relief planes were still landing. The war went on. The radio said there would be no surrender.

Ifakala lived its days poised for flight. If there were prolonged firing or rumours of an intended attack, everyone packed their loads or removed some belongings to the further outskirts of the village. Again, we wondered what to do, this time if the invaders decided to link with those on the other tarred road at Ubomiri, along the bush road that ran from Ogbaku through part of Ifakala. Our car was finished. The battery had been looted (or liberated) by passing Biafran soldiers, and although we had recovered the car, which disappeared with the battery, the vehicle was now useless. It was propped on pieces of timber with the wheels off. If we had to run again, it would be on foot with whatever we could carry. As soon as we came out of the bush, John had travelled by bicycle to see our friends the Reverend Fathers at Awo-Omamma to let them know where we were and to ask them to get a letter out to reassure my family in England that we were still alive. The Fathers offered to transport us if we wanted to move anywhere, so John decided to send me with my children to Alaenyi Ogwa. His mother, his late brother's wife and her children were to remain for the present at Oboro Ifakala. And so it happened. The Father came and we loaded his small car with children, cooking pots, sleeping mats, boxes, bundles and all the untidy odds and ends that made up all we had in the world and came ten miles or so along bumpy bush roads to Alaenyi Ogwa.[2]

Although I had never been to Alaenyi before, we knew several families there. Some were people we had known in England and others were friends from Enugu. Some were in their homeland, others were like ourselves, refugees—once, twice, even three times over. For a while we seemed to be constantly meeting people whom we hadn't seen for two or three years. Friends had found us somewhere to live— two rooms in the junior family quarters attached to a fine modern house. The furnishing was spartan, one wooden armchair without cushion, one ordinary chair, one large table, one small table and one plank bed. But the beautiful compound was quiet, with plenty of room for the children to play and a good patch of trees for them to take cover in while planes were passing. The big house itself was empty and shuttered since the owner was stationed elsewhere with his family. There was only a caretaker living in the compound at first, then a young nurse and her husband came to the room next to ours. So after the very noisy and public way we had been living at Ifakala we were now enjoying more privacy than we had known since Enugu.

Of course, we had not left the war behind. The guns sounded all around us and in the first week we learned that this direction meant Okigwe and that direction Owerri. The sombre thud of the heavy guns was, at least, further away but several times the *cok-cok-cok* of the automatic fire seemed to swell close then recede. Rumours flew, and local people buried their iron pots and surplus crockery and prepared to run with the remainder. Ogwa was a more prosperous and advanced place than Ogbaku. Even in the area where we were lodging there were several well-built two-storey houses (upstairs, as everyone called them); their compounds were enclosed in concrete block walls with wrought iron gates. There was a piped water system with public pipes but this was seldom working because of the shortage of diesel to work the pump. Best of all, just along the road there was the Community Hospital where a clinic was held twice a week. As soon as we arrived, Osondu fell sick with a high fever. This was really my first experience of serious illness with any of the children when there was no car to put them in and no emergency doctor to rush them to, and I was particu-larly alarmed since she was so young. Quite by chance we had come to one of the few places where there was a functioning clinic and we quickly took advantage of it.

We located the Owerri branch of Barclays Bank, where it was hiding about nine miles from Ogwa, but there was still an extreme shortage of money. Banks were only paying out £2 or £3 per customer and mak-ing payments one or two days each week. There were five shilling notes again, but cash was scarce. Traders were willing to give one Biafran pound note for six Nigerian shillings, since they wanted the coins for buying goods from smugglers. A tin of rubber solution for mending bicycle punctures could be bought for three shillings at Oguta and sold for four 10-shilling notes. For a time two prices might be quoted. A packet of sugar was offered to me for 15 shillings cash or 30 shillings in notes, a cup of salt for five shillings cash or 25 shillings in notes. In markets it was difficult to get change for anything bigger than a shilling. If you bought three shillings worth of goods and tendered a five shilling note, you could not get change. To get over this, either something else had to be taken to bring the sum to an amount divisible by five, or else a form of barter was used. A bottle of cough medicine was bought for seven shillings and the change taken as three M and B tablets.[3] A bicycle pump cost 12 shillings, and instead of three shillings change, the pur-chaser accepted an exercise book.

John was kept busy riding about on his old bicycle, which was the only form of transport we had left. He went regularly to the bank or to visit the rest of the family at Ifakala. Days when he did not ride out seemed to be spent having the bicycle repaired. One time he came back very late, having received the full treatment at an Army checkpoint. A crowd had gathered in the hope that a sabo had been discovered, while the soldiers read their way through every scrap of paper in his briefcase. At last they became sympathetic and advised him that the whole suspicion was caused by his 'longsleeve' and tie. Certainly you didn't see many people wearing English-type shirts and long ties, even those who once used to dress quite formally and still had such clothes to wear. Instead men were wearing cotton sports shirts, or since cotton cloth was getting very expensive and hard to find, a 'Biafra shirt'—a cotton slipover with a wide neckline, short sleeves, and a tabbed breast pocket. This was economical in cloth, time and sewing cotton and needed no buttons.

John returned from Ifakala one day and told us some soldiers had promised him Ogbaku would be cleared within a week. Somewhat sceptical, he had promised to buy them palm wine if it were true. Fortunately he went back with some money, because the Nigerians had in fact been driven out from Ogbaku, then from the next villages, then all the way back to Owerri.[4] The villagers began to return as soon as the army allowed them, first the men, then the women and children. They found the village that they had left three months before overgrown, cold and lonely, with a colossal amount of damage. Thatched houses had been burned while 'zinc' houses, built of concrete blocks with zinc roofs, were looted and damaged. Those houses on the main tarred road had suffered most. Our own little house, which was some distance away, had only minor damage, with a few bullet holes in the roof. The doors had been broken open but then there was nothing inside worth stealing. The mission church roof had been shot full of holes 'like a grater'. The statue outside was smashed, and church books had been heaped up and burned. At the Technical College, buildings had been damaged in the fighting. The pump that used to bring up the water from the well had been looted and taken away, as had the electricity generator and all the school machines for wood and metal working. The Maternity Home had been cleared of everything useful, and what couldn't be carried away had been destroyed. Orie Ogbaku market sheds had all been burned, and everywhere crops had been destroyed—even the young cassava plants of that year's planting which had nothing at all at their roots. Rumour said two white mercenaries had been killed in the area. One was said to have fallen into an *umi* and drowned, another to have been bitten by a snake.

The people at once began to clear the overgrown roads and compounds, repair the roofs and damaged buildings. They planted more cassava while the guns pounded from the direction of Owerri.

12

THE PATCH-PATCH LIFE

We celebrated the second Christmas of the war even more quietly than the first. We did have a Christmas card, though it arrived late, but there were no presents or new clothes for anyone. By saving here and there, we managed to produce something extra to eat. For lunch there was rice and dried peas with a sauce made from tinned meat, our last tin of tomato puree and an onion, for which we paid £1. At tea time there were biscottes, some with cheese, some with apple jam, biscuits, and a cake with some raisins in it, all sent by the Father at Attah from his personal supplies. All this was received by the children in impressed silence, then a burst of excited chatter which was reward enough.

In contrast, the New Year was celebrated at midnight so noisily with shouts and the firing of guns that jittery people packed once again and prepared to run. 'What were you all shouting?' I asked Angelina. 'Oh, we were chasing away the old year and telling it to take the war with it.' Then it was the Harmattan season again, a time when once curtains had fluttered and billowed in the strong dry wind, when the familiar line of hills was lost and trees and houses swam in the haze, and when a film of dust dimmed the polished furniture and the green tiled floor, however often it was rubbed and brushed away. Now Harmattan for us meant the cold weather, when we were glad of our blankets and the roof above our heads even though there was no ceiling and the chill air drifted down from the four-inch space between the top of the walls and the edge of the roofing sheets. To wake at night meant to listen to the unfamiliar sound of the wind roaring in the tree tops and the noise of the heavy lorries passing in the dark, taking troops down to the fighting lines round Owerri. The glorious sound of the singing brought back memories of those who practised their drill in the Queens School compound and sang their way back from their training runs in the days of our inexperience.

> Remember, children of Biafra,
> Remember Aguiyi-Ironsi, Biafra,
> Remember Ojukwu, Biafra,
> Remember those who have died, Biafra.

There were more and more to remember.

In that cold, dry air the last leaves clattered from the umbrella tree to lie crunching underfoot. Biafra pomade, like Marmite, was fixed inaccessible at the bottom of the bottle. Palm oil congealed like red gravy. Harmattan was always an unhealthy season, with the very chilly nights, often with heavy dews and damps, then hot afternoons. Every year there would be coughs, colds and epidemics, usually measles. This year any epidemic was likely to be more severe because of the shortage of medicines and because so many children were undernourished and would have little resistance to the post-measles complications, bronchitis, pneumonia. Waking before dawn, shivering in the cold at 4 a.m., we thought of the refugees in camps trying to keep warm in open school buildings with half walls, no ceilings, open window spaces without glass. In the morning we happened to go by one of the refugee camps. In an attempt to keep out the cold, the refugees had put palm branches in the wide window openings. Groups of children were playing dancing games, clapping their hands and singing rather breathlessly, trying to get warm again. Older people were gathered round fires of fast burning twigs which looked bright but gave out little heat. Most of them looked cheerful, if only because the long night was over and the sun was breaking through the early morning mists. For one old woman, the sun had risen too late. The men were digging her grave at the edge of the field.

There were many refugees in Ogwa. Every school seemed to be a camp with 500 or more people, and the refugee population of the area ran into many thousands. Typical was a camp I visited in Alaenyi. There were two long, bleak school buildings with no partition walls or ceilings. One was completely bare, with half walls and window spaces. The other was more enclosed, with solid wooden shutters to close over the window openings. All down the room there was a clutter of bamboo beds, old suitcases, cardboard cartons, enamel bowls, sleeping mats, children (including twin girls the size of dolls and completely silent), odds and ends of blankets and clothes, ragged *lappas* and personal possessions, battered now but too cherished to abandon. The scene was overlooked at one end by a large chalk drawing of the sower sowing the seed of the Word, at the other by details of some long-forgotten entrance examination for which this had been a centre, and exquisitely inappropriate posters:

'Even a little alcohol makes you less safe on the roads';
'Remember, always be kind to animals.'

People who lived in such places were called Camp A refugees. The camps were organised by officials appointed from outside and by committees formed among the refugees themselves to try and ensure equitable divisions of food. Supplies were collected for the camps from relief stores. Some camps had a resident nurse, and most were visited more or less regularly by a doctor. In this respect they were better off than the Camp B refugees, who did not live in camps at all but in private compounds with friends or relatives. They were often people technically in receipt of salaries, if only the banks were paying out any money and if there were anything much to be bought with it. During January 1969 beans and rice cost 10 shillings a cup in the market. Salt in Ogwa was £3 a cup, in Ogbaku £3.10s.

In the more remote places there were no medical facilities. Sick people found it difficult to travel several miles on foot and most got better or died without ever seeing a doctor. Camp B refugees were sometimes given a tiny allowance of protein food too. Feeding centres were still being established and hundreds of children were being fed two or three times a week with a small but valuable high protein meal, usually containing stockfish. Kwashiorkor sickbays were also being set up. There was now one in a wing of the community hospital. At first many of the patients died because they were in a hopeless condition when admitted, but gradually more were recovering. It was always a long business. The patients needed both treatment and feeding, and if the supplies of either fell, it was useless admitting them. They had better stay at home and die there.

I found it a terrible responsibility to have sick children brought to me by relatives or friends of relatives and to know that I must be the one to help them, since the hospital had little food or medicine and such children did not yet meet the standards for admission. I did what little I could, and found it hard to forget the children who stood and looked at me like little lost souls, frail and thin with the signs of kwashiorkor coming—the feet just beginning to swell, the fading skin loose and wrinkled where the arm joined the shoulder. I would count out the vitamin tablets, iron tablets, and give some advice and milk powder— plenty of one, little of the other. They would go but I could not stop thinking of them long after the sun lay disturbed across the doorway. The BCB gave some statistics early in January. They said a million people had died in the war so far, 95 percent of them civilians. Two million had been injured in some way or other, with seven million displaced. At the same time, they said, 2,000 square miles of Biafran territory had been liberated between 27 October and 31 December 1968. The people were naturally optimistic and resilient. They had always expressed this quality in their proverbs, in the slogans they painted on lorries: 'Every day is not Christmas'; 'Every disappointment is a blessing'. Even 'Nothing without end,' and 'No condition is permanent' were just as much promises for the future as warnings about the present.

It was an instance of this optimism, we felt, when it was announced that the primary schools were to reopen. They had closed with the rest of the schools in July 1967, opened for a few days in September, and closed again because of the threat of air raids. Now they were to open again, not in the regular school buildings, most of which were being used for some other purpose, but in temporary buildings in out-of-the-way places. Before long I was taking some of my children down past the place where the market used to be held, past the new place safe under the cover of trees where it was now being held, to a very temporary building of thatched roof supported on poles, larger but no better than our shelter on the farmland. All the children already there flocked out to see us, and I decided I would be less conspicuous if I went in and sat down on one of the battered old school benches. A teacher arrived and wondered quite loudly, 'Where did this white woman come from?' I explained myself, handed over the boys, and came away leaving them in that well-known confusion of excitement and apprehension of the first morning at any new school. Over the next few weeks more and more children registered. Classes became enormous, especially Elementary One. Besides refugee children added to the local children, there were all those who had reached school age (six years) since the war began.

No longer did the children go to school in droves along the main roads, all with tin suitcases or raffia bags with books, pens, ink, neat in their school uniforms of bright blue, bright green. Now they went corner-corner along the bush roads, wearing anything or nothing. Most had no textbook, and it was difficult to buy exercise books or pencils. An 80-page exercise book now cost 15 shillings; I took one to pieces and made the children books of a few pages at a time. Even the thin, blue exercise books which had once cost twopence were now two for five shillings, as were pencils. Lucky children had small pieces of blackboard to write on with chalk. And somehow with all these difficulties the primary schools began to function again even in places, like Ogbaku, within the near sound of the guns. It was easier for the children to start school because they all now spoke Igbo fluently, although (as some Ogwa people told me with amusement) all spoke in Ogbaku dialect. As one place was only ten miles from the other I was surprised to hear there could be such marked differences in the language.

However, even I had noticed many other differences besides the large, affluent houses that had caught our attention when we arrived. The area seemed even more densely populated and there appeared to be little farmland, so the ground was planted over and over and not left for some years to recover its fertility. As a result, the few local yams we saw were all very small. People stored them in enclosures in their compounds instead of on the farms. Most compounds were walled with thick mud walls five or six feet high, or with fences made wholly from palm fronds. The whole area was full of palm trees which provided firewood. In Ogbaku, after the harvest, the dead wood that had been used to stake the yams provided the next year's firewood. But in Ogwa, they mostly staked the yams with pieces of bamboo trees, which grew here but rarely in Ogbaku. There was hardly any bush in which ordi-

149

nary stakes could be cut or firewood gathered, and so dry palm fronds had to suffice. Ogwa was well provided with water; sometimes the taps would run for half an hour or so, but generally people went down to the streams to bathe, wash clothes and take water. After the dryness of the land round Ogbaku, it was strange to see a wide stream flowing. And in Ogwa there was some religious rivalry between Church Missionary Society (CMS) and Catholic Missions, both of which were established in the area. There were also many Gospel or Spiritual churches, singing, clapping hands, and making a joyful noise. At Ogbaku the choice lay between Catholic and pagan, with the Cherubim and Seraphim a later arrival.

Before long the anticipated measles epidemic arrived, beating the Ministry of Health immunisation team to the area by several weeks. Eze had had measles in England but Uzoma and Iheoma went down with it and were ill for several days. Measles was always a serious illness here because the high fever could lead to convulsions and death and to the post-measles complications of pneumonia, eye troubles and even blindness. Many people did not even have aspirin to bring down the fever. As the epidemic spread, we sent aspirin and vitamin tablets to children we had heard were sick. Our own two were having a mixture of European and local treatment. This included mopping with cool water, and a wet cloth on the forehead. The children were painted with *uri*, a medicinal black dye obtained from a fruit the size of a small lemon, but dark green in colour with slight fluting.[1] When cut and soaked in water it was used to paint the children in horizontal zebra stripes. Particular care was taken to see that the stripes went across the joints, knee, ankles, elbow, wrist, and across the eyes. A drop or two of the dye would be put in the eyes to stop the infection there and in the mouth to kill the germs inside. And I used aspirin and penicillin eye ointment too.

When the immunisation team from the Ministry of Health came to the district I took along Nwaneze and Osondu for their injections. The very next day, Nwaneze began to develop chickenpox, a disease that was always taken very seriously because of smallpox, and the high fever. The first signs appeared on the morning; the Reverend Sister Doctor was due to hold a clinic nearby and so we went down to meet her. When we arrived, everything was already well organised. St.

Joseph's was quite a large church and the pews were full of a nightmare congregation of very sick people. Three-quarters of them, both young and old, had kwashiorkor or some other deficiency disease. They sat packed closely together waiting for the doctor. She arrived promptly with her assistants: nurses to give injections and dispense medicines, and a laboratory assistant to perform blood and urine tests in other parts of the compound. The doctor herself came into the Church, serene and efficient. A blue overall was fastened on top of her white habit, her veil was clipped back. The table and benches were quickly arranged to her liking, so that fresher air could blow in through the open door, and the clinic began. Something like 500 people would be attended to before the team left in the late afternoon after working continuously in the noise and heat. Next day they would go to some other clinic in another district and repeat the whole performance. They gave me VIP treatment. I felt more guilty than ever. After we had seen the doctor, we went over to the 'dispensary', a small room overflowing with medicines, worth hundreds of pounds even by outside prices, and here just incalculable. There were large polythene containers of pills, tablets and capsules and laboratory size jars of lotions and potions. All the foreign language labels spoke eloquently of sympathy and concern to those who wanted to read them that way. As someone said wistfully, 'Caritas have medicine enough!'

There was some relief food for distribution to those who needed it most—milk and salt particularly. In one corner someone was carefully cutting a bar of laundry soap into small pieces. Every now and then he scraped the powder and flakes into a pill envelope so that nothing was wasted. As we waited for our prescriptions to be dispensed, we sat on a bench outside and watched the steady stream of people out of the Church across the field, some to join the line for medicine, some to go for injections or tests. Nwaneze broke in with a stage whisper, 'Look at this man's feet.' Beside her, an old man was sitting, his feet very swollen, the skin flaking and peeling like old sunburn. 'Tell him sorry,' I said inadequately. 'Ndo,' she said—the universal word of sympathy. 'My child, thank you,' he said, smiling. In years, he was not even very old.

By the time Nwaneze, Iheoma, and even the baby Osondu had worked their way through chickenpox, the new year was not so new again. I had always heard that African children suffered more severely from these diseases than 'European' children. Maybe the Europeans sought medical advice more quickly; if they were living in Africa they could afford it more easily than most of the indigenous people, while in Europe it was mostly there for the asking, and the problem of payment rarely arose. Perhaps the better nutrition of European children helped them to combat infection; European children seemed on average to be heavier at birth than African children and tended to stay ahead in height and weight. But then I had heard African mothers comment that back home their children weighed five to six pounds at birth, but while in England they delivered children weighing eight pounds. Perhaps climate as well as nutrition had an influence on birth weight? European children were certainly slower in their development than African children. I had always thought this was caused by the restrictions on infants imposed by living conditions and climate, such as blankets, layers of clothing, pram harness, high chairs, play pens, even the lengthy performance of blocking the draughts that whistle across the ordinary English floor, needed to allow a baby even half an hour's free play on the floor—not to mention the working mother's difficulty in sparing half an hour in an overflowing day.

To this catalogue of excuses, Angelina added another. 'You don't teach your children,' she accused, and, to my alarm, she sat up the baby—who promptly folded in half like a flower with a wind-snapped stem. I explained I wanted Osondu to follow the usual procedure and advance at her own pace, from rolling over front to back, back to front, to pushing herself up, to sitting, to crawling. If she were forced onto the next step it would strain her back because the muscles are not strong enough. That was what all the books said, didn't they? But despite my protests, Osondu was soon sitting up straight and strong, bouncing on her buttocks, flailing her arms in an attempt to reach something beyond her grasp, and at four to five months trying to crawl.

The number of people in our household was constantly changing, as people came and stayed overnight while on their way from some other place or came visiting and stayed some days. Early in February we had the second of several children to stay to recover their health. Colly was fourteen years old, very tall, very thin, very weak. I felt a pang of genuine alarm at the sight of him nearly falling from the carrier of John's bicycle. The inside of his eyelids was waxy with anaemia. I began administering some super-quantity vitamin and iron capsules and gradually he progressed from lying on his mat with his face to the wall, to lying watching the other children, to sitting, to performing a few odd jobs, sweeping the floor, washing pots, until at last he was well and strong enough to rejoin his parents.

Many people continued to call for medicine and advice. Sister Doctor sent me simple medicines to give to those I could reach—headaches, fevers, and diarrhoea were the most common complaints. I sent urgent requests to sympathetic friends in England for iron tablets, vitamins, aspirin, whatever they could send. It was more difficult than ever to get mail, particularly parcels, and those few that were delivered took three months or more to arrive. Friends packed strips of patent medicine in newspaper cuttings and sent them in envelopes. A packet of medicine that arrived in February 1969 had cuttings dated August, September, and October of the previous year—all burying Biafra. That was how we heard that Uli airstrip had been occupied by Nigerian forces; that the final military push had begun, and the remainder of the area was expected to be captured within a few weeks; that Col. Ojukwu was personally conducting a last stand at Umuahia; that he had been chosen by the 'Igbo tribal chiefs' (that word again!) as head of a resistance movement they would form once hostilities ended; that he was preparing to flee to Gabon....

Still the guns resounded on all sides, and in the middle of the night we would wake to the sound of a heavy attack and a pale bar of moonlight marking the top of the bedroom walls. When the firing by day was too prolonged or near we would begin to look at our loads, wondering what to take up if we had to run again, wondering how we could leave behind the odd bottles, tins and rags which made the difference between having something and owning nothing. We had gone into the bush with a number of cups and saucers, though only one cup had a handle and nothing matched. We arrived in Ogwa with only one cup. Previously we had used empty tins as general purpose cups for transferring water to the kettle, or while cooking, but for a while they had to be used for drinking. There was nothing else until Reverend Father, returning from São Tomé, brought us some Hong Kong white enamel mugs. Many of the children attending feeding centres used the flat brown bullybeef tins as their cups and bowls, and sickbays also made use of them to feed their patients until enough plates could be provided. Soon neat bowls were being made with a handle and lid and put on sale, all made from these basic brown tins.

Shortage of money continued to be a problem. There was hardly any cash at all and everything cost a five shilling note—a bunch of vegetables, a bicycle patch, a gallon of palm wine. A new currency was 'launched' at Umuahia but the notes were slow to come into circulation, and there was still no cash. Unable to afford a minimum of five shillings for every ingredient in the soup, I brought out the sewing machine again and began to mend people's clothes, taking my payment in vegetables, pepper and palm oil. It was hard work, as many of the clothes were just disintegrating. I discovered that cotton could age in two ways. Sometimes it became as thin as tissue paper, or it could stay thick, but crumble as the needle went into it to sew on the patch. Often a garment, however carefully it was mended, would tear again next to the patch, or between the patches. 'English-made' had always been a certificate of quality; I found it hard to explain to customers that their clothes, though 'English-mended', could not be guaranteed to remain in one piece. My careful mending could not make them new again. Prices continued to go up; we continued to sell odds and ends of our possessions, to collect whenever we could get anything from the bank, and with my repairing service we managed to keep going.

Indeed, everyone around us was rediscovering old skills and finding new ones. We learned how to make coconut oil. First, take a coconut—a dry one is best. Take out the pieces of nut and grate them, including the brownish side next to the shell. Pour some clean water and wash the shavings well. Squeeze the pieces of nut as dry as possible and discard them. Boil away the water, and finally pour off the oil— very fine, clear pale yellow in colour, with only a faint and quite pleasant smell. This oil could be used for the skin and hair. If an egg could be spared (they cost two shillings and sixpence each) and beaten into the hot oil, the mixture would set like a good skin cream. The pure oil could be used to oil sewing machines. Someone we knew bought a sewing machine needle for £5. I hated risking mine across the iron hard seams of men's shorts when they came to be re-mended. Coconut oil again, mixed with Biafra gin (a spirit distilled from palm wine), was said to be a substitute for brake fluid in cars.

Second-hand car tyres cost from £40 upwards. A bicycle tyre cost £25 and an inner tube £9. All were mended over and over again. Two old tyres, which we had changed at Ogbaku and which had been hanging on one wall through the occupation, not worth anyone's effort to remove or loot, worn smooth and full of patches as they were, now could be sold for £3. The bicycle owners with tyres in reasonable condition were very unwilling to have their bicycles commandeered by the Army, in case they were changed while the vehicles were out of their hands. Certainly the soldiers did not ride their borrowed vehicles with the same consideration and knowledge of their weaknesses as the owners did, and commandeered bicycles were seldom the same again. The owners with fairly good inner tubes were well advised to sit beside them while they were patched instead of passing the time in some palm wine bar. Otherwise the next time they had to stop for repairs they might find their good tube had somewhere been changed for another, older and in worse condition.

We were coming again to the hottest time of the year. The autumn-coloured leaves were gone from the umbrella trees and the branches were bare against the dazzling sky. The work was going on to clear the land for planting. In late afternoon there were great leaping fires of dry stuff, dying away to send their last trails of smoke up to the darkening sky. As evening came the planes began their mysterious circling and circling, the last sunlight glinting on their wings as they turned overhead. As the land grew darker, lights would be hidden while the planes droned by. Doors were closed in the thick hot darkness until they had passed. Since nobody knew, nobody could be sure…

During the day, there were more cars and lorries passing on the road outside the compound. We were conscious of their noise, reminding us of how quiet the countryside had become. It always seemed to be listening to the noise of the guns, holding its breath to know the direction and the distance of the war. The small sounds near at hand seemed clearer—shrill voices raised in dispute, the thud of the pestle where palm oil was being made, the piercing sounds of grief where someone had died. All these noises were hushed by day if a plane flew over, just as if those passing might overhear as well as overlook the defenceless land. The airstrip at Uli, they said, was being attacked with bombs or rockets nearly every night. A friend who went out on a brief trip viv-

155

idly described the drama of leaving, how they had been driven in the darkness without headlights to have their papers checked, in darkness again to the airport. When a plane landed, it was unloaded in darkness with only the occasional glimmer of a torch, and the heavily laden lorries moved off without lights.

In contrast, the island of São Tomé was bright and booming with business, with sixteen warehouses packed full of relief materials, and there was only a shortage of planes.[2] He had felt confused and bewildered by the sight of shops packed with everything and people buying as much as they liked. We experienced much the same feelings whenever a rare parcel arrived from outside. Everything was impossibly bright and glossy. A cotton bra had all the dazzling whiteness the advertisements had once vainly promised. We admired the pictures on the packets, even their smooth, thick strokeable texture, and all the extravagant layers—polythene cardboard, bright printed and crackling papers—before we reached the product. The baby played with the empty packets of Quaker Oats and Italian washing powder—all splashes, streamers and whirligigs of pinks, greens and blues.

Air raids were bad again, until a reporter from outside filed his dispatches, then amid vociferous denials that they had ever taken place, they stopped again, almost completely for a while. Any time a sullen boom rolled across the sky the citizens would ask calmly, 'Is that bombing, shelling or thunder?' When will this war end?

13

A LAND ARMY

The first heavy rains of the season fell on 1 March and as soon as the weeks of dust had been washed off the roof, everyone rushed with pails and bowls to catch the water and save the weary walk to the stream and back. The nearest streams had dried and the only source of water was an hour's walk away, where the dwindling pools still trickled with water as brown and dubious as from any *umi*. It coated the bottom of a bowl with a tawny slime and rainwater, however dusty, looked crystal clear by contrast. Usually the rains would begin slowly, and a downpour would be followed by a week or more of blazing sunshine burning everything to dust again. This year, rain fell often enough to allow planting to begin almost a month earlier than usual. Another miracle, everyone said. It was more important than ever for as much food to be grown as possible and the earlier this could begin to be harvested, the better.

The Government was calling for the formation of 'Land Army' units everywhere and instructing that all available land should be cultivated to try to avoid starvation. It was clear that hardly any yams would be planted. Very few people had seed yams left to plant and where they did, hungry people and thieves often came in the night to dig up the seed yams and eat them. Everywhere cassava was being planted instead—six or eight inch lengths planted two or four to a mound in an X position. Even the sides of the road were being cultivated, generally with longer sticks pushed through the fences, so that as they grew tall and bulky the plants would not encroach on the road. Gradually, market places, out of use because of the fear of air raids, football pitches, the wide spaces around churches and schools, compounds inch by inch, all were dug over and planted. Cassava was the 'win the war' crop.

At night the bellmen went round warning everyone of heavy local penalties if anyone were to be found digging for crickets near the newly-planted cassava. Another result of the rains had been that the children went digging for crickets in the mornings to put in the soup. The insects were betrayed by a fine heap of earth like a worm cast and the children soon became experts. When I tried to help by pointing out likely heaps, I was quickly put in my place. 'Those are ants,' the children said, otherwise ignoring me. Everywhere you could see them, small children briskly digging up the insects or catching big green grasshoppers, all to put in their meatless soup. Everyone looked for snails too, no longer wanting just the very big ones but taking up any size from under the damp dead leaves and behind fences. At Ogbaku after rain the older boys and girls used to go out with lamps collecting snails. Apollonia and Angelina had gone too, until they realised their favourite hunting ground was the particular piece of bush where the family community used to bury their dead children. After that, as the darkness enshrouded the bush or the moon scattered eerie shadows skipping and dancing ahead, they did not want to go again.

After a week or so, the nearer streams came back and the further ones grew deep and ran clean again. Even at Ogbaku, dry as it was, we had always heard the thirsty croaking of frogs in the bush 'calling for rain' or giving thanks for it with a juicier voice, but I never heard anything like the frogs at the further stream. That morning, cycling down the hill, I heard the distant uproar, but as we crossed the plank bridge the noise was extraordinary: *Aaaark, ooooorrrrrk, iiiirrrrk, uuuurrrrrk* resounded from all sides in a continual shout until my ears rung with the noise. With the coming of the rains we had also started working. Last year a vegetable garden had been a pleasant and useful way of passing the time. This year it was a necessity, and we started to prepare the patch of ground allotted to us in the compound. Slowly the ridges and beds were shaped and we began to plant whatever we could find— waterleaf stalks, pumpkin seeds, corn and sweet potatoes. But the soil was poor and there would not be the exuberant growth we had enjoyed the previous year. Soon the waterleaf was putting out green buds, the tendrils of the pumpkin shoots were waving for support, and the green leaves of the corn were piercing the earth. Heads of corn for planting were costing two for five shillings. It took at least three months from planting the corn to cutting the cobs. We watched the sky, bluish grey through the trees, and listened to the thunder rumbling, praying for rain to bring everything along quickly.

And at night as the rain spattered on the roof the children sat telling stories, their eyes brimming with lamplight. There were some new songs too.

> I take my foot and trek to Enugu,
> Go and receive my gun from Ojukwu,
> This war is paining me.
> I sing a song about the Biafra war.
> The war we are fighting is getting to the end.
> If I die in bullet, I want to save my nation,
> Every Biafra soldier is fighting for survive.
> Go and tell the girl who I love,
> To and tell my parents we see no more.
> If I die in bullet, I want to save my nation,
> Every Biafra soldier is fighting to survive.

There had been some talk of the British Prime Minister, Harold Wilson, coming to Biafra, but nothing came of it. He had an extremely bad reputation there in any case. Most people believed him capable of selling his grandmother's bones for fertiliser. Radio Biafra called him the British Crime Minister, or, more bitterly, Herod Wilson.

The guns were still sounding on all sides. The best way to ignore them was to do something noisy—use the sewing machine, beat the children. The noise of shelling was heard all over your body. After half an hour your mind ached with longing for it to stop, your limbs were cramped with nervous tension. When the children began to play at Ferret cars, pushing the heavy butt end of a palm frond along the ground so it went bop-bop-bop like a machine gun muffled by distance, it was hard not to yell hysterically at them to stop it, stop it, stop it ...

One weekend when John was home he had travelled to see relatives in the next village. The sound of firing from all along the tarred road from Owerri brought every returned community within hearing trembling to its feet. On all sides people prepared to pack and run, convinced the enemy were back. A small boy went shirtless corner-to-corner to see what was going on and returned with the news that the Biafran army was jubilating because America had recognised Biafra. Later this was amended to an island near America. But when I learned it was Haiti, somehow the news failed to cheer. The Nigerians were still very close at Owerri but cut off there, said rumour, supplied if at all by parachute drop. Two relatives on leave from the army told us of the gibing cross talk between the soldiers in the opposing lines. 'Biafra, Biafra,' the voices would jeer, 'Why are you always dere for bush? Biafra be mosquito brother.' Then they would say that the Biafrans have to stay in the bush since they have no towns and no houses. They don't get paid, while Ojukwu lives comfortably. He always travels by air and doesn't even dare to come on the ground. The relief planes crossing the night sky were 'Ojukwu taxi where never allow man to rest.'

'Vandals! Vandals!'[1] other voices would taunt in reply. 'Why did Lance-Corporal Gowon drop you in this trap?' They would point out that the invaders couldn't get out or get away, while they could go on pass and visit their people. When did the Vandals last go and see their relatives? They were going to stay until they provided manure for Biafran farms. When a Biafran soldier stole a head of plantain from the kitchen that provided food for more abuse: 'Biafra! You too t'ief. Why you come and t'ief plantain for kitchen?'[2]

'Na, my Mama plantain,' was the unanswerable reply. When the sarcasm was landing too close for comfort the opposition turned to their guns. 'Too much bukri! Na here I read my Achimota.'[3] And when shots were answered by a burst of firing: 'Biafra! You craze!'

> My mother delivered me
> And called me a soldier
> Who lives in the bush.
> My hair and my beard
> Are growing all over me.
> Does that disturb me?
> I am a soldier and live in the bush.

There was a determined attempt to capture Umuahia in time for the British Prime Minister's visit to Nigeria. They failed only in the timing. One evening, calm and silver grey with moonlight, we sat out in the courtyard tuning to the foreign stations, listening to them announcing the capture of the town in tones of variously controlled glee and speculating on the effects on Biafran morale, whether the troops would revolt or the civilians reject their leaders. There were some days of extreme gloom while everyone reminded each other that the towns were not important. Biafra had been supposed incapable of surviving the loss of Enugu, then Onitsha, then Port Harcourt. But no-one could help feeling unhappy at seeing the gibe realised, that we were all mosquito brothers just living in the bush, with every town lost.

Fortunately it soon appeared that one town had been lost and another regained. Everyone had known for some months that those in Owerri were cut off and unable to get reinforcements or supplies except by air. 'Operation Wipeout' had been promised several times by rumour. On Easter Saturday the sound of the guns was particularly loud and frightening. Then it receded and died away while speculation spread about what had been happening. On 19 April a friend stopped his car at the gate and announced with a twinkle and obviously for effect that he wanted to tell us he was just on his way to Owerri. To his annoyance, he was stopped outside the town by the Army, who refused to accept the responsibility of allowing an unauthorised civilian to go in, and so he had to sit and watch soldiers streaming down the road until he could bear it no longer and came back. The BCB announced the liberation of Owerri six days later and at once everyone shrugged off the gloom and disappointment from the loss of Umuahia, telling each other that Owerri was a milestone, the first of the townships to be freed from occupation.

Our impatient friend at last succeeded in reaching his office, then his quarters, and found both looted and stripped bare. All his textbooks and official documents had been dumped outside the doors where traces lay sodden and useless. The Advanced Teacher Training College (ATTC), which lay on both sides of a tarred road, had looked untroubled from a distance and very beautiful with all its many flowering trees. But on coming nearer, the administration buildings were found to be looted, all the glass in the windows smashed out, while in the residential part houses had been looted and even refrigerators removed. Houses on the corners of the roadways through the compound appeared to have been occupied while those inside, further along the lines, had been used as latrines. All vegetables growing on the compound had been dug up, palm trees cut down and tapped for wine, while enough shells lay round to show that the visitors had been cracking kernels and eating 'Biafra biscuit'.

The Cathedral and Holy Ghost College were little damaged except for bullet holes. The General Post Office had been used, they said, as an officers' mortuary. Even before the police moved in, some civilians had already returned to begin clearing up the mess both in the town and in their own compounds. It seemed as if almost every thatched building had been burned. Several eye-witnesses spoke of seeing heaps of weapons being dug up near the court buildings—mortars, ammunition, rockets, an Oerlikon gun.[4] A Ferret armoured car was found, tested to the alarm of everyone within hearing, found to be in good condition, and sent off to be useful near Umuahia, as were boxes of ammunition found buried where Col. Ojukwu had previously been living. Another told us of seeing ammunition boxes from Britain labelled 'tea'. A French news agency was reported to have spoken of people streaming down to look at Owerri as if on a pilgrimage. Certainly when people met, the question was always, 'Have you been to Owerri? How was it?'

> Ojukwu is the leader of Biafra.
> It has been written at Aburi.
> Awolowo, Yakubu Gowon,
> You have no power on Biafra again.
> Biafra, win the war.

People were recalling incidents in their own flight from the town seven months before. I heard of one large family who were caught with their car petrol tank completely empty and no means of obtaining petrol. Nothing daunted they had loaded the young children and as much luggage as they could, and the adults pushed the car eight miles to safety.

Sedentary as always, I questioned everyone who came by, not thinking I had any chance of seeing for myself, but two weeks later I managed to beg a ride to Ezinihitte, a few miles away, to visit the Ministry of Education, whose headquarters were there. Our way led through Owerri. On the way down the tarred road our driver, who had been several times, already pointed out the damage on both sides. Only one house had been left standing in Umudagu village where there had been heavy fighting. Some seemed to have been set on fire deliberately in other areas, as stains of smoke sometimes showed where a fire had smouldered and gone out instead of destroying the building. Most eloquent to me were the bush roads leading off the tar, completely overgrown with grass, only recognisable as roads at all for a few yards before they merged with the bush on both sides. From the top of the hill the town looked a real metropolis. It was fifteen months since I had seen any township. Now Owerri, which had once seemed a poor small place after Enugu, was transformed. As we drew near, he drove more slowly and we gazed out at the scenes of destruction, incongruous on a particularly beautiful day. On the outskirts of the town the road sides were heaped with barricades of tree trunks now cleared from the highway. The car jolted over trenches across the road which had been roughly filled in where previously the surface had been undermined and booby trapped. Some palm trees were snapped off half way or drooped brownish fronds, scorched by shelling as if by lightning.

In the streets of the township were a litter of overturned and burned cars, buses, taxis. There seemed to be hundreds of them heaped along the sides of the road and covering the forecourts of petrol filling stations. Even the metal sheets had been ripped off the petrol pumps, leaving the twisted pipes exposed. It seemed that every thatched building had been fired, as they said, leaving the smoke-grimed stumps of walls. Some of the large 'zinc' buildings, shops with flats over them, were mere broken shells. As we went by, I saw a window box, once no doubt arranged with green and red plants, growing unkempt and wild while the house it had decorated sagged and leaned hideously around it. The market where we had once walked every week in search of anything to buy had simply disappeared and long grass rustled over the site. All the damage seemed twice as ugly in the smiling morning light under a sky of blue space and sun-swept clouds. It belonged properly to grimy skies, half-light and persistent drizzle. There were some people roving about the streets, but more were inside their compounds clearing up the mess and repairing as they could. Soon there was a storm of workers restoring the water system and getting electricity turned on again. There was already that morning a blackboard at the crossroads chalked with details of the next Mass in the cathedral. In the

163

excitement over Owerri, nobody talked about Umuahia again. The Government was trying to get people to move back into the town as quickly as possible, so that it could return to life.

Money continued to be a problem, even though the handsome new currency notes were now nominally in circulation. The £10 note showed an Awka woodcarver, the £5 note an Akwete weaver. The £1 and 10 shilling notes had a coat of arms. The five shilling note had retained the design of the four smiling Biafran girls, but it did not print so well on the thicker paper with its plastic texture. People were calling this kind of money 'waterproof'. By the end of May the first Biafran coins were issued—bright, lightweight metal coins that looked like aluminium. The first two values were threepence and one shilling. Both bore the rising sun and palm tree symbols and the motto 'Peace, Unity, Freedom'. At the end of the month, Nigerian coins were no longer legal tender though still in demand for the illicit border trade and smuggling.

Just before the second anniversary of independence, Radio Biafra announced with conscious pride that the Biafran Air Force had bombed Port Harcourt oil refinery and Port Harcourt airfield, destroying two fighters and a bomber. Next day there was a report of an equally successful raid on Benin airport, followed two days later by an announcement of a raid on Enugu, in which two fighters, two bombers and one Heron light aircraft were destroyed, the anti-air-craft guns had been silenced, and the control tower and terminal buildings set on fire. The BBC, which had made the first reports of the existence of a Biafran Air Force with a significant pause for the laughter to die away, now began to repeat allegations that the planes were converted training planes, light aircraft manned by Swedish mercenaries led by Count Von Rosen.[5]

By now the rains had become heavy and it was raining for hours at a time. There was fresh corn to buy, but it cost five shillings for five heads. Last year it had been eight heads for one shilling. At that price it was too expensive to be used for *akamu*. There were plenty of pears, green and buttery-fleshed, to roast in the ashes. All along the roads you saw boys climbing the tall trees to gather the fruit as it turned black and ripe. But it looked particularly beautiful when it was rosy-red in colour, catching the evening sunlight and glowing against the green. The children were not so cautious about the rain this year or so unwilling to get wet and dirty. As soon as the heavy downpour was over they would be splashing through the puddles or squelching with bare feet through the mud. One bad result was that all of them developed sores from earthworms (so they said)—very itchy and pus-filled so that sometimes a toenail came off and the places were slow and difficult to heal. I tried penicillin ointment, antiseptic powder, gentian violet, whatever I could beg from Sister Doctor on her visits.

People continued to come for medicine and advice and some of them were frighteningly ill. Usually, I would hand over a few vitamin tablets and tell my patients, 'This will help, but it won't cure you. You must go to the hospital,' and hope they would do so. Several times I was consulted by women who had stopped menstruating and were anxious and upset. The first time I had thought the woman wanted to get rid of an unwanted pregnancy, and had read a little lecture on the follies and dangers of attempted abortion. The woman explained further. She thought she might be starting the change of life and was anxious to postpone it. She already had eight children; wasn't that enough? Apparently not. It used to be the educated and emancipated wives who said they had told their mothers-in-law that six children were enough. A doctor confirmed there were many cases of amenorrhea among women of all ages due to anxiety, poor nutrition, and anaemia. 'Nature is being kind enough not to waste the little they have.' After that I would give iron tablets to such women who came to me, and repeat the doctor's remarks. Another service I regularly performed was writing petitions for women who wanted to apply for relief. They all seemed to think a 'paper' from me would work better than any other, although I tried to persuade them that I had no authority or influence over the relief agencies. I would write the paper for them, but so could any other literate person, and it would be up to the relief agency to agree or no.

Mrs O had returned from Lagos, she said, with her husband and six children. Since her husband had joined the army she had heard no news of him. Three of the children had died. She was living with the rest in the house of her married sister and needed help.

Mrs U had lost her husband and five of her six children. She was living with her nine younger brothers and sisters. Her parents had died. She needed help.

Some came directly to me for 'help'. We hated to turn anyone away even though all we could give might be a handful of milk powder or cornmeal, or a teaspoon of salt. Some of those who came regularly would bring me a 'dash' of pepper, oil, vegetables or firewood, still keeping up the old courtesies. Begging was not usually an Igbo custom. Even women with no outside financial help had managed to put children through secondary school through sheer hard work. It went very much against the grain for many of them to have to come, hand outstretched, to beg for food. We ourselves were still managing to exist through the kindness of the Reverend Fathers. It was no longer possible to throw out any food that was not completely spoiled. Even from Ogbaku we had used rat-nibbled packets of soup mix and if we had any flour with insects in it, we used to get out as many as we could and ignore the rest. 'Look on it as so much more protein,' we said briskly.

A kind of beetle much the same size and shape as a wood-louse used to live inside and eat away the stockfish. Before cooking, the fish would be knocked together to dislodge the insects. Any chickens nearby would eat them up as fast as they fell out. Most flour products used to harbour insects very quickly—noodles, spaghetti, macaroni, rice too. They were black with long pointed jaws and they ate holes in the polythene bags from the inside out. I always assumed these were weevils and dealt with them as briskly as any others. Once I received some biscuits, of all things, which had been badly stored for a few days and become damp. Some were mouldy and most had stockfish beetles in them. Unable to bear to throw them away, I sat in the kitchen beside a low fire, discarded the biscuits that were completely green with mould, and dried the rest a few at a time in a clean frying pan. The heat brought out and killed the beetles, crisped the biscuits, and we ate them to the last crumb. Rats too were a nuisance and nothing was safe from them unless it was kept in a tin. At night they ran everywhere scratching, nibbling and squeaking, even running over the family asleep on the floor. It never seemed to occur to the children to more than protest when the rats disturbed them. When they became too troublesome, a hunt would be arranged. Someone we knew caught twenty-one in her two rooms, but this included two nests. Our highest score was ten large ones—large for these mouse-sized creatures. The compound children gleefully collected a double handful of silky heads and twitching tails and sold them at the gate for £1.

Some of the relief supplies were being sold in markets. However they obtained them, people showed great ingenuity in making these strange foods into something more familiar. The first attempts to prepare cornmeal like *garri*, by soaking it with hot water, had been conspicuously unsuccessful. Now people knew it had to be cooked in a pot and stirred with a stick until it was done. They also used it to prepare *akara*, fried cakes usually made from beans, *moi-moi*, also made from bean pulp but wrapped in plantain leaves and steamed, and *agidi*. The cornmeal resembled the raw material of *agidi* more than anything else. This was maize meal pounded, sifted, cooked over the fire until it was thick, then wrapped by spoonfuls in leaves and left to cool and stiffen while the soup was being prepared. Quaker oats could be used to make rather tough fried cakes as well as porridge. But if it had become sour through long or bad storage, then it was better used with stew. It would be prepared as stiffish porridge, then pounded together with prepared *garri* until the two were blended together.

People were making use of local bush vegetables that grew wild by the roadside and had been neglected while farm and garden varieties had been so plentiful. The refugees introduced the use of new kinds since the inhabitants of the area would see refugees gathering and preparing leaves and would copy them. Cassava leaves were also being recommended as a source of protein, once they had been properly prepared to remove a harmful juice. 'We never used to eat those,' said John, looking at a heap of prickly bush green. The garden variety known as white green is smooth stemmed and has lighter-coloured leaves and probably less iron. 'And how much cornmeal did you eat before this war?' we asked him. But some restrictions in diet were actual taboos and so much more difficult to break. Women traditionally did not eat certain wild creatures, though the varieties might differ from place to place. In Ogbaku, women did not eat monkey, snakes, owls, and those nocturnal animals that only creep slowly by daylight. In some areas near rivers, fish could not be caught in certain streams. In other places, snakes were venerated and never injured or driven away. Someone told me how he saw a large snake in one village and seized a stick to kill it. The people shouted him down and a woman took a lamp and talked to the snake as she conducted it away with the light, until it slipped away into a hole.

The third scarcity that harassed the people was a shortage of cloth-ing. Here the Biafran ingenuity could do so very little. Empty relief flour bags that were made of tough cotton, not sacking, were made into boys' shorts, shirts and women's blouses, complete with their blue printing about relief food in several languages. The teenage girls made shift dresses from *lappas*. New *lappa* cloth was already £5 a yard and soon even a second-hand two yard length was being priced up to £10 and refused. Sometimes small girls could wear an old wrapper blouse as a rather short dress—the old-fashioned style with a deep frill of cloth joined to the blouse at the waist so it extended down to a wom-an's hips. Many women went about in rags, some because it was the obvious thing to wear when begging, others because they were wid-ows. If they had no black wrapper to wear, they wore tatters until their year of mourning was over and they could 'wash'.

Some had just nothing else to wear. One morning we went to inves-tigate the sound of weeping near the door. A patient soon to be dis-charged from the nearby sickbay had come to the nurse who lived next door to us. She was wearing her hospital blanket for want of anything else and she had just been told she would have to give it up when she left. The idea of going naked at her age reduced her to tears. I gave her the remaining piece of one of the old *lappas*. Five of those I had brought from Enugu were now either worn out or given away piece by piece. Most of those that were left were party-going wear, with broad bands of silk embroidery or elaborate sleeves, not daytime wear at all unless for a wedding, and just not suitable for going about in wartime. Anyone who dressed up was likely to be asked whether the war had ended. I had no ordinary dresses at all. Oh, the old fabric stalls at Ogbete—all the patterns and colours in cotton. Autumn leaves, little goats, rosettes, numbers and letters, trailing vines, fish and umbrellas, horses, records, cups, drums, palm trees, pineapples, flowers, houses and palm fronds, whirligigs, hooks, zigzag whirls and swirls, bold or subtle, brilliant or sombre, all the geometrical and abstract prints, one pattern overlap-ping and blending with another …

Now it was 30 May again. The anniversary of independence was marked by a day of prayer and rededication. The second year was over. The third began.

14

WAITING IT OUT

Early in June, a Swedish Red Cross relief plane was shot down. From listening to the foreign radio stations, it appeared that the plane, an unarmed transport, marked with Red Cross signs, had been flying in early while it was still daylight. First reports said all four crew members were alive, then that one was missing, then that all were dead. Other reports said that the plane had been shot down after refusing to reply to radio calls, while others again said those monitoring had heard no radio messages until the pilot of the relief plane signalled that he was being fired on.[1] The first reactions of the head of the International Red Cross were sufficiently forthright and indignant, and then became steadily more diplomatic. The Red Cross did not seem particularly well liked by either side. There seemed to be so much manoeuvering that the noble image of a heroic organisation, selflessly bringing aid wherever it was needed without taking political sides, had been rather tarnished. There had been reports in foreign papers that on the Nigerian side of the lines Red Cross planes were ferrying troops for the federal forces.

Nigeria had several times claimed that the Red Cross were carrying arms into Biafra. Early in February the BBC had a report that an unidentified plane had bombed federal territory near Benin and Calabar and then quoted Nigerian sources saying that the attacker had been a returning relief plane. A couple of months later came a story that a box marked with the Red Cross had been found at Ututu con-

169

taining high explosive. But the BBC added that another similar box which had been claimed to contain arms actually held water purifying equipment and followed up its first story with the information that the explosive turned out to be gas for inflating weather balloons to be used at Obilagu, formerly an airstrip for the Red Cross. The various church organisations seemed to be much more efficient. At the end of March 1969 Caritas International had passed its first year in Biafran relief and reported more than 900 flights, carrying 15,000 tons of food and medicines at a cost of £5 million. By all accounts the Red Cross began its operations later and did less, although its base at Fernando Po was much nearer the mainland than the Joint Church Aid headquarters at São Tomé. Supposedly under the influence of the new American administration, flights also began from Dahomey early in February 1969. Four months later, the bringing down of the Swedish Red Cross plane brought all Red Cross aid to a complete stop.

The nights seemed darker without the sound of the old planes chugging overhead. By the end of the month, Joint Church Aid resumed its flights. Once again we began to listen hopefully as darkness came down for one or two planes to pass. It was like going back to the weeks after the fall of Port Harcourt the previous year. Obviously the same kwashiorkor situation was going to develop, since the interlocking system which had been built up over the months entirely depended on the supply of relief from outside and the reduced flights would be inadequate to maintain it. Only someone with detailed information could give a complete account of the whole relief programme and how it was organised, and with what degree of co-operation and independence among the three organisations: World Council of Churches, Red Cross and Caritas. But there were stores to which the supplies were delivered in bulk for distribution to refugee camps, sickbays and feeding centres, with special provision for clergymen and others to help the destitute. There were still many refugee camps and since the end of 1968 Camp B refugees had also been allowed some relief. Sickbays mostly treated kwashiorkor and other deficiency diseases and varied in size. Some had only a few dozen patients, while others had hundreds. Many of these sickbays were set up in the empty school compounds and were inspected and approved by the Government no matter which organisation was running them. All had a resident qualified nurse and a visiting doctor. A visit to a sickbay was a haunting experience. Here were the children from the Oxfam posters, puffy with kwashiorkor or shrivelled with marasmus—severe malnutrition. The silent pictures lack the worst detail. When reduced to bones loosely wrapped in faded tattered skin, children stay so horribly alive. In those skull-like faces the mouths gape, continually moaning and whimpering.

With centres now organised in every area, feeding hundreds of children several times a week, it was just enough to keep them from developing kwashiorkor. Discharged sickbay people also attended so that they would not relapse. Apart from the sickbays there were also the hospitals, including mobile clinics, which regularly visited villages treating every imaginable human condition and giving out relief to many with malnutrition. Everything they used, from stockfish and salt to injections and pills, depended on the airlift.

The BBC at once began to estimate the food stocks remaining in Biafra and announced several times that the people would begin to starve in ten days. All the organisations at once began to contract their operations and conserve stocks. Gradually, as the weeks passed, feeding centres closed and sickbays discharged all but the worst cases. Soon enough, children were being carried past the gate of our compound to the nearby hospital and they had those familiar signs again. There had been many reports on the foreign stations of the misuse of relief materials and inside the country most people seemed to believe that there were relief officials trafficking in these supplies. The situation would look worse to someone unused to the country. With every passing week it was less possible to buy whatever one needed in the markets. Except for the relief, the supplies were just not there any more after more than two years of blockade. And then everyone expected the others would be looking after themselves, 'Hand washes hand' was the proverb, while the local children sang:

> Do you want to know those who benefit from kwashiorkor?
> Shall I tell you those who benefit from kwashiorkor?
> Leonard is number one,
> Vincent is number two,
> The store keeper number three,
> and the Red Cross number four.

As most people had large and clamorous families dependent on them, however upright they were, it was hard not to agree that charity began at home. It was the old prewar nepotism problem all over again. Committees were always reputed to 'chop all', and that included those who organised feeding centres.

> Dorothy, give me my own uncooked.
> Dorothy, give me my own uncooked.
> When you cook, you cook for kwashiorkor,
> When you roast, you roast for kwashiorkor,
> So Dorothy, give me my own uncooked.

And again:

> The Sergeant finished all the stockfish.
> The Sergeant finished all the stockfish,
> And left us only the milk to purge our stomachs with.

For this reason there was a proliferation of committees and everyone wanted to be on one and wrote petitions against those who were appointed, even before they had had the chance to prove their incompetence and general unsuitability for the office.

Some relief materials found their way to the market as a result of fairly legitimate exchange. Since the Biafran traditional diet was generally starch of some kind, like *garri*, yam or rice, with soup, refugees had for a long time been selling or exchanging part of their protein relief to obtain carbohydrates. Similarly there were exchanges in return for petrol when this was scarce, to obtain enough to allow the relief workers to discharge their duties and get round their districts. Trading was in the blood. In former times everyone seemed to do a little trading, from the village housewife who bought and resold salt and dried fish, to the minister's wife who dealt in expensive lengths of Akwete cloth or elaborate head ties and gold jewellery from Lagos. At a time when all legitimate opportunities for trading were at a standstill, the chance of making money was just too much temptation for some. As the proverb said, 'The animal that doesn't eat another animal doesn't grow fat.' And so there would be a brisk underhand bit of business with imported vegetable seeds or medicines, perhaps those marked, 'Free medical sample, not to be sold'. While appreciating those who did their duty by relief food and medicine honestly and conscientiously, ordinary people would still be a little surprised that such an opportunity for gain could be allowed to pass by. It was not the misuse so much as the excessive

prices which were resented. The situation was a good deal more complex than it appeared at first sight. Nearly a year before, when I had
displayed some high-minded principles on the subject, I had been told
quite plainly: 'Your brothers [i.e., the white Reverend Fathers] will
help you and your family. But if we don't care for ourselves, who will
care for us?'

> Chairman-oh, Supervisor,
> Store-keeper, Supervisor,
> Don't finish all the stockfish.
> Stockfish, move ahead.
> Children, take heart.
> The sickness is going to leave you.

Definite attempts were being made to shake people from a dangerous reliance on relief. One Sunday, instead of a sermon, there was a
lecture on doing our best to feed the children using palm oil, insects,
bush-meat, cassava leaf, and so on, instead of folding the hands and
waiting for an angel from heaven. I tasted fried insects for the first
time; fried in palm oil and dusted with a little salt, they tasted like
crispy bits of fried bacon. Others still put their trust elsewhere. A
notice along the road to the next village promised, 'Kwashoka sickness
cured here'.

We hoped in vain for something to happen. The tiny voices talking
to themselves deep inside the radio were all concerned with the
Americans' flight to the moon. Though we could sympathise with anyone's desire to escape the mess on Earth, it seemed a sterile achievement. Radio batteries now cost £4–£6 each, and more people than
ever were tuning in to the Voice of Rumour. I was travelling around a
little more than usual, every time the illegal conscription became
troublesome.[2] Unauthorised soldiers would pretend to conscript men
on the roads and allow them to buy their way past with money, food or
cigarettes. Whenever John was backing me (or towing me), that is
whenever I was a passenger on the carrier of his bicycle, we sailed
through such obstructions with a shower of comments, waves and
greetings. Sometimes I could sit there and watch the heartbreaking
beauty of the countryside flow smoothly past, everywhere lush and
green and sprinkled with wayside flowers, pinky-mauve and yellow.
Greetings would come from all sides, even from the air, from men

picking pears, cutting palm fronds or palm nuts, tapping wine. Children dashed out to wave and shout: 'Dash me money.' 'Where do you see money?' 'We always thought you people were so rich.'

They were even more astonished the few times I rode a bicycle myself. There were plenty of hazards already—loose sandals, entangling wrapper skirt, an unfamiliar bicycle that was too heavy for me and kept going out of gear, patches of loose, skidding sand on the roadway. The worst were the other travellers, who turned in a leisurely way at the sound of the bell to see who was coming, and then were too astonished to move out of the way. The heavy rains tore up the dirt roads so much that I no longer felt safe riding; I preferred to be a passenger and hold on for dear life while we skidded and jolted along. Sometimes it was hard to decide whether it was better to look over John's shoulder and see what was coming or to hide behind his broad back and just hold on tight. The passenger always had a rougher time than the rider, since the bicycle saddle was sprung but the metal carrier most certainly was not. At times, deep pools of rainwater stretched completely across the road. Generally we would swish our way through, leaving a wake like a boat. It was easy to tell when such a pool had become too deep for riding. A way round would have been beaten down at the side of the road, the undergrowth trampled down and worn away where travellers had dragged their loaded bicycles up onto the bank along the side of the pool and down again. For the first time I knew what it was like to get soaked to the skin miles away from home. If the road were fairly flat we could always look for shelter in some wayside palm wine bar until the storm passed. But if the way we were going was uphill it was better to keep going, since for hours after heavy rain such steep tracks were turned into torrents as all the water drained down, not gently trickling but roaring and shouting in a dozen different levels and voices. As the deep water swirled across the whole road, masking the deep ruts and pot holes, it was better to take off sandals altogether, hoist a wrapper up to the knee and paddle instead of risking losing a slipper forever in the flood.

Distance was measured in poles. I tried to remember the length of a rod, pole or perch. It appeared it was the distance apart of the telegraph poles if, of course, there had been any. It was an unreliable measure, and when walking I found distances very elastic. 'Is it far?' I asked as we set off. 'It is not far,' they answered encouragingly. After half an hour of walking, I asked again. 'Is it far now?' 'It is a bit far,' they answered with a note of warning. After another half an hour of walking, I asked, 'Is it still far?' 'Yes,' they said. I had to make a journey many times before I was able to recognise the bush road and then usually, just as I had learned it, someone would cut bush, plant cassava, put up a fence and hopelessly change its appearance once again.

One result of the increasing hardship was a decline in traditional standards of behaviour, particularly of honesty. On our travels we would often hear a voice eloquently lamenting from the farms the loss of cassava, or meet women showering abuse on thieves who had ripped up immature plants. At one time anyone caught stealing was likely to be paraded round the village, hung around with yellow-green, young palm branches and wearing a crown of dried grass with the stolen articles hung around the neck, while children flocked to yell and jeer. Now even the extended family system itself was under pressure. There were orphanages instead of children being cared for by relatives, who may have thought the children could be fed by the Government more easily than by relations. Certainly if a child was found a foster home, an indignant relative seemed to appear from somewhere to make sure it had not been sold.

Salt reached £12 a cup. Pre-war it had been 11 shillings for a bag and a large family hardly used £2 worth in a year. People were making black shoe polish out of old radio batteries ground very fine between stones and mixed to a cream with kerosene. Someone found a way to re-ink old typewriter ribbons so they could be used again. Second-hand shoes for men cost anything between £12 and £25. We all wore sandals made from old Volkswagen tyres, and paid the shoemaker with a second tyre. Some women replaced the worn out straps of their sandals with pieces of their leather or plastic dress belts. We paid £2 for a plate to eat from. The acid for car batteries that had once been two shillings and sixpence a bottle now cost £30.

In Ogbaku the *juju* was running again, though more cautiously this year because of conscription and the soldiers stationed nearby. Few people could afford a chicken to use for their personal sacrifice and snails were being used instead. 'Next year, a lizard,' people said.

I had finished the two bottles of shampoo I had been managing with since January, and began to wash my waist-length hair with shampoo soap intended for the treatment of head lice. A piece still remained from the previous year when—my scrubbed and holy-stoned North Country soul revolted by the whole subject of bedbugs, lice, and fleas—I had managed to get some disinfectant soap and lotion and a fine toothed comb for hunting them out.

The children were now completely bilingual, even talking Igbo among themselves. In English they were now making all the typical mistakes, confusing he/she, him/her, yesterday/tomorrow and forgetting how to make the 'th' sound. I grew tired trying to correct Doratee, Sammel, Massey, Jemmiss, Eeeedit, Jennatan. In moments of stress I could manage a weird mixture of Igbo and English, but generally my self-consciousness and unwillingness to make mistakes still kept me tongue tied.

Meanwhile, it was a long rainy season. It had begun early and it rained steadily week by week, without even the usual two-week break in August. Several months passed without our hearing the sound of the guns. BCB said 203 towns and villages had been cleared in Owerri, Port Harcourt and Yenagoa provinces. But one night the village was alarmed by hearing occasional shots, not from a hunter's gun, but unmistakably the cok-cok-cok-cok of automatic firing very near. It turned out to be a soldier son firing off his gun in respect and honour to his dead father. The vague rumble of distant thunder still made people stop and ask each other what it was. 'Natural shelling' was the usual reply.

The Pope, on a visit to Uganda, tried to start peace talks but nothing came of it. The Government was encouraging late season planting of crops to use the end of the rains. As cassava was harvested, the same ground was dug over again, the cane cut into lengths and replanted using leaves and ashes as fertiliser.

> Gowon to Ojukwu said,
> 'Can you agree to sell your fatherland to me?'
> Ojukwu to Gowon he took this stand:
> 'Even at Jehovah's own command,
> I would not sell my fatherland.'

I was always looking for something to read and about this time I began to get old copies of *Time* magazine. They looked unbelievably bright and gay; even though some were up to five years old, and the news was well out of date, I read every word, including the advertisements, until they nearly fell to pieces. Outside our world some truly extraordinary things had been happening. As I read more up-to-date copies, the news seemed to get even more fantastic. As every part of the world seemed to be engaged in its own particular madness, it was no longer so inexplicable that no-one could succeed in curing the madness here.

The children were fascinated by the magazines. To them every pictured aeroplane was a Nigerian bomber. Every soldier in the picture from Vietnam was either a Nigerian or a Biafran, depending whether he was flat or upright. The advertisements showed a life of such triviality, with heavy emphasis on display and insecurity, eating, drinking, travelling by particular airlines, making money, proving status to oneself and others, by wristwatches and choice of hotels. We peered wistfully into the coloured pictures, where stewards were cutting wedges from whole hams and stewardesses balanced trays of croissants, salad, ice cream and peaches. But the elegancies of Japanese hors d'oeuvres disturbed us less than the simplest picture of a rye loaf, gold, freckled brown. After looking at it long enough we could nearly smell it, and just about pick it from the page.

Some of the more recent had items about Biafra. No wonder those abroad continued to beg for news of their families through Caritas, and were unable to believe that anyone was left alive. Some enquiries came to the local Reverend Father and we helped to find the people concerned. It was very easy if the family name were known in a district where the people had not had to run. Sometimes the news that had to be passed on was bad, of people dead a couple of years or sick. Sometimes it was good, that all were alive and well. At least one who returned from outside found it difficult to believe the good news and came to ensure that his people were decently buried. When the people had had some months in which to get really hungry, the overseas stations announced the defection of Dr Nnamdi Azikiwe to the Nigerian cause.[3] But for the moment nothing came of it.

During August I made another rare journey by car and admired all the cars and lorries on the road. The 'kitchen cooker' system of refining petrol had certainly helped to solve the shortage.[4] In some places on the road to Orlu the surface of the tarred road was pocked and rutted—by strafing, people said. Moving vehicles were then a favourite target for attack and in a car it was not possible to hear the sound of a plane. People walking would wave and point in warning and then it was wise to get the car under a tree until the plane had passed. There was plenty to see along the roads, such as people setting their face towards markets, hospitals or banks that were ten, twenty miles off, and walking there. Some made half-hearted attempts to hitch a lift in cars, but most were already packed full. Some of the wayside shops had surprising spreads of goods for sale, most (so people said unkindly) either looted from war areas or stolen at the airport. There were many wayside bars and 'hotels', from palm-thatch shelters with chalked signs to shining names and notices. There were many called Freedom Bar, Biafra Bar. Back to Land—a popular name in 1967—was less frequent, but as many as before seemed to be called Hope Rising. There was the Hotel Casablanca and the California Bar, Tanzania Hotel, Hotel de Gabon and my favourite of them all, the Hotel de Survival.

The OAU met again but nothing came of it except another resolution that there should be peace negotiations on the basis of One Nigeria.

The rainy season went on and on. The trunks of palm trees in the compound were as full of ferns, mosses and small plants as an old damp wall. We stacked firewood in the kitchen. Some pieces of tree trunk were full of ants and now and then the wood gave out a dry rustle like the purr of a thirsty cat. We planted more waterleaf, more seeds of beans and cabbage and encouraged the pumpkin vines to grow up again after we had cut them down so far. Some of the relief food was still finding its way to the market, at the usual exorbitant prices. The Government issued stiff orders against the misuse of relief and unjust enrichment. Even palm oil was £1 5s a bottle and no-one could afford to use it in a Biafra lamp. There was kerosene again from the home refineries, liable to go whump with a blue flame, if you poured it into a lamp already lit.

The International Red Cross issued details of a new agreement with the Federal Government for a three-week airlift of relief by day to Uli. One clause of the agreement specifically allowed military operations along the relief flight route and everyone came to see what that could mean. It was no use waiting until the airport had been bombed to bits or captured, and then loudly crying that it wasn't fair. So nothing came of it. For a while the foreign news broadcasts were saying that the chances of peace were brighter, but these hopes also died away in a welter of contradictions.

I went to a wedding. The bride wore a white lace dress with a full length veil. Her little attendants had white shift dresses and carried white baskets of flower heads and wore white and blue head-dresses. A photographer took two pictures. The dress and veil were second-hand, the bridesmaids' dresses made from a couple of sheets. Their head-dresses were from a length of bandage, with a paper white-and-blue bow tied on. The baskets had newspaper wrapped round them, and the photographs cost £7 for each exposure. The Reverend Father was an Army chaplain; he wore camouflage battledress under his vestments.

When will this war end?

15

THE END IN SIGHT?

Early in September, two Reverend Sisters arrived in the compound looking for me. Visitors and new faces were now very rare and those we had we talked about for a long time afterwards. There was the day when two white wives came unexpectedly with their husbands, and the morning when a white man drove in looking for somewhere quite different and drove away with a hasty note to post 'outside' to my family. This visit was a pleasure in itself. Secondary schools were to open wherever possible and the Sisters had come to invite me to join their staff. A fixed timetable would almost be alarming after so many timeless days, but the prospect of actually doing some work would keep away the moments of lonely private despair. The next morning I was there, late of course.

The school was at Umueze Ogwa, a nearby village. There were two classroom blocks, two or three dormitories, the convent with armed sentries at the gate in the fence, a line of two-roomed teachers' quarters. At the end there was a splendid 'Peace Corps House', which had been built to meet the requirements of that organisation and to attract their expatriate staff. After living so long among the trees, it seemed strange and unprotected to be under the wide sky of an open compound. Much of the compound stood deep in long grass. In other places the land was being 'farmed', with cassava growing everywhere, untidily challenging the palm tree for a place of honour on the currency. The dormitories were being used as a sickbay with rows of beds, some with bright patchwork blankets from some overseas charity, and the dank smell of sickness held at a distance for an hour or two by the sharp reek of disinfectant. The staff of the school consisted of three Sisters, two Seminarians, a nurse from the sickbay and myself. The students came from all corners for classes I to III. All had been in school before the war, but the standard ranged from one of the Government Boys' Schools to an undistinguished Commercial College, so there were boys and girls of all levels of ability. A few were even in their own school buildings but most were attending the school nearest to wherever they happened to be living at the time. Lessons began at 7:30 a.m. Some of the students walked up to seven miles each way every day.

All the problems of the primary schools were there and made worse. Some had textbooks, but most didn't, and those who did had usually been using different texts in their previous schools. French textbooks were on sale in the village bookshop at £2 or more, and a copy of *The Merchant of Venice* was £1. Exercise books cost many times what they had cost before the war; a pencil went for five shillings and a ballpoint pen for £3. We shared the available books round the class and if this could not work, we taught from the blackboard. 'Thanks be to God,' said the Sisters, 'We do have chalk.' School began early and Umueze was a mile or so away. Each day I tried to set off before 7 a.m. (it was difficult to be sure of the time) into the grey morning to meet surprised people starting on their own day. Most were palm-wine tappers, or women going to market or to their farms. The first day everyone asked each other where I was going. After the second day, everyone seemed to know and to excuse my haste I had learned to say in Igbo: 'I am going to school.' 'Na so!'[1]

It was good to be out and going somewhere with a definite purpose. I waved to small children, picking my way round the deep pools of rainwater across the paths that wavered and wandered, ran straight and divided. I soon learned to check my way by the shell of a building, half-built and abandoned roofless, with the bush growing thickly inside the piers of the walls. At every gate there seemed to be a thatch palm wine bar. At the end of the way was a market, then a wider road and down the road the school compound and the sound of singing.

Late again. It was still raining quite often but on most mornings the thick cloud cover melted, broke and streamed away across the lightening sky. As I stood before the blackboard, teaching the cases with classical detachment, the sound of shelling could roll any moment over the horizon. The door stood open to the clean-swept sand and someone near the door or window would keep an eye open for marauding conscriptors. At the first sign of the press-gang entering the compound, the well-grown boys dived out through the window. Still, we were learning.

> In Belmont is a lady richly left
> And she is fair, and, fairer than that word,
> Of wondrous virtues.[2]

They liked the adventurous part better and we took the courtroom scene in an uninterrupted rush to a conclusion that delighted Class III.

School ended early, about 12:30 p.m., and I would walk back to Alaenyi along that spider web of paths linking houses, villages, and markets across the country. Usually many of the students walked with me out of the compound, posing the kind of questions that needed an answer and then a long explanation. 'Do you farm in England?' 'We do. Not as people do here'... and then there is the world of difference to describe. As we talk, groups turn off here and there from the main path and troop away, waving, through the young cassava. Children are coming the other way from a primary school, a book in hand or blackboard neatly balanced. 'Good affnoo, Ma,' they said in chorus or solo, except for one clear voice that said 'Good morning, Sah,' and was hushed by everyone.

These blackboards were made from pieces of ordinary wood. The natural colour was covered by being painted with charcoal, ground smooth and mixed with a little water. Then the wood was dried in the sun. After that it was well rubbed with a handful of leaves whose juice would stain the fingers a blackish green. When it was dried again, the black surface of the board would not rub off to dirty one's clothes, and if the process were repeated regularly the blackboard would be really black. This was the 'poor man's slate', because if it fell down it wouldn't break. The other kind belonged to the children of richer parents who could afford to replace them.

Sometimes on the way we found soldier ants 'going on attack', pouring endlessly across the path like a trickle of blue black liquid running furiously down a channel worn through the loose sand. Sometimes we saw people digging up an edible variety of termite from the earth at the side of the path. At one stage of its life it used to fly, and people talked of its white feather, meaning its gauzy wing.

Within a couple of weeks, there was an air raid, the day after an attack was reported by the radio on Mbano Joint Hospital.[3] They said 50 had been killed, 200 injured. Something black flashed over, then the scream of the jet sent the school rushing for the scanty cover of the long grass. The Sisters pulled coloured overalls and headscarves over their white habits. Everyone was far too near the buildings for any safety, but between the grass and the sheltering trees the ground had just been cultivated and the fragile new plants offered no cover. We all kept still and watched the plane repass, heard its scream recede … then heard it returning. The muffled explosions rolled across from Alaenyi.

School was dismissed early, in a twitter of nervousness. Those of us from Alaenyi hurried back. On the way I was shown a couple of brass shell cases picked up in the family compound. If Umueze was anxious, Alaenyi was terrified. The rest of the day was spent by everyone retelling the story to each other, where they had been and what they had done. Col. Ojukwu now had a headquarters in a fine well camouflaged house at one end of the village. Had the news been spread somehow, and was the plane looking for the house? Did they know they had found it? Could the attack be repeated with force? In a straight line along one side of the bush road lay the church, used during the week as a school, the big house and compound where we were living, the hospital and sickbay, another larger house and at the end, the headquarters. The plane had searched from end to end several times, or so it seemed. We decided hastily to take up the offer already made and move down to the Peace Corps house. The children wanted to know where we were going. I described the house as best I could.

'How many people are living there?'
'Nobody. It's all empty.'
'How many rooms?'
'Big living room, three bedrooms, bathroom and toilet.'
'You mean a toilet like the one we had at Enugu?'
'Yes. The house is just like the one at Enugu.'

The answers were repeated in Igbo to the younger children amid growing excitement. The next afternoon was spent carrying loads by bicycle and on foot, our cardboard boxes, one disintegrating suitcase, the pestle and mortar, the cooking tripod, a bottle of palm-oil, the sewing machine. We were back to head-loads again. We took time off to call in at a birthday party being given for a friend's one-year-old son. It was village style, with drummers, palm wine and kola, and, with the chin-chin (fried pastry biscuit, a great luxury just now), they passed from hand to hand more of the shell cases from the previous day's raid. Quite often when we visited friends, we would be handed a battered photograph album or a thick handful of rather faded postcard-sized photos. There were always neat school groups, faces arranged in tidy pyramids, pious white dresses for first communion, weddings and par-ties, all beer bottles and glasses topped by shining, beaming smiles. Or there were individuals stiffly posed in front of wrought iron gates or stylised photographers' backgrounds of palm trees or sunsets. Or they stood self-consciously in front of new cars, or arranged themselves so that no-one could miss the real point of interest, the wrist watch or the portable radio. These were glimpses back on an older world.

When they reached the school compound, the children behaved in the Peace Corps house exactly like Saxons taking over an abandoned Roman villa—with a mixture of curiosity and suspicion. They looked in cupboards and drawers for anything that might be useful, but there were only Peace Corps circulars from 1966 about collecting data for local history books and about the political situation ('It is not antici-pated that any emergency will last long.') I took the old paper to use the blank side for making notes. For the first time in so long we had ceilings, glass windows, curtains and cushions. There was a big book-case, so I spread out my few paperback books, the Latin texts and the painstaking word lists. Still, the many doors and spacious rooms were almost disturbing me too, until I recalled we had been two years and a month away from such a large building.

Outside our front door was a tall whistling pine tree, and beyond it the footpath from the main road to the convent, just wide enough for a car to pass along. This was the way visitors came—soldiers, desti-tutes, sickbay outpatients, the doctor in her Volkswagen, the Sisters in their battered Peugeot, a visiting priest to say Mass. One evening under the oil-bean tree we saw a man riding a bicycle with a tyre on the rear wheel only. 'What are you riding?' people asked. 'An armoured car,' he replied, clanking past.

You never knew who might pass on the road and who could be asked for news. But even rumours were scarce. After a long silence, there had been shelling on Osondu's first birthday. A 21-gun salute … 22… 23. We bought a newspaper for the first time in months. It was called the *Biafran Nationalist* and cost two shillings for a double sheet of lined exercise book paper. Some letters came in and even the occasional parcel. For a while there were Biafra air-letters, which cost half a crown in foreign exchange, obtained by a complicated process. They were on very pale blue foreign-looking paper with the Rising Sun symbol in the bottom left hand corner. The system did not last long.

Enugu still haunted everyone. It was named at every news broadcast. I heard that it was stamped on the passports in the Customs office at Uli airstrip. All Army addresses ended 'Enugu', and the Bank of Biafra was at 'Enugu'. You wrote letters to the various Ministries at 'Enugu' and the Post Office forwarded them to the present month's addresses.

Meanwhile our school work was going on. Behind the scenes, the timetable was juggled day by day to ensure that each class had a teacher at all times despite the recurring crises. The children tried to recall what they once knew among their own personal problems, still with no pen, no pencil, no textbooks, too few exercise books for the subjects, even when they used rat-nibbled, second-hand books passed down from elder brothers now away in the army. There really seemed to be more than enough to do. But then someone reminded the school that it would be Reverend Mother's feast day very soon and whatever else might happen, it could not pass without celebration.

The day began with early Mass in the convent chapel, which was crowded with everyone who could get inside—soldiers, students, sick-bay patients. It was a cloudy morning with the last rags of the rainy season bringing sudden flurries of wind and dark rain to bang at the shutters and brighten the glow of the candles. Lessons continued with difficulty. The concert was scheduled for 12 o'clock. The day had brightened. A plane was seen passing away to the right, threading through the breaking cloud. The sounds of the raid came only faintly, and the plane did not return. A classroom had been cleared of desks.

Chairs were arranged, with a table for the guest of honour and the Chairman of the occasion. We began in style, with songs proper to the occasion. After that, the students, who had obviously remembered their party pieces more readily than their school work, had a programme of eighteen very assorted items. They dressed up in the less practical odds and ends to come in with relief clothing, and made frequent use of a tinselly, lace negligee and a very long white celanese (rayon) petticoat, both worn on top of ordinary clothes.

The soldiers joined in and sang for us. Then they led a party of small, Class 1 boys with charcoaled faces and twigs tied round their heads in a desperate display of field craft. The audience flocked out into the sun for a better view of the ambush laid in the long grass on both sides of the path. An empty oil drum was well whacked with a stick—it was a 'mortar'—and when it was captured, it was triumphantly displayed while the prisoners were interrogated: 'Why you come harass we Biafrans, hey?' 'We no de come for fight. Dey done tell we come and occupy!' The audience yelled. Later the same group showed us how to take cover during an air raid. More planes had been passing lately. Osondu was learning to talk and 'plane coming' was one of her first phrases. Luckily it was a well-rehearsed kite that appeared next, and soared in those menacing circles that still scattered markets in panic.

The sickbay children also joined in. Two came and gave a brief display of French conversation. The nurse had been coaching them in her spare time 'to keep them happy,' she explained. They enquired of each other, 'Comment allez-vous?' and remarked 'Enchanté de vous voir,' with painful incongruity between the words and the speakers. But the scene was really stolen by a singing group from the sickbay. There were about twenty of them, not prettied for the occasion but wearing the only clothes they had. They were aged from four or five years to nine or ten, and they sang in the traditional way with great assurance, with a solo leader and a chorus answering her. Before many minutes most of the adults in the audience were surreptitiously using their handkerchiefs:

Children of Biafra, follow me and ask
What did we do?
Children of Biafra, follow me and ask
To suffer like this, what did we do?

And then we went down to see the presents. There were several reels of cotton, a dozen eggs (10 shillings each), pawpaws and oranges, several good china dinner plates, a blanket and a sheet, some dresses, two beautiful baskets—a large one with a lid, painted and patterned, and a small one almost handbag size with a design woven in fine strands of polythene unravelled with skill and patience from a relief salt bag. Then there was palm wine from stone jars, more talk, more good wishes, and everyone went home under the brilliant afternoon sky with the air raid hawk still circling.

A week or so later, a plane came. It caught me halfway back to the school block, at the beginning of the long, steep path past the sickbay. I took cover in the ward with the nurse. We sat on a bed in that still breathlessness that fell whenever a plane came. The plane crossed and re-crossed the sky, quartering and searching. At last it made away and we heard the explosions and saw the column of smoke rolling round and up without end. The plane had found the refinery and within days a gallon of petrol at Mbano cost £28 and a seat in a car travelling from Owerri to Orodo cost up to £2. Money by now was a token only, without reference to reality. A razor blade was ten shillings; four yards of wrapper cloth were offered for £65; a new head tie would cost you £12. A bicycle tyre was £85. Where could it end?

Everyone was still making use of the little they had. When battered umbrellas fell to pieces, people wove coolie hats to keep off the rain. Those women who still wanted to tie their hair used raffia as hair thread, dyed black with vegetable juice. Holes that appeared in concrete floors and walls as the blocks crumbled away were patched with well-trodden mud. I helped to search through the school staff room, trying to salvage school records, useful text books, unused envelopes, scrap for notes. The room hadn't been opened for two years, and everywhere there was thick, ropey dust and cobwebs. Some cupboards and drawers were inches deep in shredded paper, and as we opened the doors the insects scurried away from eating books. The damage was not a modest worm-hole but hollows inches across, gnawing a gaping hole through scores of pages. We searched grimly through the sticky, dirty, creeping mess. It was a distasteful job, no more dismal than the knowledge that this would be the reality everywhere, with the grass grown tall around familiar buildings and the sand shifting under the doors.

To advocate surrender would be to announce oneself a 'sabo', but the increasing weariness was having an insidious effect. Perhaps to encourage morale and combat this feeling of exhaustion, there were constant rumours that Chinese troops were coming, even that they had arrived. The idea of defeat was like the thought of death—to be pushed aside for as long as strength might last. What might come after was for both experiences a matter of faith and hope, not knowledge.

There were going to be promotion exams, since this was by the calendar the third term of the year. There was no writing paper and the children had to provide their own. Lined foolscap cost five shillings for a folded sheet, and the cheapest exercise books was now 15 shillings, so they came with old calendars, circulars, minutes of long-dismissed meetings to write their answers on the empty sides. There was no way of printing examination papers. Questions had to be written on the blackboard and we still had plenty of chalk. People were making ink from the same leaves that were used to complete the transformation of a piece of wood into a blackboard. The children pinned their answer sheets together with splinters of palm-fibre broom. We finished and marked the exams, and wrote reports—the report books were there still in cartons from pre-war. In a frenzy of improvisation, we even held an entrance examination for the new school year beginning January 1970.

And so it was the Christmas holiday. The children brought home their reports from the Primary School up the road. I chopped a bushy branch from the whistling pine, trimmed it to shape and planted it in a pot. We all decorated it solemnly with gold and silver icicles, stars and snowballs, all made from cardboard, cigarette foil, the inner side of soup packets, the lining of a tea-chest, and we kept it on top of the bookcase. The children thought it was beautiful and so did I, particularly at night when we lit the bush lamp and it cast along the ceiling a fantastic shadow of gauzy branches and sharp star shapes. In this unreal existence we were connoisseurs of shadows. The glow-worms in the grass outside were hundreds of tiny yellow-green lights. Peace on earth.

16

AND SO WE SURVIVED

The news was very bad, so far as we admitted its existence that Christmas. There was frequent shelling from new directions with that new and frightening sound: five or six rapid explosions instead of a single '*bim*'. It seemed to be coming nearer. The BBC had been talking of new guns with a range of 30 miles. The road at the end of the compound was crowded again with refugees moving both up and down ... a particularly depressing sight. One could see that some people about to take one lateral route might need to go up the road and some taking another would need to go down but still it seemed to exemplify the vain hopelessness of flight. If it came to running again, where was left?

The school reopened as scheduled, but overnight there were refugees in the compound from Owerri disputing for possession of the buildings. I awoke to lights passing and loud urgent voices from the darkness outside the windows. Next day we discussed soberly whether to attempt to escape or not when the choice became immediate, and decided at last to stay where we were. The Fathers made a hasty visit to share some of their own supplies and to tell us the end seemed to be near. They had also decided to stay. To my mind, Biafra had become one of those corn fields so often seen at harvest time. The machines move noisily round the edges, knifed blades turning, and all the small creatures move steadily in away from the clatter, the fear and the danger. The reaper moves in also, gradually circling nearer to the centre. Now the field was almost cut. Whatever might happen, let it come quickly.

On Saturday we heard the sound of heavy machine gunfire not very distant, most probably moving down a road from Owerri. By late afternoon the rest of the family had arrived from Ogbaku together with other members of the family-community. Twenty-two of them, tired and frightened, they packed in and slept on the floor of the living room. In the night, local thieves entered the compound talking Hausa in loud ostentatious voices to discourage any possible resistance and broke into the store to the convent sickbay. In the morning the frightened Sisters packed out from the compound.

By Sunday the bursts of shooting had moved far away to the right. Someone called hurriedly to report the whole area was cut off. Nigerians had been seen at Atta and now at Orodo. The firing so far beyond us had already made the situation fairly plain. A group of civilians arrived on the doorstep and informed us that they were 'breaking all the stores'. With some difficulty they were persuaded there was no store in the house but we knew they must return at night or others of the same mind would come. We decided to move out of the lonely compound, back into Alaenyi where the people lived more closely together. Someone agreed to take in all the party, now about forty in number. I found I had become a lucky charm, a safe conduct. No-one wanted to make the short journey unless I came with them. The people in the compound wanted me to stay with them to protect them. We plodded the bush path between Umueze and Alaenyi, too emotionally exhausted to talk. One of the palm wine sheds was already named 'One Nigeria Bar', with the name chalked in capitals on a small blackboard at the open door.

That night I sat out in the darkness listening to the radio with the new batteries I had just been given, listening to the BBC and the VOA to find out what was happening elsewhere.

Locally there was a state of anarchy. All over the district, stores had indeed been broken into and the supplies carried off by looters, both Biafran soldiers and civilians. Feeding centres, hospitals and sickbays lost their staff, stores and patients overnight and the empty buildings were stripped. Missions were also robbed of church plate, vestments and furniture. The school compound we had just left and the Peace Corps house were burgled. The convent lost its tabernacle for the sake of the thin gold lining.

The thirty months had ended in complete collapse. Optimism and confidence turned to the frantic grabbing of whatever could be gained. Many people ran the risk of poisoning. I was asked openly to advise on a basketful of bottles and injections. Some had no identification at all. Those with packets in a language I could guess included tablets for diabetes and cardiac conditions, contraceptive pills, and hormone injections. I knew the owner would not take my urgent advice either to destroy them or hand them over to a hospital whenever one might begin to function again. Did 'capsules' always contain antibiotics? People always thought so. Even the food stores had their dangers. I heard later that sacks of fertiliser were mistaken for coarse cooking salt.

Even in the fear and confusion of these few days, farce was never very far away. The two Fathers from Mbieri described how a large consignment of stockfish had just been received in their store and the big church was crowded with local people. The priests tried to hand over the relief to the needy while keeping away the menacing 'Artillery Boys'—ragged, shell-shocked soldiers, genuine or not you never could tell: 'And what did I see at the other end of the Church? A bride in white, a groom complete to white gloves and silk socks! And with all that fearful noise and tumult there was Father Carney marrying somebody. Then, with an Irish roar: "DO YOU TAKE THIS WOMAN ..."'.

By the time the Nigerian soldiers arrived, the Fathers had been ready to greet them with a cheer. And many of the Artillery Boys, they said, slipped the bandages off their heads, dropped their falsetto ghostlike voices and quietly vanished with the crowd. But soon the Fathers themselves had been removed from the scene to Port Harcourt for deportation. A visitor described with a touch of envy a resourceful man in his own village: 'And seeing that he had some relief materials stored in his compound, when things fell apart he fell on what he had,' a remark that gained point from the fact that everyone knew at least the title of Chinua Achebe's famous novel.

The panicky rumours were at first of rape and wholesale looting, the abduction of children and young girls and of casual murders, mostly found later to be untrue. Some days the girls were afraid to go out of the compound to the stream for water and no-one at all went very far. There were frequent loud bursts of shooting but generally it sounded too rhythmical and exuberant to be really terrifying, though it was always cause for sudden alarm. Gradually the flying tales modulated to harassment and robbery. Sometimes people who had kept their possessions all through the running and the raids lost their valuables, particularly cars and radios, at the end.

The refugee family staying in the next house hid their own car by removing part of the high palm branch fence around the back yard and pushing the car inside. Only a thorough search would have found it, since there was no entry into the back yard except through the house and no open space through which a car could pass. They replaced the fence, rubbed out the tyre marks and walked the smooth sand back to the normal dappled appearance. Since we were all staying quite a step from the road, the ruse was never put to the test.

We ventured as far as Mbieri, and there nervously saw the first Nigerian soldiers face to face. Looted goods were on sale in the market and Biafran money was still being accepted there. I bought some primary school textbooks for the children from a pile obviously taken recently from some good book store since they were neat and new, not second-hand or dirty.

A few days later we had the chance to travel to Owerri. As we passed through Mbieri, the Volkswagen had to squeeze past the corpse of a looter who had been killed on the job. The nearly naked body lay sprawled across the road and no-one seemed disposed to claim it. In Owerri there were other strange sights. At the side of one road there was actually a small herd of once-familiar long horned cattle. In one area you could see long lines of shuffling destitutes, hoping now for Red Cross relief. In another, there was a busy market crowded with all those who had something to sell. You could buy fine gold trinkets very cheaply if you had money to spare for such things. Biafran money was not accepted here and very few people had much Nigerian money. We had some pennies, once offered in vain to the traders who found coppers too bulky and were only interested in shillings for their smuggling. It was inexpressibly strange to move about, hearing prices quoted in pennies instead of in pounds, seeing salt sold from a full headpan poured in the measuring cup and heaped up once more, looking at piles of onions, many full bars of yellow soap, stacks of tinned goods, whole packets of biscuits. We had no money to spare and bought only basic foods, but we added a few groundnuts which the children had not seen for so long. All the time the big green army lorries roared past, full of soldiers.

Gradually as confidence increased and the days passed without massacre, people stopped 'taking cover', venturing a little way and then returning to base where they felt safer. They began to move out at last, still cautiously. It was not until weeks later in Enugu that I heard the loud and cheerful greeting everywhere: 'Happy Survival!'

Wherever the end of the war had found them, whether 'nearly at Port Harcourt' or not, Biafran soldiers had taken off whatever uniform they had, disposed of their arms and melted away. Now they were returning to their families. Or day after day they did not come, and their families began to go about asking those who had safely returned whether they had seen them. Some of the people who had been cut off by the war and were thought to be long since dead came in looking for their relatives, if any could be still alive. Those who had been caught inside Biafra and had their homes far outside set off to rejoin their own people. We decided it was time to move also, back into that world, first from Ogwa to Ogbaku then, sometime, when somehow we could find a way, back to Enugu.

Many were setting off on foot. I did not see how we could attempt the 100 mile journey with five children, and it had become almost an article of faith that we should not be separated. And so one morning we left Alaenyi and walked down the path to Umueze, past the empty school, past the abandoned checkpoint under the oil bean tree, over the plank bridge where the tankers from Amandugba had churned the mud into crumbling ruts, past Orodo where the excited bursts of firing had signalled the end.

The main tarred road from Owerri was busy with convoys of Red Cross lorries speeding past in the direction of Orlu. We walked on our own way. John had loaded the smaller children on the carrier of his bicycle. I took my turn carrying Osondu and noticed quite often scores of pages from someone's carefully preserved files, abandoned at the last, torn out and thrown away along the roadside in the dust.

PART III

S. Elizabeth Bird

17

AFTER BIAFRA

With the war officially over in January 1970, the Umelo family were eager to get home to Enugu. Many had feared what would happen with the arrival of Federal troops; the stories of massacres and rapes were still fresh, and there is no doubt that some abuse of civilians took place. However, in the wake of Gowon's 'No Victor, No Vanquished' decree, the much-feared retaliations against the defeated Igbos did not happen. Rose's friend and fellow Nigerwife, Wendy Ijioma, believed that Gowon's orders saved her in one particularly fearful moment:

> I was briefly abducted by a soldier with two soldiers sitting in the back of the car with guns ... he muttered something about Gowon forbidding them to behave badly. Eventually I said my baby would be very hungry. Unwillingly he let me out of the car. I had quite a long walk home through the bush and I really had no idea how to get back ... But I arrived home safely.[1]

Rose and her family experienced no violence or harassment, but she remembers this as a difficult and chaotic time, when normal behaviour broke down:

> The war ended with complete anarchy. Talk about a free-for-all ... there was no law, no nothing, people going around breaking into the stores, into the hospitals, into the sick bays, stealing the food ... looting, frankly. I mean presumably you felt you had the choice of being

looted by soldiers so you had better do it now … after three years of struggling to survive you take what you can, I suppose.

Rose has trouble remembering exactly when and how they travelled back to Enugu, but thinks they must have got home in February or March. Their car was long gone, and they took whatever transport they could find: 'Uzo says he remembered being on the front seat in a wooden sided lorry for the first time and being scolded by John for standing up to look at the rattling bonnet of the vehicle. So John must have got us transport through his contacts.' Her official staff house in Queens School was a ruin, with the roof torn off and scraps of belongings scattered everywhere:

> Luckily I found the papers which were the ownership of a piece of land we'd bought. It was lying there, trampled over you know … But we had left behind and lost a lot of things. All my prizes, all my books, my stamp album, my collection of beads, you know that kind of thing …

The school was also seriously damaged:

> thoroughly looted, all buildings roofless, classrooms and staff houses, the library a wreck, books gone, big smoky stain up a wall, many trees cut down. During the war schools were in regular use for something— sickbay, hospital, barracks. I don't know what Queens might have been used for.

But throughout the former Biafra, people began to repair and rebuild, and schools reopened, often in makeshift conditions. Rose and John lived temporarily in the boys' quarters belonging to her house, and were able to use the recovered documents to secure title to their land and build up a new home. Rose returned to teaching at Queens School, but the calm and orderly world of pre-war education had changed. She felt the students no longer wanted to learn, but just wanted to pass somehow, get on and make up for lost time, and she gradually became disenchanted with teaching. After serving as vice-principal for a couple of years, in 1975 she moved to a position as principal at St. Catherine's Girls' Secondary School, in Nkwerre, about 90 miles south of Enugu. 'There, you had to not only hold down some of the students, you had to hold down some of the teachers, and I wasn't happy a bit.'

A New Career

Rose had been writing for years, and was an award winner from the BBC for a short story in 1966. In 1973 she won First Prize from Britain's Cheltenham Literary Festival for a short story, followed by a second place award in 1975. It was time for a career change, and in 1979 she was offered a position as an editor with Macmillan Nigeria, where she worked for the next nine years, while building her own reputation as a writer. A collection of her short stories, *The Man who Ate the Money*, was published in 1978 by Oxford University Press, Ibadan, and over the next two decades she published over a dozen short novels, mostly aimed at young Nigerians. Perhaps her best known were under Macmillan's Pacesetter brand—an extremely popular series of about 130 books, 'written by established African authors who write on societal realities, personal concerns, contemporary issues and problems faced by Africans ... it is the only novel series written by Africans.'[2] The series was marketed as an engaging English as a Second Language (ESL) experience; writers from all over Africa contributed, including such well-known names as Buchi Emecheta and Helen Ovbiagele.

Although Rose explored publication of her civil war account, there was little interest in revisiting this national trauma in the 1970s, and she put it aside. Later, she found ways to address the war in some of her fiction, such as *Soldier Boy* and *Waiting for Tomorrow*, and most notably in her Pacesetters novel, *Felicia* (1978), described in 2002 as 'beautifully written, poignant, and often hilarious'.[3] Her teenage heroine, the studious Felicia, finds herself pregnant in Biafra by a book-loving young man who is killed in the war. She returns home to face the disapproval of her family, but she perseveres, returns to her education, and is eventually embraced by the baby's father's family, as well as her own. The book's descriptions, from Felicia's return to her ruined school, to life in her village, draw directly from Rose's personal experiences. And the novel holds a special place in published women's writing about the civil war. As noted by Virginia Coulon, men had begun publishing creative work on the war almost immediately after it ended, while by 1990 only eight fictional works by women had appeared. The first was Flora Nwapa's *Never Again*, in 1975; the second was *Felicia*.[4]

As Lee Erwin notes, the Pacesetters books were striking in the way so many of their protagonists were making 'complex, often conflicted attempts to assimilate traditional sources of authority with the new forms thrown up by modernization' and they often featured strong, independent women, who nevertheless had to negotiate traditional structures.[5] Felicia 'illustrates the way patrilineal system benefits women above all through the solidarity it offers them with other women'.[6] Rose's books, which another scholar described as filled with 'upstanding, self-sufficient, individualist protagonists'[7] reflect her own sense of independence, coupled with an unswerving embrace of local Nigerian values.

Rose became a Nigerian citizen in 1972. During her time in the village, she had developed close ties with John's family, especially her mother-in-law, Ukwuaru, usually called Ukwa, who had supported her through her pregnancy and lain with her after the birth of her daughter in the makeshift bush shelter. Even though Ukwa spoke no English and Rose hardly a word of Igbo, they grew to love each other across the barrier of language:

> You know she came to me several times after the war when she was not well and lived with me. I would sometimes take her hospital for treatment, but the only thing is I had to promise that I wouldn't ever leave her there, because, as she said, people died in hospital.

Rose's last child (and fourth daughter) Nkechi, was born in 1971, and Rose decided that six children was enough. Igbo society values all children highly, but sons above all else, and John wanted more sons, especially as his extended family was quite small by Igbo standards. As she moved into her 40s, Rose made an important decision:

> I wasn't prepared to keep on having children. I thought, 'I don't want to die on my eighth.' You know, you don't get better at it. I knew from observation that you can't tell a man to stop having kids, he would just get another woman outside, and I wanted to know the opposition, so I looked around the available talent.

Her suggested choice for John's second wife was someone who had been well known to them for years: 'I thought—she's a very nice woman. She's pretty, with a sweet nature, and she knows us so well.' While taking a second wife was not uncommon in Nigeria at the time, Rose agreed that this rarely happened when the first wife was white: 'They usually say "Never!" and pack and go.' But, as she put it, 'I was unconventional all the way,' managing an unfamiliar situation in a matter-of-fact manner that allowed her to retain control.

For the next few years, Rose's career with Macmillan took her to various places, and in 1988, she was moved to their head office in Ibadan in Western Nigeria. Over the years, the couple had grown more distant: 'I was still the earner but he would not move to do anything he thought contrary to his idea of himself.' After Rose left teaching, John had moved back to Ogbaku, where he tried to establish several businesses, such as a petrol station and lorry service. Rose recalls that as the senior man in the extended family he was responsible for many relatives, and that some took advantage of him. But in the end, 'He really had no head for business. Nigeria had moved on while he was in England for so long and after the war it went faster.'

When in-house reorganisation ended Rose's Macmillan job, she took a temporary editing position at the International Institute of Tropical Agriculture, a non-profit organisation that seeks to use agricultural innovations to address hunger, poverty, and natural resource degradation. She stayed there for 27 years. John and Rose remained married, and on polite terms, although the relationship was effectively over, and the couple's six children remained with Rose. She built a house in Moniya, just outside Ibadan, with her son Uzoma Anthony (Uzo), in which she lived for 20 years:

> I liked my house, I got on well with local people. I tended to accumulate lots of books, most of them second hand, and I was very happy. In the end, he went his way, to his second wife and family, with my blessing, and I suppose I went my way, concentrating on getting all the children educated.

She very much succeeded; all Rose's children went on to higher education. Four now live in Britain: her oldest son Eze recently retired from his job as a financial accountant in London, Uzo became an administrator in a London medical school, Anne teaches in Dagenham, and Iheoma is a manager at a primary school in Hackney. Elizabeth (Osondu, the 'baby born in bush') earned her PhD in bio-science in Canada, and now does research and development for a company in the United States, while the youngest, Nkechi, teaches in Owerri, Imo State. For years, Rose never seriously considered returning to the United Kingdom, although her children insisted on her coming for a month's holiday every year. John died in 2010; Rose noted that at his funeral she told his second wife to also wear white, which was usually reserved for the first wife. In 2015, in her mid-80s, she finally decided to retire and move back to England, where her four children were eager for her to join them. She agreed, securing a freelance arrangement with IITA, for whom she still edits documents from her home computer. 'I gradually had to dispose of a lot of stuff ... I packed everything up and that was it. End of story.'

In Hindsight

Looking back on Biafra after fifty years, Rose has few regrets about the choices she made:

> I think every woman has the moment when she thinks she could have done differently, (and in times of exasperation, better). Things didn't work out as expected for either of us. ... I still think Nigeria was a better option than the UK in 1964 to bring up double-heritage children ... Being a writer in Nigeria at that time was an advantage, and I was lucky in making contacts in publishing after the war. And during the war, if the idea of leaving had ever occurred to me, there was always the thought, 'How would I ever get back?'

She recalls that many Biafran Nigerwives had decided not to stay when the war heated up; evacuations of expatriates began when the war started, and by late 1968, most had left. For instance Catherine Onyemelukwe, an American Nigerwife, wrote that by August that year, she felt it was impossible to remain, and she left with her husband's approval, 'flooded with relief that the children and I were among the people getting out, mixed with sadness at leaving Clem behind'.[8] But Rose believed there was no choice: 'I was brought up with this idea that marriage is forever and though we didn't marry in a church, I made the promises ...'

None of the women who stayed had an easy time in the war. However, most were married to higher-status Biafrans, who were usually able to lead more comfortable lives than people in the villages. For instance Wendy Ijioma, a teacher, and her husband Sam supervised a food distribution centre; towards the end of the war, they were also forced to retreat to the villages, but kept the centre running. Leslie

Ofoegbu, who later wrote a memoir of her experiences, spent most of the war under the protection of the Holy Ghost Fathers, while her engineer husband worked on development for Biafra. As Rose explains,

> The others ... they were graduates. Yes, so was I, but they had husbands with professional jobs, one her husband was a lawyer, another one was an engineer. They moved in a different society to us, and also we were in our own village and they were not.

Rose received help from the Fathers, as she describes, but she lived throughout the war in much the same way as many Biafrans—experiencing constant uprooting and uncertainty. In John's village, where white people had been rarely encountered, she was received with kindness, but with a degree of scepticism about her ability to survive. With a smile, Rose recalls,

> My mother-in-law, bless her, always had the idea I was some kind of albino; she used to say it was wonderful the way Rose can see in the sunshine, when that one along the road can't see anything. Of course that would be in Igbo because she didn't speak any English. A lovely lady!

Wendy Ijioma, who knew Rose, and saw her occasionally during the war, commented that 'she experienced more hardships than any of us ... She is an amazing person whom I greatly admire'. Wendy recalled that she and her husband helped Rose when they could:

> several times we travelled quite a distance to take food to her. One day when we visited she was so pleased because Sam had brought her some soap. She had just given her last piece of soap to a lady she knew with a new born baby ...

Today, living in East London with four of her children nearby, Rose would never describe herself as 'amazing', and declines to characterise her life as in any way remarkable, insisting that she simply did her best to keep her children and family together. As her extended family eventually learned, 'I was never a delicate flower!' Rose credited her wartime ability to manage to her upbringing in Northern England, and the resourcefulness of her mother:

> I was eight or nine when the Second World War started ... my mother was a domestic servant from a constrained background but she knew how to manage. Very calm, very efficient, very good cook, could bring food out of the air I think. Knew how to use offal and marrow bones

and sheep's head and things like that, which were off-ration in World War II and often unfamiliar. Cooking them needed more knowledge and special skill.

Throughout the war, her goal was to allow her children to feel safe from the violence that was so close every day. Her daughter Anne, born in 1964, remembers only flashes of life in Biafra, but recalled that she rarely felt afraid, even though, 'my God, it must've been horrible!' Instead,

I remember the moonlight ... games and clapping and running around, and telling stories ... I remember the fun bits ... You leave the worry to the adults and even when it's really bad they protect you from that ... we could be dead any time now, but they wouldn't say that ... I'm not sure I've seen Mum panic about anything really. When she talks about things in retrospect ... we didn't know they were happening ... that's just her nature you know.

Wendy Ijioma agrees:

She never complained, though we did talk about the difficulties ... She was always calm and just coped with all the problems that occurred ... But it must have been very hard to find enough money to feed and clothe not only her own children but so many others, too.

Indeed, Rose's education and basic medical and nutritional knowledge, combined with her calm personality, proved invaluable, and the extended family came to depend on her. John, as the oldest surviving brother, was responsible for more than his immediate family, and Rose took their duty seriously. As her daughter Anne explains,

You wanted to help everybody, Mum. There were people depending on us, and you felt you would be abandoning them if you just took your five children and just left everybody else. If it weren't for you, my auntie said to me, a lot of our cousins would have died. They lived with us, our house was always packed with people throughout the war and everywhere we went our cousins all went with us. Mum and Dad just absorbed everybody so we were like a huge family—we never moved as five. My grandmother, and then my uncle's wife, Alice's mother and all of Alice's family, and many more distant from us, they all came along. This huge crowd, all depending on Mum really.

Rose remembers that when she offered her story for publication soon after the war, one response was that it seemed 'too calm'—that readers would expect panic and terror:

Well I didn't have any panics actually and there are no panics in the manuscript. There's a good deal of war weariness towards the end but there were no panics ... I mean they all got measles or chicken pox, and they had malaria up and down but I always had this feeling we were going to see the end of it.

In the end, no-one in the Umelo family died, for which Rose is deeply grateful. Other families were not so fortunate; her daughter Anne's husband, eldest of six children, was the only one among them to survive. Rose knows she was lucky; she had advantages that most Igbo families did not have, such as personal help from the Holy Ghost Fathers and other Nigerwives. Even in the worst of times, the Biafran government continued to function, and as a government teacher, she was among those who continued to receive salary payments throughout the war—at least on paper. Actual cash came whenever banks were open, and currency was available. The irregular two or three pounds she was able to pick up did not go far with so many depending on her, but they made all the difference.

Too Weary to Weep

Today, Nigeria is still one nation, although its unity continues to be precarious, threatened by Islamist terrorism in the North, resistance movements in the Niger Delta, and a desperation rooted in years of government misrule and corruption. It is a nation of contrasts—vast wealth coupled with grinding poverty; a vibrant culture of brilliant writers and artists coupled with chronic unemployment and urban squalor.

After the war, the name of Biafra was wiped off the map, and the former Eastern Region now covers several of the thirty-six Nigerian states, undermining any sense of a common identity for the area. Although Gowon's policies of 'reconciliation, reconstruction, and reintegration' prevented violent retaliation against the Igbo, the former Biafra was deeply changed by the war, with much of its infrastructure damaged or destroyed. Missionary orders, condemned by the Federal Government for their support of Biafran people during the war, were expelled from the country. Many of the best schools had been church-run, and these were now turned over to the state, which did not have the funds or the will to make them what they once were.

Policies such as the 'abandoned property' rule prevented many Igbo from retrieving assets they had been forced to leave behind in the war, and these were deemed 'abandoned'. With the post-war state reorganisation, even property within the former Biafra, such as in the newly-created Rivers and South Eastern states, was forfeited to other ethnic groups who now controlled it.[9] The government also decreed that those holding Biafran currency of any amount could exchange it for no more than a total of £20 (Nigerian). Such policies were widely viewed as attempts to prevent the Igbo middle class from re-establishing their important roles in business and civil service, prompting many well-to-do Igbos to migrate to Europe or the United States.[10] For the less affluent majority, the end of the war meant returning to villages and farms that were often devastated by the war, and rebuilding kinship networks that had been decimated, a burden that speeded the flight of many into swelling cities like Lagos.

Meanwhile, the central government made a concerted effort to 'forget' the conflict that nearly tore the nation apart; the war became a footnote in the official history curriculum. Nevertheless, it kept reasserting itself in Nigeria's consciousness, most recently in Chimamanda Ngozi Adichie's acclaimed 2007 novel, *Half of a Yellow Sun*, and in the memoir *There was a Country*, the last work by Chinua Achebe, who had spent the war in service to Biafra. Fuelled by years of resentment, a Biafran resurgent political movement has grown in power, protesting against what is perceived to be continued Igbo marginalisation. And in Britain, which once played such a major and problematic role in the war, Biafra gradually receded into a foggy memory of starvation and suffering.

And what of the two young men who presided over the tragedy that was Biafra? After years in exile, Biafran leader Emeka Ojukwu returned to Nigeria in 1982, where he became active in politics and gained the status of elder statesman. He died in London in 2011, and was buried in Nigeria with full military honours. In 1975, Gen. Yakubu Gowon was overthrown in a military coup by his war-time Division commander and rival, Murtala Muhammed. After years abroad in Britain, he also returned to Nigeria; he never again became politically active, but wields influence as a former head of state. In 2016, I met and interviewed Gowon. As he consistently has done, he reiterated that the war was only to keep Nigeria united, and that his government never had genocidal intent against the Igbo.[11] He pointed to the way the Igbo were welcomed back, and he preferred not to dwell on the many who died from the long starvation. He spoke of Ojukwu almost fondly, recalling him as an erstwhile comrade-in-arms:

> I went to see him years later in his home town … I saw him in his uniform looking like Castro, and I said, 'Who is that rebel?' and we laughed.[12]

For those at the top, personally unharmed and rehabilitated, it must have been easier to forgive and forget, and celebrate the future of Nigeria. And the new Biafran resurgence movement, which glorifies an idealised independence, does not generally attract those who lived through the thirty months of suffering and wish never to revisit it. That is why stories from survivors are so important. For Rose Umelo, like her family and friends, the end of the war had brought little excitement—just relief: 'It was all over, and it had all been for nothing.' Looking back, she is reluctant to place blame, whether on Ojukwu, Gowon, or her native country, which she believed 'behaved very badly'.

Her greatest sorrow was that so many, in a worse situation than she was, died unnecessarily:

> I got a lot of privilege, simply by being white … After the war, you know, I won't claim to having had post-traumatic stress, but I did lot of brooding on why I survived, and bought extra soap and sewing cotton.…

Today, she reflects that the war was not noble or heroic, but rather 'the slow grinding down and wearing away of expectation, resources, hope, and innocence', exemplified by both the suffering and strength of women. And so we end with a short poem, which Rose wrote some years ago and titled 'After a War':

> Sitting round palm wine, the men out-shout the storm to celebrate their lives.
>
> Their wives,
>
> Too weary to weep, under the machine-gun rattle of the rain,
>
> Make songs for dead children and rock them asleep.

NOTES

PROLOGUE: LIVING FROM HOPE TO HOPE

1. Bird, S. Elizabeth and Fraser Ottanelli, *The Asaba Massacre: Trauma, Memory, and the Nigerian Civil War*, Cambridge: Cambridge University Press, 2017.
2. I received my first email from Rose on 9 Dec. 2016, after which we corresponded regularly. We met at her home in Dagenham in March 2017, and talked for several hours over two days, sometimes joined by her daughter Anne. All direct quotes from Rose are drawn from those meetings and/or the dozens of emails we have exchanged before or since then.
3. Adimora-Ezeigbo, Akachi, 'From the Horse's Mouth: The Politics of Remembrance in Women's Writing on the Nigerian Civil War', in *Body, Sexuality, and Gender: Versions and Subversions in African Literatures 1*, ed. Flora Veit–Wild and Dirk Naguschewski, Amsterdam: Rodopi, 2005, p. 223.
4. Harneit-Sievers, Axel, Jones O. Ahazuem and Sydney Emezue, *A Social History of the Nigerian Civil War: Perspectives from Below*, Enugu: Jemezie Associates and Hamburg: Lit Verlag, 1997. See also de Lame, Danielle, 'On Behalf of Ordinary People: Bridging the Gap between High Politics and Simple Tragedies', *African Studies Review*, 48, 3 (2005), pp. 133–41.
5. Harneit-Sievers, *A Social History*, p. 12. For a discussion of Nigerian Civil War novels by women, see Nnaemeka, Obioma, 'Fighting on all Fronts: Gendered Spaces, Ethnic Boundaries, and the Nigerian Civil War', *Dialectical Anthropology*, 22 (1997), pp. 235–63.

1. FROM COLONIALISM TO WAR

1. There are several good, recent accounts of Nigeria's history, which the

reader can consult to understand the full story, and I draw heavily on these sources. They include works by Toyin Falola and Matthew M. Heaton; Richard Bourne; and Stephen Ellis. All are listed in the bibliography.

2. See Lugard, Frederick John Dealtry, *The Dual Mandate in British Tropical Africa*, London: William Blackwood, 1922; Hetherington, Penelope, *British Paternalism and Africa, 1920–1940*, London: Frank Cass, 1978.

3. Achebe, Chinua, *Home and Exile*, New York: Anchor, 2000, p. 18. The spelling 'Ibo' was commonly used until about the 1970s; throughout we use the modern, preferred spelling 'Igbo' unless quoting original sources.

4. Bourne, Richard, *Nigeria: A New History of a Turbulent Country*, London: Zed Books, 2015.

5. Baker, Pauline, 'Lurching toward Unity', *The Wilson Quarterly*, 4 (1980), p. 76.

6. Ibid.

7. Achebe, Chinua, *There was a Country*, New York: Penguin, 2012, p. 40.

8. Bourne, *Nigeria*, p. 95.

9. See Omaka, Arua Oko, *The Biafran Humanitarian Crisis, 1967–1970*, Fairleigh Dickinson University Press, 2016, p. 33.

10. Garrison, Lloyd, '300 Ibo Tribesmen Killed by Troops and Nigerian Mob', *New York Times*, 2 Oct. 1966, pp. 1; 17. Garrison reported that soldiers, defying the orders of their officers, opened fire on a large group of Igbos trying to board an aeroplane at Kano.

11. See Anthony, Douglas, *Irreconcilable Narratives: Biafra, Nigeria, and Arguments against Genocide, 1966–1970*, in Moses, A. Dirk and Lasse Heerten (ed.), *Postcolonial Conflict and the Question of Genocide: The Nigeria-Biafra War, 1967–1970*, London: Routledge, 2017, pp. 47–71. Bourne argues that the 30,000 was an inflated figure, and that the real numbers were smaller.

12. Cruise O'Brien, Conor, 'Condemned People', *New York Review of Books*, 21 Dec. 1967, 14.

13. The new country was named after the Bight of Biafra, the most eastern part of the Gulf of Guinea, closest to Eastern Nigeria.

14. Harneit-Sievers et al. devote a chapter to the attitude of non-Igbo minorities to Biafra, showing that many were ambivalent or opposed to the new state: Axel Harneit-Sievers, Jones O. Ahazuem and Sydney Emezue, *A Social History of the Nigerian Civil War: Perspectives from Below*, Enugu: Jemezie Associates and Hamburg: Lit Verlag, 1997.

15. Anthony, Douglas, 'Resourceful and Progressive Blackmen': Modernity and Race In Biafra, 1967–70', *Journal of African History*, 51, 2010, p. 43.

16. Oil had first been discovered in Nigeria in 1956 by a Shell-BP consortium, and pumping began in 1958. While the consortium retained sole rights until Independence, after that rights were sold to other international companies to explore areas in the Niger Delta. Soon oil became the main source of income for Nigeria.

17. The name by which the war is known is contentious. Depending on viewpoint, it is known as the Nigeria-Biafra War (which suggests a conflict between two sovereign entities), the Biafran War (which places the emphasis on the struggle for Biafra), or the War of Nigerian Unity (underlining the purpose of keeping Nigeria one). I will use the term Nigerian Civil War because it is the most common, and arguably the most neutral. The first account of the war, written soon after its end, was by John de St. Jorre. Later accounts include books by Michael Gould (2012); Lasse Heerten (2017); A. Dirk Moses and Lasse Heerten (2017). Full details and other sources are listed in the Bibliography.

18. Shepherd, Jack, 'Memo from Nigeria: Old Headaches for our New President', *Look*, 26 Nov. 1968, p. 74. Shepherd wrote that 'perhaps 8,000 Ibo civilians died when the Midwest was "liberated" by troops under Col. Murtala Muhammed'.

19. For a full account of the Asaba Massacre, its causes, consequences, and place in the history of the war, see Bird and Ottanelli, *The Asaba Massacre*.

20. *Newsweek*, 'Nigeria: Setting Sun', 9 Oct. 1967, pp. 41–2.

21. For an account of the technological achievements in Biafra, written by one of its chief scientists, see Oraguwu, Felix N.C., *Scientific and Technological Innovations in Biafra: The Ogbunigwe Fame 1967–1970*, Enugu: Fourth Dimension Publishing, 2010.

22. Joint Consultative Assembly of Biafra, letter to Third Committee of the United Nations on Human Rights, 15 Feb. 1968. Clearing House for Nigeria/Biafra Information, 'Nigeria/Biafra Information Collection', Reel 5. Center for Research Libraries, Chicago.

23. M.T. Mbu, Commissioner for Foreign Affairs and Commonwealth Relations, Republic of Biafra, to His Excellency U Thant, 24 Feb. 1968. Accessed in Clearing House for Nigeria/Biafra Information, 'Nigeria/Biafra Information Collection' Reel 5. Center for Research Libraries, Chicago.

24. Heerten, *The Biafran War*, p. 107.

25. Sherman, John, *War Stories: A Memoir of Nigeria and Biafra*, Indianapolis: Mesa Verde Press, 2002, p. 72.

26. See Uwechue, Raph, *Reflections on the Nigerian Civil War*, New York: Africana Publishing Corporation, 1971. Uwechue, a Midwest Igbo,

supported Biafra, but became disenchanted with Ojukwu's leadership style.

27. Akpan, Ntieyong U., *The Struggle for Secession 1966–1970: A Personal Account of the Nigerian Civil War*, London: Frank Cass, 1972, p. 157.
28. Harneit-Sievers et al., *A Social History*, p. 68.
29. Uzokwe, Alfred Obiora, *Surviving in Biafra: The Story of the Nigerian Civil War*, New York: Writers Advantage, 2003, p. 78.
30. Harneit-Sievers et al., *A Social History*, p. 95.

2. BIAFRA AND BRITAIN: A POSTCOLONIAL TRAGEDY

1. *Runcorn Weekly News*, 'Mail from War-torn Biafra', Spring 1968 (exact date and page number unknown; source is Rosina Umelo's collection of clippings).
2. *Runcorn Weekly News*, 'Letter from Biafra: Former Frodsham Woman's Graphic Account of Suffering', Oct. 1968.
3. See McNeil, Brian, '"And Starvation is the Grim Reaper": The American Committee to Keep Biafra Alive and the Genocide Question during the Nigerian Civil War, 1968–1970', in Moses and Heerten, *Postcolonial Conflict and the Question of Genocide*, pp. 278–300; Farquharson, James, 'Black America Cares: The Response of African-Americans to Civil War and Genocide, 1967–1970', in Moses and Heerten, pp. 301–326.
4. Otigbah, Dominique, 'Nigerwives 1936–1970s: Locating the History of Expatriate Wives in Nigeria with the Context of Race Relations, Gender and Colonial/Post-colonial Encounters', Independent Study Project, School of Oriental and African Studies, London, 2014.
5. Young, John W., *The Labour Governments 1964–1970, Vol. 2, International Policy*, Manchester: Manchester University Press, 2004, p. 193.
6. Waugh, Auberon and Suzanne Cronje, *Biafra, Britain's Shame*, London: Michael Joseph, 1969, p. 117.
7. de St. Jorre, *The Brothers' War*, p. 304.
8. Quoted in Curtis, Mark, *Unpeople: Britain's Secret Human Rights Abuses*, London: Vintage, 2004, 170.
9. Omaka, *The Biafran Humanitarian Crisis*, p. 50.
10. For a more detailed discussion of the British position in the early months of the war, as well as British media coverage, see Bird and Ottanelli, *The Asaba Massacre*.
11. Young, *The Labour Governments*, p. 203.
12. Reports of talks with British High Commissioner Sir David Hunt, 3 Aug. 1967, UK National Archives, FCO 38/284, file 78 and file 114.
13. Cronje, Suzanne, *The World and Nigeria: The Diplomatic History of the Biafran War 1967–1970*, London: Sidgwick and Jackson, 1972.

14. T.J. Allison, Note to Press Officers, 22 Dec. 1967, UK National Archive, FCO 38/269, file 388.

15. For text of the Code of Conduct, see Kirk-Greene, Anthony H.M., *Crisis and Conflict in Nigeria: A Documentary Sourcebook, 1966–1970*, Vol. 1, London: Oxford University Press, 1971, pp. 455–57

16. Memo from David Hunt, 8 Feb. 1968, UK National Archives, FCO 38/285, file 309.

17. Memo from Michael Newington, in British High Commission, 31 Jan. 1968, UK National Archive, FCO 38/285, file 303.

18. Memo from David Hunt, 7 Feb. 1968, UK National Archives, FCO 38/285, file 305.

19. Memo on situation in 'liberated areas' from Michael Newington in British High Commission to Peter McEntee, West and General Africa Departments, 28 Jan. 1968, UK National Archive, FCO 38/285, file 292.

20. Memo 25 Jan. 1968, Lagos to Commonwealth Office, UK National Archive, FCO 38/285, file 294.

21. Jonathan Derrick, interview with Elizabeth Bird, 20 April 2017, London.

22. Quoted in Harrison, Paul and Robin Palmer, *News out of Africa: Biafra to Band Aid*, London: Shipman, 1986, p. 16.

23. Forsyth, Frederick, *The Biafra Story*, London: Penguin, 1969.

24. Rosa, Matthew, 'Schools and Hospitals Bombed, says Biafra', *The Observer*, 3 March 1968, p. 4.

25. Telegram from David Hunt, 5 March 1968, Lagos to Commonwealth Office, UK National Archives, FCO 38/285, file 327.

26. Norris, Bill, 'Media Ethics at the Sharp End', in David Berry (ed.), *Ethics and Media Culture: Practices and Representations*, Oxford: Focal Press, 2000, p. 331.

27. Ibid.

28. Ibid., p. 332.

29. For discussions of the relationship between the British government and the press, see Bird and Ottanelli, *The Asaba Massacre*; and John De St. Jorre, *The Brothers' War*. De Jorre, p. 354, describes how at least one British journalist, under direction from Nigerian authorities, reported on events in Biafra while never leaving Lagos.

30. Memo, West and General Africa Department, 4 March 1968, UK National Archives, FCO 38/285, file 325.

31. Young, *The Labour Governments*, p. 205.

32. Blank, Gary, 'Britain, Biafra and the Balance of Payments: The Formation of London's "One Nigeria" Policy,' *Revue Française de Civilisation Britannique*, 18, 2 (2013), pp. 66–86.

33. Smith, Karen E., 'The UK and "genocide" in Biafra', in A. Dirk Moses and Lasse Heerten (ed.), *Postcolonial Conflict*, p. 143.
34. Ibid., p. 144
35. Waugh and Cronje, *Biafra, Britain's Shame*.
36. Douglas Anthony, '"Resourceful and Progressive Blackmen": Modernity and Race In Biafra, 1967–70', *Journal of African History*, 51, 2010, pp. 41–61.
37. Cronje, *The World and Nigeria*, p. 84.
38. Smith, 'The UK and "genocide"', p. 150.
39. Letters to the Editor, 6 March 1969, *The Times*, p. 11.
40. *Blue Peter*, 5 Dec. 1967, audio recording posted on Youtube: https://www.youtube.com/watch?v=wExun5aTyfI, last accessed 16 Nov. 2017.
41. 'Matthew', The Tragedy of the Biafran War', 7 August 2013; http://www.workersliberty.org/story/2013/08/07/tragedy-biafran-war, last accessed 17 Nov. 2017.
42. O'Sullivan, Kevin, 'Humanitarian Encounters: Biafra, NGOs and Imaginings of the Third World in Britain and Ireland, 1967–70,' in Moses and Heerten, *Postcolonial Conflict*, p. 263.
43. Omaka, *The Biafran Humanitarian Crisis*, 95.
44. 'Biafran Aid—via Market Stall', *Runcorn Weekly News*, 10 April 1969.
45. O'Sullivan, 'Humanitarian Encounters', p. 264.
46. Ntieyong U. Akpan, *The Struggle for Secession 1966–1970: A Personal Account of the Nigerian Civil War*, London: Cass, 1972, p. 150.
47. Ibid., p. 151.
48. Anthony, 'Resourceful and Progressive Blackmen', p. 49.
49. Adam Curle and Walter Martin, Notes on Visit to Biafra-Eastern Nigeria, 6–11 March, 1968. Archives of American Friends Service Committee, Philadelphia, p. 5.
50. Akpan, *The Struggle for Secession*, p. 169.
51. Emeka Ojukwu, *The Ahiara Declaration: Principles of the Biafran Revolution*. Speech delivered June 1, 1969. Downloaded 10 Dec. 2017, from http://www.biafraland.com/ahiara_declaration_1969.htm, p. 5.
52. Ibid., p. 6.
53. Uwechue, Raph, *Reflections on the Nigerian Civil War*, New York: Africana Publishing Corporation, 1971, p. 93.
54. Morris, Roger, *Uncertain Greatness: Henry Kissinger and American Foreign Policy*, New York: Harper and Row, 1977, p. 20.
55. Ibid., p. 124.
56. Leapman, Michael, 'British interests, Nigerian tragedy', *The Independent*, 4 Jan. 1998. http://www.independent.co.uk/voices/british-interests-nigerian-tragedy-1136684.html, last accessed 20 Nov. 2017.
57. Morris, *Uncertain Greatness*, p. 122.

58. Heerten, Lasse, *The Biafran War and Postcolonial Humanitarianism*, Cambridge University Press, 2017.
59. Ibid., p. 139.

3. BECOMING A NIGERWIFE

1. Dominique Otigbah, the daughter of a Nigerwife, surveyed the scant literature on Nigerwives, and conducted twenty interviews. ('Nigerwives 1936–1970s'). There is no equivalent terminology for a foreign man married to a Nigerian woman, although many such marriages do exist. Nigerian ethnic groups are deeply patrilineal—a woman marries into the kinship structure, and bears children for the male line, which explains the emphasis on intercultural marriages by male Nigerians.
2. Asuni, Judith Burdin and Tolani Asuni, 'Towards the Success of Intercultural Marriage: A Nigerian Example', *Practicing Anthropology*, 9, 3 (1987), pp. 12–14.
3. *The Lawyers Chronicle: The Magazine for the African Lawyer*, 'Who is a Niger-wife?' Online at: http://www.thelawyerschronicle.com/who-is-a-niger-wife/, last accessed 10 Nov. 2017. The term is now often spelled 'naijawife.'
4. Asuni and Asuni, 'Towards the Success', p. 12.
5. Otigbah, 'Nigerwives', p. 25.
6. See, for example Ofoegbu, Leslie, *Blow the Fire*, Enugu: Tana Press, 1985; Onyemelukwe, Catherine, *Nigeria Revisited: My Life and Loves Abroad*, Peace Corps Writers, 2014. White people are often referred to as *oyibo* (Yoruba) or *onyeocha* (Igbo).
7. Ryeland, Kenneth C., *The Up-Country Man: A Personal Account of the First One Hundred Days Inside the Secessionist Biafra*, Oguns Fire, 2012.
8. Asuni and Asuni, 'Towards the Success', p. 12.
9. Otigbah, 'Nigerwives', p. 32.
10. While many feared the fall-out from the Cochrane murder would lead to increased racial tension, in hindsight it is now seen as turning point in race relations, which is sometimes credited with being a catalyst for the now-famous Notting Hill Carnival.
11. Many Igbo children are given both Igbo and English (Christian) names. For instance, John's full name was John Emerenwa Umelo. The couple's eldest son is Ezenwa Charles, known in the family as Eze.

4. BEFORE THE STORM

1. Enugu was the capital of the Eastern Region, with a population of just over 138,000 in 1963.

2. The second institution on that hillside, along with Queens School, was the Women's Training Centre (WTC), which trained students to teach in primary school, focusing on general education, rather than specific subjects.

3. The dormitories (houses) were named for eighteenth- and nineteenth-century British explorers of West Africa: Hugh Clapperton, Dixon Denham, John and Richard Lander, and Mungo Park.

4. During colonial days, 'Senior Service' referred to high-ranking government administrative positions, which were almost exclusively held by Europeans. As Independence approached, 'Nigerianisation' began, and more Nigerians moved into coveted senior positions. As a government-employed teacher, Rose was a civil servant.

5. The main campus of the University of Nigeria was at Nsukka, about 60 km. to the north; the university also had a branch at Enugu.

6. Tilley and Aladdin were brands of kerosene pressure lamps. Fuel, poured into a tank at the base of the lamp, is pressurised by using an attached pump to pump in air. When a valve is opened, the fuel is forced up into a chamber, where it is ignited by a pre-heated mantle.

7. Kingsway was a chain of department stores owned by the United Africa Company, which grew out of Niger Company (formerly Royal Niger Company). The UAC became a subsidiary of Unilever, and was eventually absorbed by that company. In the 1960s, Kingsway stores catered primarily to European expatriates and more well-to-do Nigerians. Retailers Chanrai and Chellaram have both since grown into major Nigerian conglomerates.

8. Farex was a food for babies made from flour and enriched with vitamins. It was made by the British company Glaxo.

9. *Udara* is sometimes known as African cherry or African star apple.

10. *Garri* is a staple food of West Africa, made from cassava tubers, which are peeled, washed and grated to create a mash. This is pressed for a day or more to ferment slightly and, for excess starchy water to be removed, then sieved and dry fried, resulting in a granular product. Palm oil can be sprinkled while frying goes on to give a yellow colour if desired.

11. Akwete cloth is a hand-woven Igbo textile originating in the town of Akwete (in present-day Abia state). George is a luxury cloth featuring embroidery on lace, silk, satin, or other fabric.

5. NIGERIANS ALL?

1. This was indeed the coup of 1966, as described in Chapter 1.

2. The extended family, generally including the descendants (through the

male line) of one great-grandfather, was (and still is) the building block of Igbo society. All Igbo people have a natal village, of which they are 'indigenes', and in times of crisis, they can expect to be welcomed home. Even if they have lived years elsewhere, they will return for marriage and burial. See Uchendu, Victor Chikezie, 'Ezi na ulo: The Extended Family in Igbo Civilization', *Dialectical Anthropology*, 31, 1–3 (2007), pp. 167–219.

3. 'A World of our Own' was a popular hit song by the Australian group The Seekers, first released in 1965.

4. Hail Biafra, our country.

6. WE ARE AT WAR

1. The Nigerian pound, set at parity with the pound sterling initially, was Nigeria's currency until 1973. Like the British pound before conversion to the decimal system, the Nigerian pound was made up of 20 shillings, each comprising 12 pence (thus 240 pennies to the pound). In 1967, the pound was worth approximately the equivalent of £16 today. However, as Rose describes, comparisons gradually became meaningless, as prices spiralled out of control as the war went on.

2. This was the result of advances by the Federal troops, which were forcefully pushing the Biafrans back; they retreated across the River Niger in early October.

3. More likely this was actually the approaching troops of the Federal 1st Division.

7. RUNNING FOR HOME

1. Typical of Igbo social organisation, the town of Ogbaku is made up of four distinct communities, each of which comprises small, named villages based on patrilineal kinship, totalling eighteen in all. John's home village was Umudogu.

2. The *iroko* tree, a large, durable hardwood that can live hundreds of years, is revered in Igbo culture. It can be used for boat-building, flooring, and furniture, as well as firewood, and in many villages a massive *iroko* serves as a focal point, where people gather under its shade.

3. Kinshasa is the capital of the Democratic Republic of Congo, once known as Belgian Congo, and (from 1971–97) as Zaire. Biafra had requested that the OAU consider its case at the 1967 summit; the OAU appointed a committee, while also reaffirming respect for 'the sovereignty and territorial integrity of member states' and condemning secession, thus making its support for a united Nigeria clear.

8. IN THE VILLAGE

1. Sandflies do not actually carry dengue fever, but the bites can indeed be dangerous, as they carry 'sandfly fever' (phlebotomus fever), and may also transmit leishmaniasis, which produces sores and ulcers that can take weeks or months to heal. Neither condition is fatal, but both are painful and unpleasant.
2. Several members of the Holy Ghost Fathers, an Irish order, remained in Biafra, coordinating food distribution and missionary work, and also facilitating communication among expatriate wives. Father Donal O'Sullivan, one of those Rose mentions, maintained a list of twenty-one Nigerwives, eighteen of them British or Irish, and he kept in regular touch with them. The Fathers also developed a system to get letters in and out of Biafra. Nigerwife Leslie Ofoegbu kept the list, as well as Father O'Sullivan's short diary about his time in Biafra.
3. Awgu Market, just over 100 km. northeast of Ogbaku, was bombed on 17 Feb. 1968. Many other air-raids on civilian targets followed.
4. The Federal Military Government hired mainly Egyptian mercenary pilots (with Nigerian crews) to fly its Soviet-made fighters and bombers. British and South African pilots were also recruited, and were generally regarded as much more effective. According to John de St. Jorre (see Bibliography), 'There were usually never less than a dozen pilots, sometimes rising to 20, with a rapid turnover' (p. 316).
5. Many things which nature has made difficult, good management renders easy.
6. 'In times of adversity and slender hope, the bravest counsels are safest.'
7. 'It is said that the truth is often eclipsed, but never extinguished.'
8. 'Nothing is left anywhere for us unless we protect it.'

9. LEARNING TO MAKE DO

1. Here, Rose is referring to the widespread perception in Biafra that the BBC, while a useful source of news, was heavily biased in favour of Nigeria, and was eager to report Biafran defeats, even before they happened.
2. The more common spelling now is 'machete', but in Nigeria these tools were generally called 'matchets'.
3. Cocoyams are plants grown primarily for their edible roots, although other parts of the plant can also be eaten.
4. Waterleaf (*Talinum fruticosum*) is a fast-growing plant grown primarily for its edible green leaves.

5. Rose is referring, of course, to Rachel Carson's influential book *Silent Spring*, first published in 1962, which documented the detrimental effects of widespread pesticide use on the environment.
6. Port Harcourt was captured in May 1968.

10. THE HUNGER

1. The term *juju* seems to have emerged as a hybrid term for a broad range of indigenous religious and ritual practices. Each distinct local Igbo variation had its own traditional name, varying by district—*omenala* in Owerri Igbo. By the time of the civil war most educated Igbo had officially converted to some form of Christianity, but traditional practices were still widely followed, especially at important festival times. The new yam festival was (and still is) one of the most important events of the traditional calendar.
2. Piperazine was used to treat pinworms and roundworms, both common parasites.
3. *Egusi* is made from the seeds of plants like squash, melon, and gourds. The seeds are dried and ground and used in cooking, especially soup, and are quite rich in fat and protein.

11. THE WAR CLOSES IN

1. The Vono company, founded in the UK in 1896, makes spring mattresses and beds, and has long been a popular brand internationally.
2. Ogwa, like other Igbo communities, was made up of a number of distinct villages, of which Alaenyi Ogwa was one. Another was nearby Umueze Ogwa, the location of a school where Rose taught later in the war.
3. M and B was the common name for sulphapyridine, a sulfonamide antibacterial, made by the British firm May and Baker. While widely used for many years, it had a range of side-effects, and eventually gave way to improved drugs.
4. Biafran troops re-entered Owerri in December 1968.

12. THE PATCH-PATCH LIFE

1. *Uri* dye is extracted from a podded plant (*Rothmania hispiola*), and has many uses among Igbo people. As well as being used in childhood ailments, it is believed to alleviate rheumatism. For more information on this and other plant uses, see Agbasiere, Joseph Therese, *Women in Igbo Life and Thought*, London: Routledge, 2015, pp. 59–61.

2. São Tomé, a Portuguese-owned island in the then Bight of Biafra, was used as a base for relief flights into Biafra, with Portuguese permission. The flight from the island to Uli airstrip was about 600 km. São Tomé became independent in 1975.

13. A LAND ARMY

1. 'Vandals' was a term used widely by Biafrans to describe the Federal Nigerian troops.
2. This back-and-forth was in pidgin English, commonly used in Nigeria as a way to communicate among the many different ethnic and linguistic groups.
3. Rose explains this comment: 'Achimota College was founded (as Prince of Wales College) in 1927 in the then Gold Coast (now Ghana). The name and reputation were well known throughout West Africa. So the intruder is saying warfare provides all the education he wants. Similarly Bukri is pidgin, and means "book learning". He means he's a hard man who knows how to fight; that's enough and his opponent talks too much.'
4. The 20mm Oerlikon 'cannon' was a famous gun, one of the most effective anti-aircraft weapons in World War II.
5. Count Carl Gustaf von Rosen was a Swedish aviator. As a mercenary pilot he flew relief missions in a number of conflicts, but is best known for his role in Biafra. He flew relief missions for aid organisations into Biafra, often from São Tomé to the Uli airstrip. He also trained Biafran pilots to use the small Malmö MFI-9 in a ground attack role, resulting in some success later in the war, when the squadron destroyed several Nigerian fighting and bombing aircraft on the ground.

14. WAITING IT OUT

1. The Nigerian government confirmed that it had shot down the Red Cross plane on 5 June after intercepting it over Eket, thirty miles east of Calabar. Nigeria claimed that the plane had been carrying arms. The incident was widely reported in the international Press, e.g. 'Nigeria admits downing Red Cross plane' (Reuters), *Chicago Tribune*, 7 June 1969, p. 18.
2. By 1969, the supply of volunteers for the Biafran forces had dwindled, and many men and boys were being forcibly conscripted, causing great resentment among the civilian population. John Umelo was past the normal age for fighting, but the need for soldiers was so intense that he was vulnerable.

3. Azikiwe, an Igbo and the first President of Nigeria, was a nationalist who had long believed in the concept of a united Nigeria. During the war he advised Ojukwu, and travelled to other African nations seeking their recognition, believing that this would allow Biafra to negotiate peace from a position of strength. By 1969, defeat seemed inevitable, and he returned to his position that unity was the only way to avoid continuing bloodshed. Although this decision was viewed as a betrayal by many Igbo, it is also often credited with helping to end the war.

4. With the capture of Bonny Island and Port Harcourt, Biafra lost its access to oil refineries. However, the Biafran government formed a Petroleum Management Board, which helped coordinate the production of oil in local refineries, often coordinated by Western-trained scientists. Some of these grew quite large, and serviced the military and government, while others were constructed by private citizens to keep their own families in petrol and kerosene.

15. THE END IN SIGHT?

1. 'Na so' is a common pidgin phrase that roughly translates as 'Is that so!' or 'Really!'
2. From Bassanio's speech in Shakespeare's *Merchant of Venice*, Act 1, Scene 1.
3. Mbano was just over 15 km. from Ogwa.

17. AFTER BIAFRA

1. Quotes from Wendy Ijioma are drawn from emails to Elizabeth Bird, 16 and 18 Dec. 2017.
2. http://www.pacesetternovels.com/, last accessed 10 Dec. 2017.
3. Erwin, Lee, 'Genre and Authority in Some Popular Nigerian Women's Novels', *Research in African Literatures*, 33, 2 (2002), p. 92.
4. Coulon, Virginia, 'Women at War: Nigerian Women Writers and the Civil War', *Commonwealth*, 13, 1 (1990), pp. 1–12.
5. Erwin, 'Genre and Authority', p. 82.
6. Ibid, p. 95.
7. Christensen, Matthew J., 'Managed Risk and the Lure of Transparency in Anglophone African Detective Noir', *Textual Practice*, 29, 2 (2015), p. 332.
8. Onyemelukwe, Catherine, *Nigeria Revisited: My Life and Loves Abroad*, Peace Corps Writers, 2014, p. 137.
9. Okonta, Ike, 'Biafra of the Mind: MASSOB and the Mobilization of History', *Journal of Genocide Research*, 16 (2014), pp. 355–78.

10. See, e.g. Reynolds, Rachel R., 'An African Brain Drain: Igbo Decisions to Immigrate to the US', *Review of African Political Economy*, 29 (2007), pp. 273–84.
11. For the most part, history has agreed that there was no genocidal intent on the part of the Federal Military Government. At the same time, its relentless blockade policy, and the actions of some of its commanders and soldiers, particularly in the first year of the war, fed Biafran claims that they must continue to fight or die. For an even-handed discussion of the genocide issues, see A. Dirk Moses and Lasse Heerten (ed.), *Postcolonial Conflict and the Question of Genocide: The Nigeria-Biafra War, 1967–1970*, London: Routledge.
12. With colleague Fraser Ottanelli, I interviewed Gen. Yakubu Gowon, 10 Oct. 2016, Abuja, Nigeria.

SOURCES CONSULTED

In addition to the bibliographic sources, several archival collections were consulted:

African Collections at Michigan State University Library, East Lansing, USA.
American Friends Service Committee Archive, Philadelphia, USA.
Bodleian Library, University of Oxford, UK.
United Kingdom National Archives, Kew, UK.
Imperial War Museum, London, UK.

BIBLIOGRAPHY

Achebe, Chinua, *Home and Exile*, New York: Anchor, 2000.

Adimora-Ezeigbo, Akachi, 'From the Horse's Mouth: The Politics of Remembrance in Women's Writing on the Nigerian Civil War', in *Body, Sexuality, and Gender: Versions and Subversions in African Literatures 1*, Flora Veit-Wild and Dirk Naguschewski (eds), Amsterdam: Rodopi, 2005, pp. 221–31.

Amoba, Mohibi, 'Background to the Conflict' in Joseph Okpaku (ed.), *Nigeria, Dilemma of Nationhood. An African Analysis of the Biafran Conflict*, Westport, CT: Greenwood, 1972, pp. 14–75.

Agbasiere, Joseph Therese, *Women in Igbo Life and Thought*, London: Routledge, 2015.

Anthony, Douglas, *Irreconcilable Narratives: Biafra, Nigeria, and Arguments against Genocide, 1966–1970*, in Moses and Heerten (eds), *Postcolonial Conflict and the Question of Genocide*, pp. 47–71.

Anthony, Douglas, 'Resourceful and Progressive Blackmen': Modernity and Race in Biafra, 1967–70', *Journal of African History*, 51 (2010), pp. 41–61.

Asiegbu, Johnson U. J., *Nigeria and its British Invaders, 1851–1920: A Thematic Documentary History*, New York/Lagos: Nok Publishers, 1984.

Asuni, Judith Burdin and Tolani Asuni, 'Towards the Success of Intercultural Marriage: A Nigerian Example', *Practicing Anthropology*, 9, 3 (1987), pp. 12–14.

Baker, Pauline, 'Lurching toward Unity', *The Wilson Quarterly*, 4 (1980), pp. 70–80.

Bird, S. Elizabeth and Fraser Ottanelli, *The Asaba Massacre: Trauma, Memory, and the Nigerian Civil War*, Cambridge: Cambridge University Press, 2017.

Blank, Gary, 'Britain, Biafra and the Balance of Payments: The Formation of London's "One Nigeria" Policy', *Revue Française de Civilisation Britannique*, 18, 2 (2013), pp. 66–86.

BIBLIOGRAPHY

Bourne, Richard, *Nigeria: A New History of a Turbulent Country*, London: Zed Books, 2015.

Christensen, Matthew J., 'Managed Risk and the Lure of Transparency in Anglophone African Detective Noir', *Textual Practice*, 29, 2 (2015), pp. 315–33.

Coulon, Virginia, 'Women at War: Nigerian Women Writers and the Civil War', *Commonwealth*, 13, 1 (1990), pp. 1–12.

Cronje, Suzanne, *The World and Nigeria: The Diplomatic History of the Biafran War 1967–1970*, London: Sidgwick and Jackson, 1972.

Cruise O'Brien, Conor, 'Condemned People', *New York Review of Books*, 21 Dec. 1967, pp. 14–21.

Curtis, Mark, *Unpeople: Britain's Secret Human Rights Abuses*, London: Vintage, 2004.

de Lame, Danielle, 'On Behalf of Ordinary People: Bridging the Gap between High Politics and Simple Tragedies', *African Studies Review*, 48, 3 (2005), pp. 133–41.

Davis, Morris, *Interpreters for Nigeria: The Third World and International Public Relations*, Urbana: University of Illinois Press, 1977.

De St. Jorre, John, *The Brothers' War: Biafra and Nigeria*, Boston: Houghton Mifflin, 1972.

Ekwe-Ekwe, Herbert, *The Biafra War: Nigeria and the Aftermath*, New York: Edwin Mellen Press, 1990.

Ellis, Stephen, *This Present Darkness: A History of Nigerian Organised Crime*, London: Hurst, 2016.

Erwin, Lee, 'Genre and Authority in Some Popular Nigerian Women's Novels', *Research in African Literatures*, 33, 2 (2002), pp. 81–99.

Falola, Toyin and Matthew M. Heaton, *A History of Nigeria*, Cambridge: Cambridge University Press, 2008.

Farquharson, James, 'Black America Cares: The Response of African-Americans to Civil War and Genocide, 1967–1970', in Moses and Heerten (eds), *Postcolonial Conflict and the Question of Genocide*, pp. 301–326.

Forsyth, Frederick, *The Biafra Story*, London: Penguin, 1969.

Garrison, Lloyd, '300 Ibo Tribesmen Killed by Troops and Nigerian Mob', *New York Times*, 2 Oct. 1966, pp. 1; 17.

Geary, William N.M., *Nigeria under British Rule*, New York: Barnes and Noble, 1927.

Gould, Michael, *The Biafran War: The Struggle for Modern Nigeria*, New York: I.B. Tauris, 2012.

Harneit-Sievers, Axel, Jones O. Ahazuem, and Sydney Emezue, *A Social History of the Nigerian Civil War: Perspectives from Below*, Enugu: Jemezie Associates and Hamburg: Lit Verlag, 1997.

Harrison, Paul and Robin Palmer, *News out of Africa: Biafra to Band Aid*, London: Shipman, 1986.

BIBLIOGRAPHY

Heerten, Lasse, *The Biafran War and Postcolonial Humanitarianism*, Cambridge University Press, 2017.

Hetherington, Penelope, *British Paternalism and Africa, 1920–1940*, London: F. Cass, 1978.

Kirk-Greene, Anthony H.M., *Crisis and Conflict in Nigeria: A Documentary Sourcebook*, 1966–1970, Vol. 1, London: Oxford University Press, 1971.

Leapman, Michael, 'British interests, Nigerian tragedy', *The Independent*, 4 Jan. 1998. http://www.independent.co.uk/voices/british-interests-nigerian-tragedy-1136684.html

Lugard, Frederick John Dealtry, *The Dual Mandate in British Tropical Africa*, London: William Blackwood, 1922.

McNeil, Brian, 'And Starvation is the Grim Reaper': The American Committee to Keep Biafra Alive and the Genocide Question during the Nigerian Civil War, 1968–1970', in Moses and Heerten (eds), *Postcolonial Conflict and the Question of Genocide*, pp. 278–300.

Momoh, H.B., *The Nigerian Civil War, 1967–1970: History and Reminiscences*, Ibadan: Sam Bookman Publishers, 2000.

Morris, Roger, *Uncertain Greatness: Henry Kissinger and American Foreign Policy*, New York: Harper and Row, 1977.

Moses, A. Dirk and Lasse Heerten (eds), *Postcolonial Conflict and the Question of Genocide: The Nigeria-Biafra War, 1967–1970*, London: Routledge, 2017.

Newsweek, 'Nigeria: Setting Sun', 9 Oct. 1967, pp. 41–2.

Niven, Rex, *The War of Nigerian Unity*, Towata, NJ: Rowman and Littlefield, 1970.

Nnaemeka, Obioma, 'Fighting on all Fronts: Gendered Spaces, Ethnic Boundaries, and the Nigerian Civil War', *Dialectical Anthropology*, 22 (1997), pp. 235–63.

Norris, Bill, 'Media Ethics at the Sharp End' in David Berry (ed.), *Ethics and Media Culture: Practices and Representations*, Oxford: Focal Press, 2000, pp. 325–38.

Okonta, Ike, 'Biafra of the Mind: MASSOB and the Mobilization of History', *Journal of Genocide Research*, 16 (2014), pp. 355–78.

Omaka, Arua Oko, *The Biafran Humanitarian Crisis, 1967–1970*, Fairleigh Dickinson University Press, 2016.

O'Sullivan, Kevin, 'Humanitarian Encounters: Biafra, NGOs and Imaginings of the Third World in Britain and Ireland, 1967–70,' in Moses and Heerten (eds), *Postcolonial Conflict and the Question of Genocide: The Nigeria-Biafra War, 1967–1970*, pp. 259–77.

Otigbah, Dominique, 'Nigerwives 1936–1970s: Locating the History of Expatriate Wives in Nigeria with the Context of Race Relations, Gender and Colonial/Post-colonial Encounters'. Independent Study Project, School of Oriental and African Studies, London, 2014.

BIBLIOGRAPHY

Reynolds, Rachel R., 'An African Brain Drain: Igbo Decisions to Immigrate to the US', *Review of African Political Economy*, 29 (2007), pp. 273–84.

Rosa, Matthew, 'Schools and Hospitals Bombed, says Biafra', *The Observer*, 3 March 1968, p. 4.

Shepherd, Jack, 'Memo from Nigeria: Old Headaches for our New President', *Look*, 26 Nov. 1968, p. 74.

Smith, Karen E., 'The UK and "genocide" in Biafra', in Moses and Heerten (eds), *Postcolonial Conflict and the Question of Genocide: The Nigeria-Biafra War, 1967–1970*, pp. 137–55.

Stremlau, John J., *The International Politics of the Nigerian Civil War, 1967–1970*, Princeton: Princeton University Press, 1977.

Uche, Chibuike, 'Oil, British Interests and the Nigerian Civil War', *Journal of African History*, 49 (2008), pp. 111–35.

Uchendu, Egodi, *Women and Conflict in the Nigerian Civil War*, Trenton, NJ: Africa World Press, 2007.

Uchendu, Victor Chikezie, 'Ezi na ulo: The Extended Family in Igbo Civilization', *Dialectical Anthropology*, 31, 1–3 (2007), pp. 167–219.

Venter, Al J., *Biafra's War: 1967–1970*, Solihull: Helion, 2015.

Waugh, Auberon and Suzanne Cronje, *Biafra, Britain's Shame*, London: Michael Joseph, 1969.

Young, John W., *The Labour Governments 1964–1970, Vol. 2, International Policy*, Manchester: Manchester University Press, 2004.

Civil War Memoirs

Achebe, Chinua, *There was a Country*, New York: Penguin, 2012.

Akpan, Ntieyong U. *The Struggle for Secession 1966–1970: A Personal Account of the Nigerian Civil War*, London: Cass, 1972.

Alabi-Isama, Godwin, *The Tragedy of Victory: On the Spot Account of the Nigeria-Biafra War in the Atlantic Theatre*, Ibadan: Spectrum Books, 2013.

Alli, M. Chris, *The Federal Republic of Nigerian Army: The Siege of a Nation*, Lagos, Nigeria: Malthouse Press, 2000.

Idahosa, Patrick E., *Truth and Tragedy: A Fighting Man's Memoir of the Nigerian Civil War*, Ibadan: Heinemann Educational Books (Nigeria), 1989.

Obasanjo, Olusegun, *My Command: An Account of the Nigerian Civil War, 1967–1970*, London: Heinemann, 1980.

Ofoegbu, Leslie, *Blow the Fire*, Enugu: Tana Press, 1985.

Onyemelukwe, Catherine, *Nigeria Revisited: My Life and Loves Abroad*, Peace Corps Writers, 2014.

Oraguwu, Felix N.C., *Scientific and Technological Innovations in Biafra: The Ogbunigwe Fame 1967–1970*, Enugu: Fourth Dimension Publishing, 2010.

Oyewole, Fola, *Reluctant Rebel*, London: Rex Collings, 1975.

Ryeland, Kenneth C., *The Up-Country Man: A Personal Account of the First One Hundred Days Inside the Secessionist Biafra*, Oguns Fire, 2012.

BIBLIOGRAPHY

Sherman, John, *War Stories: A Memoir of Nigeria and Biafra*, Indianapolis: Mesa Verde Press, 2002.

Soyinka, Wole, *The Man Died: Prison Notes*. London: Rex Collings, 1972.

Uwechue, Raph, *Reflections on the Nigerian Civil War*, New York: Africana Publishing Corporation, 1971.

Uzokwe, Alfred Obiora, *Surviving in Biafra: The Story of the Nigerian Civil War*, New York: Writers Advantage, 2003.

INDEX